CONTEMPORARY BIBLICAL HERMENEUTICS

Contemporary Biblical Hermeneutics

An Introduction

MANFRED OEMING
Ruprecht-Karls-Universität, Heidelberg, Germany

translated by
Joachim F. Vette

ASHGATE

Published by
Ashgate Publishing Limited
Gower House
Croft Road
Aldershot
Hants GU11 3HR
England

Ashgate Publishing Company
Suite 420
101 Cherry Street
Burlington
Vermont, 05401–4405
USA

Ashgate website: http://www.ashgate.com

British Library Cataloguing in Publication Data
Oeming, Manfred
    Contemporary Biblical Hermeneutics: An Introduction.
    1. Bible – Hermeneutics. I. Title.
    220.6'01

US Library of Congress Cataloging in Publication Data
Oeming, Manfred
    Contemporary Biblical Hermeneutics: An Introduction / Manfred Oeming.
      p.   cm.
    Includes bibliographical references and index.
    1. Bible – Hermeneutics. I. Title.
    BS476.O3913 2006
    220.601–dc22   2005031999

ISBN 0 7546 5659 4 (hardback)
ISBN 0 7546 5660 8 (paperback)

This book is printed on acid-free paper.

Printed and bound in Great Britain by TJ International Ltd, Padstow, Cornwall.

Contents

PART III: Summary: Fullness or Food of Meaning?

List of Figures

Preface to the English Translation

The term 'hermeneutics' in the title of this book may well convey a wrong impression. It may indicate that this volume is concerned with complicated theoretical problems not connected to practical everyday application. Yet hermeneutics is anything but a distant non-practical mind game. Hermeneutics is concerned with the scholarly analysis of an elementary problem: how does understanding work? When can I say that I have understood something or someone? This book offers a model of understanding that is universally applicable, not only for understanding the Bible. Understanding a text is a complex process involving several different aspects: the author, the text, the reader and the subject matter contained in the text. Each of these aspects is connected to its own discourse and set of rules. If a theory of understanding is to take these various aspects seriously, we are confronted with a need for a 'multiplicity of approaches' and a continually intensifying discussion between them ('hermeneutical spiral'). Thus, there is a great deal of overlap between hermeneutics and the science of communication.[1] A sender attempts to communicate a message on a certain subject matter to a recipient and perhaps evoke a certain response by this recipient. The recipient must use all available resources to understand the meaning of this message. Empathy and imagination are as important in this endeavour as linguistic competence and specific expertise.

Following the lead of thinkers such as Martin Heidegger and Hans-Georg Gadamer, it is safe to say that hermeneutics starts at birth. Every new-born sends out meaningful signals that must be understood by its parents and that require certain responses (such as the demand for food, crying due to indigestion, joy evoked by a dry diaper). Similarly, the new-born receives signals that answer its attempts at communication while providing guidance for its future actions (the singing of its mother or the rocking of its father). Over the course of a life-time, the hermeneutic process continues to grow more complex and differentiated. Learning one's own language as well as foreign languages is an important part of this process. No matter how complex hermeneutics becomes, however, it always retains its connection to the very practical aspect of providing guidance and meaning for everyday life. 'Biblical hermeneutics' is thus a very elementary topic. It too often begins at birth, when parents utter their first 'thank God', or when they pray or have their child baptised. The child is able to see a church or a cemetery filled with crosses. This wealth of symbols speaks a vague but complex language.

---

[1] The word 'hermeneutics' derives from the name of the Greek god Hermes. It is his task to relay the messages of the gods to human beings. Hermeneutics thus is the art of conveying information as well as the interpretation of the information conveyed.

On this very elementary level, the child comes in contact with a basic message: 'God exists, he reveals himself and lets himself be known. Relationship with him leads to a certain conduct in life; he grants joy and strength and provides guidance and meaning.' In time, the perception of God's Word in its various expressions expands and deepens as we develop a 'mother-tongue' of our own faith and learn and interact with various theological 'foreign tongues'.

Even if biblical hermeneutics is a science that often makes use of complicated terminology, it is something that remains imminently practical at its core. It speaks of what we all engage in and what we can observe about ourselves when we attempt to understand a human being or a text as 'other'. In all understanding, we must be concerned with overcoming ignorance and avoiding misunderstanding.

The Bible is the book of life, one foundation of the church and of all Christian faith – so it is stated in the tradition of the church. The Bible is a confusing and obscure book closed by seven seals, a mere historical document with no relation to current issues – so it is stated by many today. Many today are at a loss to combine how they experience these texts with the immense claim that the Bible is the 'Word of God'. They despair when attempting to decipher the message contained in its pages. This present book is concerned with the various methods, offered by modern scholarship, that may overcome ignorance in the face of the Bible and misunderstanding when engaging with its texts. I hope that this introduction into hermeneutics in its English translation may contribute to the goal of understanding how we understand, as well as increasing our delight in reading the Bible. (For the English speaking readers it may be especially interesting to see the more German – philosophical way of approaching the text.)

I owe much gratitude to Joachim F. Vette, who has diligently translated the German original. When I first met this young doctoral student in a seminar on New Literary Criticism, I did not imagine that he would one day become a translator of one of my books.

MANFRED OEMING
Heidelberg, 23 October 2004

Chapter 1

Introduction:
The Topic and Procedure of this Book

Biblical hermeneutics is the discipline of understanding biblical writing. It gathers discussions on a wide range of topics. On the one hand, it analyses how, and by what means, academic biblical interpretation proceeds and did proceed and subjects this process to critical examination. In this sense, it is a necessary part of basic methodological reflecton within the discipline of theology. On the other hand, biblical hermeneutics examines how the Bible is and was understood and applied outside of the university. Several so-called 'alternative methods' are used by various groups within church and society. Their strengths and limitations must also be considered.

In a strict sense, biblical hermeneutics could originate only after the entire Bible existed as a closed canon, i.e. from the 4th century A.D. In a wider sense, however, we find earlier attempts, more implicitly practical than theoretically reflected, to develop new understandings of older biblical writings conditioned by ever-changing historical circumstances. There are traces in the Old Testament of how the oldest creedal statements (dating back to the 10th century B.C.) were continually rewritten and expanded intertextually, thus providing interpretation through contextualisation.[2] The approbation of early statements of faith by later generations can be seen quite clearly following the (relative) closure of Israel's holy writings, e.g. in the Pesher-method of the Qumran community[3] or in the allegorical approach of Philo.[4] In a certain sense, the combined theological voices

---

[2] See Fishbane, M. (1985), *Biblical Interpretation in Ancient Israel*, Oxford. Fishbane, M. (1996), 'Inner-Biblical Exegesis', in M. Saebø (ed.), *Hebrew Bible, Old Testament. The History of its Interpretation*, Vol. I/1, Göttingen, pp. 33-48. Graf Reventlow, H. (1990), *Epochen der Bibelauslegung, Vol. 1: Vom Alten Testament bis Origines*, München.

[3] See Fabry, H.-J. (1996), 'Methoden der Schriftauslegung in den Qumranschriften', in *Stimuli. Exeges und ihre Hermeneutik in: Antike und Christentum*, JAC.E 23 (FS E. Dassmann), Münster, pp. 18-33; Stemberger, G. (1996), in Ch. Dohmen and H.-J. Fabry, *Hermeneutik der jüdischen Bibel und des Alten Testaments*, Studienbücher Theologie 1,2, Stuttgart, pp. 47-50; Maier, J. (1996), 'Early Jewish Biblical Interpretation in the Qumran Literature', in M. Saebø, *Hebrew Bible, Old Testament*, pp. 108-129.

[4] See Stemberger, G. (1996), *Hermeneutik*, pp. 67-74. Siegert, F. (1996), Early Jewish Interpretation in a Hellenistic Style, in M. Saebø, *Hebrew Bible, Old Testament*, pp. 162-189.

of the New Testament are also an attempt to understand what was said 'to our fathers' in the radical new light of God's salvific action in Jesus Christ. Certain books of the New Testament can actually be understood as a biblical hermeneutics of the Old Testament. We find tightly knit connections to the Old Testament already in the sermons of the historical Jesus and definitely in the witnesses to the resurrected Christ – especially with Matthew, Luke, Paul (mainly in his letter to the Romans) and Hebrews.[5] Such inner-biblical hermeneutics will not be part of our present discussion.

With good reason, G. Ebeling has described the history of the church as a history of interpreting the Bible.[6] A book on biblical hermeneutics could therefore present the history of how the Bible was understood from the early church up to the present. This sort of overview will not be possible here.[7] It is also not the intention of this book to present case studies of exemplary interpreters of the Bible.[8]

I will instead concentrate on *how Scripture is interpreted in the present.* This will not merely include a survey of current approaches (some of which may lead to dead ends) for accumulative purposes,[9] even if this may be a secondary effect. My primary goal is the development of a system based on an analysis of fundamental phenomenological processes of understanding as an aid to discerning and assessing the current plethora of hermeneutical methods.

This task again can be approached in different ways: as I will show, no exegesis operates without certain a priori assumptions; each method of biblical

---

[5] Koch, D.A. (1986), *Die Schrift als Zeuge des Evangeliums,* Tübingen; Söding, Th. (1995), 'Heilige Schriften für Israel und die Kirche. Die Sicht des "Alten Testamentes" bei Paulus', in *MThZ* 46, pp. 159-181; Childs, B.S. (1994+1996), *Die Theologie der einen Bibel,* Vol. 1+2, Freiburg; Hübner, H. (1996), 'New Testament Interpretation of the Old Testament', in M. Saebø, *Hebrew Bible, Old Testament,* pp. 332-372.

[6] Ebeling, G. (1996), 'Kirchengeschichte als Geschichte der Auslegung der Heiligen Schrift (1946)', in: G. Ebeling (1996), *Wort Gottes und Tradition,* 2nd edition, Tübingen, pp. 9-27.

[7] See Diestel, L. (1869), *Geschichte des Alten Testamentes in der christlichen Kirche,* Jena (NP Leipzig 1981); Gunneweg, A.H.J. (1988), *Vom Verstehen des Alten Testaments. Eine Hermeneutik,* ATD.E 5, 2nd edition Göttingen; Stuhlmacher, P. (1986), *Vom Verstehen des Neuen Testaments. Eine Hermeneutik,* NTD.E 6, 2nd edition, Göttingen; Karpp, H. (1992), *Schrift, Geist und Wort Gottes. Geltung und Wirkung der Bibel in der Geschichte der Kirche: Von der Alten Kirche bis zur Reformationszeit,* Darmstadt; Graf Reventlow, H (1994), *Epochen der Bibelauslegung, Vol 2. Von der Spätantike bis zum Ausgang des Mittelalters,* München.

[8] Such a case study can be found in Seebaß, H. (1974), *Biblische Hermeneutik,* UB 199, Stuttgart.

[9] See Berg, H.K. (1991), *Ein Wort wie Feuer. Wege lebendiger Schriftauslegung,* Stuttgart; Dohmen, Ch. (1992), 'Vom vielfachen Schriftsinn – Möglichkeiten und Grenzen neuerer Zugänge zu biblischen Texten', in Th. Sternberg (ed.), *Neue Formen der Schriftauslegung?* CD 140, Freiburg.

interpretation is necessarily dependent on specific philosophical predilections. Biblical hermeneutics must therefore give an account of the axioms that shape it. Reflecting on the basic philosophical premises of one's hermeneutics can occur in one of two ways: either we attempt a *concise presentation of the main developments in the history of philosophical hermeneutics*, or we seek to understand the epistemological ideals of each method in its specific place and time. The latter avoids repetition in the discussion of individual methods yet it tends to tear apart topics that by their nature belong together. In this book, I will proceed according to the first option and go on a stroll through the history of philosophical hermeneutics from Plato to Jean-François Lyotard while paying deliberate attention to those aspects important for understanding the methods of biblical exegesis. These aspects can then be alluded to when attending to the individual methods.

I will not deal with biblical hermeneutics on a purely theoretical level. In order to gain a vibrant impression of 'exegesis in action' I will rely on examples from *both Testaments*. Here, too, there are alternative courses of action: one could discuss the characteristics of each method by applying all of them to one or two texts.[10] It was my original idea to follow precisely this course of action based on the Exodus and the resurrection narratives; however, this procedure has the distinctive disadvantage of unavoidable repetition. It is also true that not every method is equally suited to every text. For these reasons, I will take the other route and demonstrate each method with reference to a particularly appropriate text. This will also provide a better view over the wide scope of the biblical message.

These introductory thoughts and decisions result in the following outline: I. The discussion will first present a survey of philosophical hermeneutics in search of insight into the theoretical foundations of how the Bible can be understood. II. Based on these observations, I will discuss the richness present in current biblical exegesis. This discussion will always follow the same procedure:

A) Philosophical premises
B) Theoretical presentation of the method
C) Significant example(s)
D) Critical assessment of inherent strengths and weaknesses.

A bibliography for each method is added at the end of the book. It is organised according to the same outline as the book itself.

---

[10] In this manner, Berg, H.K. (1991), *Ein Wort wie Feuer*, works with Cain and Abel (Gen 4) and the casting out of demons into a herd of swine (Mark 5:1-20). Luz, U. (ed.) (1993), *Zankapfel Bibel. Eine Bibel – viele Zugänge. Ein theologisches Gespräch*, 2nd edition, Zürich, presents a similar project based on Mark 6:30-44.

PART I:
The Philosophical Foundations of Biblical Hermeneutics

Chapter 2

The Phenomenology of Understanding: The Theory of the Hermeneutical Square

Like all other forms of understanding, the process of understanding the Bible is intimately tied to a process of communication. Four factors are involved: (1) The *author*, who aims to communicate an insight or experience from his world; (2) the *text*, which at least partially contains what the author intended to communicate; (3) the *reader*, who initiates contact with the author and his world by dealing with the text and its world (it remains to be seen whether modern readers of an ancient text are capable of re-actualising the intention of the author at all, or whether they are doomed by the 'abyss of history' to mistake the written intention within the context of their own interests); (4) the *subject matter* which connects author, text and reader. Graphically, we can portray this situation as follows:

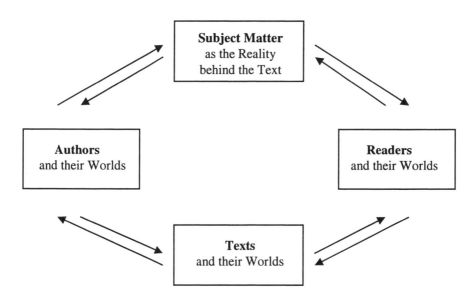

Figure 1   The hermeneutical square structured as a hermeneutical circle

We will refer to this logical structure as the hermeneutical square. The arrows are intended to highlight the dynamic movement inherent in the structure: continual movement from corner to corner *deepens* our understanding; the term 'hermeneutical circle' might thus be replaced by 'hermeneutical spiral'. We can also see that there can be no direct contact between author and recipient: understanding occurs indirectly through the medium of language.[11] In any case, both author and reader must connect with the subject matter as the world they have in common. This seemingly simple basic logical structure determines the following discussion. It is my aim to show that the various theories within both philosophical as well as biblical hermeneutics can be systematised and presented within the structure of this hermeneutical square.

---

[11] 'Language' is not limited to texts; non-verbal forms of language exist as well, e.g. the language of symbols, music, body language or the language of the spheres.

Chapter 3

A Foray into the History of Philosophical Hermeneutics with a Focus on Biblical Hermeneutics

At the beginning of Book VII of the *Republic*, in the famous parable of the cave, Plato (432-347 B.C.) unfolds his view on the status and potential of human understanding.[12] His myth describes the individual as a prisoner who, without knowing it, is chained in a deep cave. In this cave, he faces the 'wrong' way, looking only at the back wall of the cave. On this wall he sees shadows, shadows of all the things carried past the cave in front of a fire. This individual in his 'natural state' believes that these shadows are the one true reality. He does not even suspect the existence of a reality outside of the cave until philosophy comes along, frees him from his chains, and enables him to ascend to the real world (= world of ideas). Plato differentiates between things-in-themselves and their appearances not only on an ontological level, but also between varying levels of understanding reality on an epistemological level. His view of the 'normal' human being is informed by a high degree of scepticism. Even though the immortal soul pre-existed in the realm of ideas and knew of the things-in-themselves, it lost this knowledge on account of its incarnation. Driven by Eros (see his dialogue *Symposion*), the human being strives beyond the material realm back to the forgotten realm of the spiritual. Conversation is an important tool in this process of remembering (*anamnesis*). As the Platonic dialogues show, dialectical conversation acts as a process of midwifery (*maeutik*) through which the soul departs from the realm of the material and ascends to the realm of ideas. This Platonic dualism of shadowy appearance and actual being creates a tradition that must never be underestimated in its influence on hermeneutics. Plato lays the groundwork for the following attitude: good exegetes must never limit themselves to the vague and superficial literal meaning of the text; the exegete must free herself from such lowly errors and ascend to the true spiritual meaning of the work.

In the six books of his Organon (on logic) – primarily in the second book *Peri Hermeneias = De interpretatione* – Aristotle (384-324 B.C.), a student and subsequent opponent of Plato, developed a theory of statements as an alternative to the Platonic view discussed above. Behind Aristotle's dry, formal analysis of

---

[12] Politeia, 514ff.

statements lies the concept of existence outside the realm of language. Hermeneutics according to Aristotle is the art of making true statements about things. He develops a theory where truth becomes the equivalence between a thing itself and one's perception of it: *Veritas est adaequatio rei et intellectus.* Aristotle emphasises things in themselves that exist independent of language and are merely expressed by language. Even if his logic is primarily concerned with formal structures of truth, its influence on subsequent developments is very important. An optimistic view of the intellect of a human being in his 'natural state' is basic to the Aristotelian tradition; he argues that it is possible to grasp the truth of a text by a formal, logical and philological analysis of the text.

Much of the history of hermeneutics can be understood as the development of this basic opposition between Plato and Aristotle, between speculative striving for the otherworldly and sober analysis of this world itself, between poetic conversation and cool, formal logic. Exponents of both sides have ridiculed and criticised each other as dull, blind and superficial on the one side, and as effusive dreamers on the other side (even though they often were more similar than they realised).

As early as Plato, we find praise of the Rhapsodes, who were capable of interpreting Homer's old offensive myths while making the 'true intention' of the poet relevant for his readers (in Ion 530 cd). Against the harsh criticism directed at Homer by philosophical speculations on God, these interpreters understood the myths as ciphers for philosophical truths. In accordance with the Platonic teaching that things are something other than what they appear to be, the undignified actions of the gods as well as contradictions within the text are re-interpreted as ethical truths and natural laws, even if the interpretation led to adventurous and questionable results. This allegorical interpretation was used especially by the Stoics from the 3rd century B.C. on.[13] They rescued the old tradition for their contemporary setting by showing that the myths did indeed speak of logos and nature. In this manner, Zeus became the principle of life and glowing ether, Poseidon was understood as a cipher for the liquid element and Athena became the personification of the earth. As soon as the gods became elements, their love-life and their wars could be understood as the natural opposition of elements, or their combination into new forms of being. Athena was also interpreted as the personification of intelligence and prudence. When she grabs angry Achilles' hair, the poet is interpreted to say: only the moderation of intelligence is capable of controlling anger.[14] Here we find the beginnings of demythologising antiquated texts. These texts are not rejected, but instead made relevant for modern readers – even if they are violently twisted in the process.

---

[13] See Wehrli, F. (1928), *Zur Geschichte der allgemeinen Deutung Homers im Altertum,* Leipzig.

[14] Collections of stoic allegories are found in Heracleides, *Ponticus, Allegorie homerice,* or Plutarch, *De vita et Poesia Homeri.*

Hellenistic Judaism was largely able to use these allegorical hermeneutics in order to transport the world of the Old Testament into the educated circles of Greek culture. In this manner, the traditions in the Old Testament could be presented as deep philosophical truths to general society as well as to Jews, who were moving away from their heritage (compare Deut 4:6-8; Sir 24). Aristobul (ca. 160 B.C.) and the Letter of Aristeas (ca. 140 B.C.), for example, interpret the kosher food-laws as symbolic instruction (143-149). The fact than cultically clean animals had to have split hooves referred to their ability to tell right from wrong. Another example of allegorical interpretation is found in the 4th book of Maccabees (written around the birth of Christ), in which the law of Moses is said to guarantee philosophical education in accordance with natural law, as well as moderate and control desire (4 Macc. 1:14ff; 5:18-25). Biblical narratives are often understood metaphorically; the pillar of cloud becomes the wisdom of God, Jacob's ladder becomes the divine Sophia. Hellenistic Judaism's master of allegory was Philo of Alexandria (ca. 20 B.C. to A.D. 50). He explicitly separates the literal meaning of the text from its allegorical, meaning. The exciting complexity of his system of symbols cannot be discussed here.[15] For our purposes, it is important to note that his hermeneutics, influenced by the Stoa, had a huge impact on Judaism. 'In rabbinic Judaism we also find allegory, even if not as systematically applied as with Philo.'[16] The seven rules of Hillel, the 13 Middot of Rabbi Yishmael, and the 52 Middot of Rabbi Eliezer[17] all show the influence of Platonic hermeneutics when they advocate reading biblical words according to their numerical value, according to their meaning as anagrams, or even according to their meaning when read backwards. Aspects of the writings of Josephus (ca. A.D. 38-100) as well as aspects of the Talmud and Jewish Gnosis draw a line all the way to the religious philosophy and poetry of medieval Judaism (e.g. Ibn Gabriol A.D.1020-1058) and the Kabbala.

Early Christianity was also prone to retain the Old Testament as a whole only under the Platonic assumption of layers of meaning (compare 1 Cor 10:1-13; 2 Cor 3:13-18). A pluralistic view of the meaning of Scripture became mandatory as soon as Scripture was taken as proof of the highly complex philosophical speculations that developed within the framework of a systematised dogmatics. The entire early church is thus influenced by the doctrine of layers of meaning within Scripture. Augustine (345-430) was an especially influential Christian thinker. The final books of the *Confessions* contains important material that pertains to this topic:

---

[15] See Christiansen, I. (1969), *Die Technik der allegorischen Auslegungswissenschaft bei Philon von Alexandrien*, Tübingen; Mack, B. (1978), 'Weisheit und Allegorie bei Philo von Alexandrien', in *StPhilo* 5, pp. 57-105.

[16] Stemberger, G. (1979), *Das klassische Judentum*, München, p. 196.

[17] See Strack, H. and Stemberger, G. (1982), *Einleitung in Talmud und Midrasch*, 7th edition, München, pp. 40-45; Mayer, R. (1968), 'Geschichtserfahrung und Schriftauslegung – zur Hermeneutik des frühen Judentums', in O. Loretz and W. Stolz, *Die hermeneutische Frage in der Theologie*, Freiburg, pp. 290-355.

Following his interpretation of the great truths within Creation, he addresses God with the wish that Moses might have already seen the truths which he himself had found in the book of Moses (book 12, chapters 24-31):

> See with what confidence I say that Thou hast created everything by Thy unchangeable Word, everything visible and invisible; can I say with the same confidence that Moses meant nothing other than this when he wrote the words: In the beginning God created heaven and earth? I do not recognize in his spirit what he thought as he wrote this with the same confidence as a see the former truth ... No one, however, become a burden to me by saying: 'Moses did not mean what you say, he means what I say.' ... Why should we argue about the thoughts of our neighbour, which are not open to our spirit in the same manner as eternal truth? Recognize now, how foolish it is to claim to know which opinion Moses primarily held among the many fully correct opinions contained in those words. Recognize further how deeply harmful argument injures love itself. This was the very reason that Moses uttered these words which we dare interpret. ... Thus, if someone says: 'Moses meant what I mean', and another, 'no, he meant what I mean', then I believe it is appropriate in our fear of God to say: 'Why not both, if both are true?' And what if a third or even a fourth party recognizes something entirely different from both these claims? God allowed Holy Scripture to conform to the ability of many different readers, who are able to find many different and yet true meanings. ... Should it remain hidden from your spirit of gentleness what you yourself wanted to reveal to those who read your words in later times, even if the one who spoke these words may have only intended one of the many meanings?

Every premise behind the hermeneutics of the Middle Ages justifying multi-dimensional interpretation with a clear conscience can be found here: (1) The meaning intended by the ancient author (in this case Moses) may be the primary meaning, (2) but the depth of meaning in the texts was hidden from Moses (as from all the ancient saints). Not the intention of the human author is important, but rather the intention of the Holy Spirit, who was the actual author. (3) It was God's will that later generations of readers should be able to find different truths of faith in the texts than Moses did. (4) It is therefore not the primary task of exegesis to psychologically reconstruct Moses' intention (unattainable as this goal is, in any case), but to extract the truths of our faith as the true task of theology. Interpretation is more a matter of understanding God than understanding the text. (5) The pluralistic depth of meaning within the text was forseen and intended by God himself. (6) The love of truth is opposed to every self-righteous argument about the true meaning of Scripture. In his work *De doctrina christiana*, Augstine expands and legitimises this view of a divinely sanctioned plurality of meaning (book 3, 27-38).

Apart from the influences of Plato and the Stoa, we also find hermeneutical traditions much more dependent on Aristotle and his *Logic*. Aristotle argued against philosophical speculation and pursued detailed philological work, considering the 'natural' meaning of the text to be the most important. The school of Alexandria with its main exponents Clement of Alexandria (ca. A.D. 145-215) and Origen (ca. A.D. 185-253) devoted much energy to the collection and comparison of diffent manuscripts in an attempt to determine the best and the oldest text. Origen's *Hexapla* is the most famous outcome of this labour. This Aristotelian tradition reached its climax within the Judaism of the Middle Ages, especially with Maimonides (1135-1204). There always had been tendencies within Judaism (the Karaites for example) that were devoted to guarding the literary meaning of the text against take-over by philosophical or casuistic speculation.

The medieval combination of a hermeneutics interested primarily in theological matters with the doctrine of a plurality of meaning was best expressed in the following widely quoted Latin phrase:

Litera gesta docet,
quid credas allegoria,
moralis quid agas
quid speres anagogia.
('The literal meaning teaches what occurred,
the allegorical meaning teaches what should be believed,
the moral meaning teaches what should be done,
the anagogic meaning teaches what we should hope for.')

In accordance with the Pauline triad of faith, love and hope, every biblical passage contains dimensions of meaning over and above the literal: a strengthening of faith, a guide for improving or changing the world through action, and a comforting revelation for our hope in the future. These layers of meaning have to be discovered ever anew under the guidance of proper hermeneutical training.

The Reformation was also not without philosophical dimensions, even if Martin Luther (1483-1545) ridiculed Aristotle as a fool.[18] His rejection of Catholic philosophical speculation that obscured biblical intention was based on a further premise: 'Natural language is the Queen who resides over all pointed, subtle, and sophisticated interpretation. We should never stray from her, unless a dogma of faith forces us to; otherwise no letter in Scripture would be safe from intellectual charlatans.'[19] He recommends the following: 'Even though Scripture refers to things wide in meaning, we should not believe that Scripture has a split meaning, but only the one the words clearly state. All restless spirits should take a vacation, instead of hunting and searching after varied meanings beyond these words. They should in their hunt take care not to climb too high, as can happen to the hunter of mountain goats ... It is more secure and more truthful to remain with the words and

---

[18] Luther's wordplay 'Aristoteles – Narristoteles' is unfortunately confined to the German language (J.F.V.).

[19] *Wider die himmlischer Propheten, von den Bildern und Sakramenten* (1525), WA 18, p. 180, 17-20.

their simple meaning; this is the true pasture and home of all spirits.'[20] Or, more to the point: 'Allegories pull the foundation out from under us and this understanding of Scripture leads the people into a dead end.'[21] Luther allows allegory only as 'decoration',[22] as a didactic tool for simple people. Instead of using conjurer's illusions for the purpose of entertainment, he demands that Scripture interpret itself (*Sacra scriptura sui ipsius interpres*) by moving from the clear to the less clear passages and never the other way around. With his strong emphasis on the literal meaning, as well as his insistence that the Bible is a coherent cosmos capable of interpreting itself, Luther initiated a hermeneutical revolution during the Reformation.

Nevertheless, Orthodoxy's attempt to defend the results of the Reformation through didactical statements of dogma unavoidably led back to Augustine.[23] Scripture *had* to conform to basic dogmatic truth. In his work *Clavis scripturae sacrae*, Matthias Flacius Illyricus had already insisted on verbal inspiration right down to the verbal inspiration of the Hebrew consonantal text as early as 1567. Johann Gerhard (1582-1637) fully equated 'Word of God' with the Bible; God himself is seen as the *causa principalis* of Holy Scripture; human authors are not true authors, they are merely *causa intstrumentalis*, 'secretaries of God, hands of Christ, writers and notaries of the Holy Spirit.' In this view, tensions in the text, contradictions, theologically questionable material, or even criticism of the text is simply not allowed to exist – quite in contrast to the emerging rationalistic biblical criticism.

Even Pietism is not fully able to relinquish a plurality of meaning in regard to biblical texts, despite its insistence on enriching the faith through the immediate literal meaning of the Bible. Since being 'born again' is seen as a necessary pre-condition for correct understanding, every biblical text must have a 'secular' and a 'spiritual' meaning. Three Pietistic theories are especially important: (1) Pietism discovers the basic importance of the reader for the process of understanding; understanding is not the same for everybody. Texts of faith can only be understood fully by someone steeped in faith himself. (2) The involvement of the Holy Spirit and its divine power of inspiration sharpens our focus on the limitations of rational and methodical tools and possibilities. The critical distance maintained by rationalistic exegesis requires completion by a meditative approach. (3) Pietism emphasises the importance of a lay approach to the texts (especially one untainted by dogmatics and philosophy). In his work *Pia Desideria* (1675) Philipp Jakob Spener exhorts the *Collegia Pietatis* to read the Bible intensively in its breadth and

---

[20] *Auf das überchristlich usw. Buch Bocks Emsers zu Leipzig Antwort* (1521), WA 7, p. 651, 1-8.

[21] *Predigten über das 2. Buch Mose* (1524-1527), WA 16, p. 69, 28-30.

[22] *Eine kurze form das Paternoster zu verstehen und zu beten* (1519), WA 6, p. 15.

[23] Michel, K.-H. (1985), *Anfänge der Bibelkritik. Quellentexte aus Orthodoxie und Aufklärung*, Wuppertal.

richness. At a minimum, daily devotionals were seen as the basis of meditative practice (based on the model of Nikolaus Ludwig Graf von Zinzendorf (1700-1760)). Because of the central importance of the Bible, Pietism strongly promoted the scholary study of its original manuscripts, as seen for example in the works of Johann Albrecht Bengels (1687-1752).

Following Hugo Grotius (1583-1645) and Baruch Spinoza (1632-1677) in Holland, Richard Simon (1683-1712) in France, and English Deism, the Enlightenment also reached a climax in Germany through figures such as Hermann Samuel Reimarus (1694-1768), Gotthold Ephraim Lessing (1729-1781), and Immanuel Kant (1724-1804). The application of Enlightenment principles to theology was primarily achieved by Johann Salomo Semler (1725-1791) and Johann August Ernesti (1707-1781). Their hermeneutical programme consisted of an elimination of all merely historical aspects of the text in order to uncover the true centre containing eternal truths or fundamental moral values. Human reason, as understood by these proponents, was the hermeneutical sieve through which all tradition had to be pressed. Today we must recognise their eternal truths as historically conditioned propositions made during a certain era. Yet the Enlightenment goal of separating the eternal from the 'merely' historical made a large contribution towards recognising those elements of biblical texts which truly were historically conditioned.

German idealism primarily dealt with the search for an inner logic and meaning of history as such. The philosophy of Georg Friedrich Wilhelm Hegel (1770-1831) proposed an optimistic theory of a dialectically structured historical development that itself was oriented towards a goal. Even if desire more than observation fathered this theory, it must be acknowledged that this 'Hegelian temptation' remains an influential force on all who would (re)-construct 'Heilsgeschichte'. Many still believe that understanding implies organising the development of history based on the logical interaction of its various facets.

The Romantic era focused strongly on the concept of tradition, partly in opposition to the dry terminology of Idealism and Enlightenment, yet partly also in continuation of their focus on the historical. This focus once again elevated the status of the Bible. Tools for differentiated observation and assessment of differing ideologies were developed in the works of Johann Gottfried Herder (1744-1803), to name but one author. He was especially sensitive to the differences between specific peoples and times.[24] On the one hand, his postulate of specific 'ethnic natures' was connected to the strong admiration for the unspoiled, the original, the untouched, the natural. On the other hand, it showed how deeply Romanticism was steeped in the idea of intellectual progress as well as the belief that God's pedagogy could be recognised in the development of history. This focus on the historicity of the text brought the concept of the author to the forefront of interest.

---

[24] A good example of this careful separation of different ethnic traditions is found in Herder's early Romantic work *Stimmen der Völker* (1778/1779).

It was recognised that the intention of every text was determined by an individual living in a specific intellectual and spiritual context. All these great individuals were admired for their genius. Everything dogmatic, all complicated philosophy was rejected in favour of discovering the true life of a pure soul. The most important proponent of this new author-centred hermeneutics was Friedrich Daniel Ernst Schleiermacher (1768-1834).[25] Schleiermacher distinguishes between two basic types of understanding: *grammatical* understanding strives to remove obscurities in the text by means of philological analysis. This analysis can be accomplished and communicated objectively. *Psychological* understanding is of a very different nature. It requires the ability to empathise with the author. A genius can thus only be understood by a comparable intellect. Schleiermacher believed that not all understanding is possible for everyone. Empathic souls do exist, but it is equally possible that a certain author remains a closed book for certain readers. With this concept of congenial understanding as the immersion in the person of the author, Schleiermacher discovered that certain aspects of understanding cannot be described methodologically. He admits that psychological understanding does not result from grammatical analysis or from the combination of historical elements, but only from *guessing* at the individual aspects of a certain author. This element of understanding is highly speculative and depends on uncertain guesswork. It is somewhat comparable to divination and occurs when the reader is capable of immersing herself in the author's entire state of being.[26] All understanding is dependent on the risky business of somehow intuitively grasping the intentions of the author; misunderstanding is common and true understanding the result of careful deliberation about every detail.[27] Understanding requires a sensory organ for meanings and flavours that penetrates all areas of reality. One consequence of this theory is an unavoidable need for specialisation. The lay person cannot understand the Bible – or any valuable literature –easily because the lay person knows little of the soul of the author. It is never enough to reconstruct what can be understood objectively; the subjective must be attained on a psychological level.[28] Schleiermacher separates interpreters into two groups. The one group observes the authors according to their language and history; the other deals more with the observation of the person of the author. In this second group, 'an interpreter will limit himself to those authors that open themselves up most readily to him. And it is also true that these interpreters do not appear frequently in public as their art is not subject to debate and argument. The fruits of their art are enjoyed quietly.'[29]

---

[25] Schleiermacher, F.D.E. (1977), *Hermeneutik und Kritik*. Foreword by M. Frank with an Appendix on the works of Schleiermacher on the philosophy of language, stw 211, Frankfurt.

[26] Ibid., p. 318f.

[27] Ibid., p. 92.

[28] Ibid, p. 93.

[29] Ibid., p. 319.

The fact that the Bible enjoys a special hermeneutical status was emphasised strongly by the Danish philosopher Søren Kierkegaard (1813-1855) in his *Philosophical Fragments* (1844). With his emphasis on the individual, the unique, the personal and concrete, Kierkegaard can justifiably be regarded as the father of existentialist thinking. Driven by strong antisystematic leanings, Kierkegaard pursued the question: 'Who am *I*? How do *I*, as a temporal being, relate to the eternal?' This access to the transcendent and the eternal embodied in Christ cannot be gained through grammatical analysis or historical research. Both of these only produce 'scholarly trained quacks'.[30] Understanding and faith can only be attained by a 'leap'. In this respect, even the disciples of Christ were not in a better hermeneutical situation than subsequent generations. The paradox that the eternal has broken into the temporal, that God is in Christ, that the Nazarene himself is God, this paradox cannot be understood. 'If the student is to receive this truth, then the teacher must bring it to him; but apart from this, the teacher must also bring to him the conditions for understanding this truth.'[31] Understanding is not just intellectual comprehension, neither is it empathic understanding of the author. Understanding is the re-creation of one's existence by God. In continuation of the theories of Pietism, Kierkegaard believed that true understanding of the Bible and of oneself can only occur, if God, by faith, has created a new state of being for the interpreter.

The development of hermeneutics in the academic sphere went in almost diametrical opposition to Kierkegaard. Competing with natural sciences, the humanities were intent on justifying their existence as academic disciplines. Based on his own research, the historian Leopold von Ranke (1795-1886) developed the following three theories: (1) Historical research must be entirely value neutral, the beliefs and values of the historian must be left behind. (2) The historian must give up any personal judgement and only reconstruct 'how it actually occurred'. This leads to four aspects of historical understanding:[32]

- The precise knowledge of historical moments
- The description of personal moments within historical occurrences
- The creation of meaning by placing individual moments within higher contexts
- The discovery of 'leading ideas' as 'ruling tendencies within a given century'.

---

[30] Kierkegaard, S. (1976), *Die Philosophischen Brosamen*, dtv 6064, München.

[31] Ibid., p. 23.

[32] Compare Wach, J. (1933), *Das Verstehen*, Vol. II, Tübingen, p. 112.

(3) Historical research is not a court of criminal justice that must come to value judgments. It is rather the objective observation of large collations of facts.

In his work *Historik. Vorlesungen über Enzyklopädie und Methodoloie der Geschichte*, Johann Gustav Droysen (1808-1884) developed the methodological, systematic and communicative issues of historical science with greater systematic differentiation. The following is held to be true in contrast to the explanatory procedures used in the natural sciences: 'Historical research does not aim to explain, i.e. develop the later from the earlier based on laws which classify certain occurrences as necessary, as mere consequence and development.'[33] After heuristic inquiry has arranged the material and criticism has confirmed its authenticity and brought it into chronological order, interpretation must aim to 'measure the past according to its own standards'.[34] Droysen distinguishes four levels of interpretation: 1. *Pragmatic interpretation* contextualises individual sources, so that selection, analogy and correlation of sources reveal information not gained from an individual source alone. 2. The *interpretation of conditions* explores the parameters of space and time as well as the technical potential of a given period. 3. *Psychological interpretation* depicts great individuals of history in their uniqueness. 4. The *interpretation of ideas* describes varying political and ethical systems and the ideals and ideas of different eras. The goal of all these forms of interpretation is to come very close to specific historical phenomena and understand them from their own perspective. Historical thinking leaves the present and fully immerses itself in the world of the authors.

In close dependence on Schleiermacher, Wilhelm Dilthey (1833-1911) pursued a 'critique of historical reason' (analogous to Kant's 'critique of pure reason'). His basic question was how an individual could objectively understand another individual.[35] Whereas natural science describes natural phenomena, the humanities (or '*Geisteswissenschaften*', a term coined by Dilthey) aim to understand expressions of life that have been fixed in time.[36] The basic principle for such understanding is life itself: the experiences lived through by an author are reflected upon and then put into writing. This form of expression enables another to re-experience what the author has lived through. The triad of experience, expression and understanding is formative for establishing method in the humanities. The definition of understanding as re-living or re-experiencing implies, however, that only the person who has experienced much himself is also capable of understanding the experience of another. Personal experiences necessarily lead to better understanding.

---

[33] Droysen, *Grundriß der Historik*, § 38,339.

[34] Ibid., p. 156.

[35] Birus, H. (ed.) (1982), *Hermeneutische Positionen*, Göttingen 1982, p. 62.

[36] Dilthey, W. (1981), *Der Aufbau der geschichtlichen Welt in den Geisteswissenschaften*, stw 354, Frankfurt, p. 267.

The theologian and philosopher Ernst Troeltsch (1865-1923) is the main representative of this type of historicism within (liberal) theology.[37] In his work *Die Absolutheit des Christentums und die Religionsgeschichte*,[38] he proposed that absolute dogmatic statements are not possible in the sphere of theology. With Schleiermacher and Hegel he believed that revelation (for the western world) was a complex process that began in the Bible and had reached a relative climax with contemporary Christianity. This process of revelation was not fulfilled in Christ, but continued to develop throughout church history and the history of religion. For Troeltsch, understanding was a genetic phenomenon that could be organised around specific developmental lines. A historic method must thus always take precedence over a dogmatic approach.[39]

Martin Heidegger (1889-1976) presented a comprehensive phenomenological analysis of existence in his main work *Sein und Zeit* (1927). An even cursory presentation of this work would exceed the purpose of this book. In rejection of all attempts to bend, shape and deform Heidegger's thought, it must be understood that Heidegger basically pointed out that the human being in his existence is precisely concerned with this existence itself. This direct observation of human nature aims to understand what defines human existence at its core. In his analysis of existence, Heidegger first discovers its 'pre-structure': existence does not develop out of itself, it is not authentic; instead, it is thrown into a world which exists prior to it. Existence cannot choose the time of birth or its place; these are given to it by fate. Each person lives and grows up in a network of interconnectedness, in which everything has already found its interpretation. Things and their functions are already determined before the individual reflects upon them. Prior to all language and logical–rational understanding, human existence lives in a primal, original, pre-reflective, and pre-verbal network of functional connections. Heidegger refers to those items of daily life that we use intuitively as that which is at hand for us ('*das Zuhandene*'). Yet not only items of daily use, even our thinking and feeling are 'communicated' to us through the prior existing interpretation of the world, to which we initially cannot react critically. As the paragraphs 29-34 in *Sein and Zeit* explicate, this means that we must face a primal interpretation of existence prior to all reason and language, a kind a bottom layer of existence that infuses particular things and the world as a whole with meaning. 'All simple observation of that at hand for us ("*das Zuhandene*") prior to predication is already interpretive understanding' (149). Heidegger takes an ambivalent stance towards this primal interpretation and of the world. On the one hand, it is positive because it lays the foundation for who we are. On the other

---

[37] Troeltsch, E. (1922), *Gesammelte Schriften III. Der Historismus und seine Probleme*, Tübingen; Troeltsch, E. (1924), *Der Historismus und seine Überwindung*, Tübingen.

[38] Tübingen 1902 (=Siebenstern TB 138, München and Hamburg 1969).

[39] Troeltsch, E. (1922), 'Über historische und dogmatische Methode in der Theologie (1898)', in Troeltsch, E., *Gesammelte Schriften*, Vol. II, Tübingen, pp. 729-753.

hand, it is a negative seduction into laziness by the 'dictatorship of the "you should"', which can be 'mere talk' and 'non-actualness (*"Uneigentlichkeit"*)'. Existence can attain actualness (*'Eigentlichkeit'*) only by intruding into the underlying primal interpretation. The removal of the self from conventional ways of shaping existence and from the average view of the world is not a simple task and can occur only with pain and the experience of deep insecurity as side effects. A decisive role is played by the conscious awareness of the temporality of existence, caused by the experience of death. The courageous 'running ahead to death' in thought and reason enables the individual to become aware of his mortality, his uniqueness, and his individuality. This discovery also fills the individual with profound fear. How shall he shape his unique existence in the face of the limited time given to him? By deciding between various means of shaping his existence and choosing the one appropriate for him (the 'mine-ness'),[40] existence reaches its actualness. These considerations are not only one-time existential experiences of an individual, but rather the basic structure of every human existence. Heidegger refers to these basic ontological structures as existentials (*'Existentialien'*, such as deliveredness, temporality, fear, running towards death, leap into actualness).

The theologian Rudolf Bultmann (1890-1976) succeeded in systematically combining the approaches of Dilthey and Heidegger. According to Bultmann, the task of hermeutics is not the congenial understanding of a different soul, but rather an understanding of the subject matter important for both the author and reader which underlies any given text. Bultmann postulates that the precondition of all understanding is a focus on the existential relationship between the interpreter and the subject matter contained – directly or indirectly – in the text.[41] 'The interpretation of biblical literature is governed by the same conditions of understanding as the interpretation of any other type of literature. Grammatical interpretation, formal analysis and the explanation of historical context is a necessary first step. From this point on, it is clear that any further understanding is preconditioned by the bond that exists between text and interpreter. This bond is formed by the a priori existential relation between the interpreter and the subject matter conveyed in the text. A precondition of understanding the text is a prior understanding of the subject matter.'[42] The interpreter must bring everything she knows about the subject matter to bear upon her interpretation to produce an interpretation with depth and complexity. The subject matter of the Bible is understanding the human being *sub specie dei*. 'The most "subjective" interpretation becomes the most "objective". The message of the text can only be

---

[40] In German 'die Jemeinigkeit' (J.F.V.).

[41] Bultmann, R. (1952), 'Das Problem der Hermeneutik', in Bultmann, R., *Glauben und Verstehen*, Vol. II, Tübingen, pp. 211-235.

[42] Ibid., p. 231.

heard by the interpreter whose own existence is moved by it.'[43] Bultmann shows, by the example of translating a text from a foreign language, that the translation cannot be successful with out prior knowledge of the subject matter. A second pillar of Bultmann's view of understanding is the importance of the *questions* asked by the interpreter. No text can give answers unless questions are directed at it. Bultmann describes this phenomenon as the goal of questioning (*'das Woraufhin der Befragung'*). Certain questions are appropriate for certain texts, whereas others bypass the intention of a text. The appropriate question aimed at biblical texts (as is the case for all important works of literature) is the question of understanding our own existence. Interpretation of the Bible may thus *never* be reduced to reconstructing prior history or to the interests of psychology or aesthetics. Theology is only true to itself when it pursues the understanding of self, the world, and God articulated in the texts. Critical exegesis of the Bible finds the path along which its questions should be pursued in the understanding of human existence articulated in Scripture.[44] Bultmann introduced the often misconstrued term 'existential interpretation' for this view of understanding.

According to a wide consensus, Hans-Georg Gadamer's (1900-2002) *Truth and Method* is the classic modern textbook of hermeneutics. It has been, and continues to be, an influential contribution to basic research within the humanities. In continuation of issues presented by Schleiermacher and Kierkegaard, Gadamer pursues the following: 'I am concerned with examining experiences of truth that exceed the controlling mechanisms of scientific method wherever they occur, in order to test their legitimacy' (XXVII). He attempts a phenomenological analysis of the process of understanding as it actually occurs, with the aim of restoring the true scope of truth which had been reduced by the self-deceiving methodological monism within positivistic and historical sciences. Based on examples within art and play, Gadamer crystallises basic elements of understanding which cannot be grasped by method: all understanding is necessarily based on experiences which are prior to it. These experiences are most often subconscious and rooted in historically conditioned prejudice. This prejudice (or pre-judgement) – in opposition to the Enlightenment prejudice against prejudice – is not always a false judgement. On the contrary, each prejudice that determines our current thinking had to survive a long traditional filtering process in order to survive up to the present. The primary hermeneutical importance of temporal distance lies in its filtering function. We consider as 'classic' only what has survived the test of time. The fact that certain prejudices are (subconsciously) elevated to universal statements of truth is not the result of stupidity, intellectual laziness, or blind obedience to authority, but rooted in the appropriateness of a prejudice that has repeatedly been judged to be correct. We consequently must view contemporary understanding as a result of tradition. This emphasis on tradition views

---

[43] Ibid., p. 230.
[44] Ibid., p. 232.

understanding as the overlapping of one's own horizon of understanding with tradition. Understanding is immersion into a process of tradition. The interpreter cannot keep his distance when two horizons meet in the act of interpretation. Applying what has been understood to the person of the interpreter is itself basic to understanding. This hermeneutical axiom is especially true in the areas of law and theology. The meeting of different horizons is best exemplified by means of dialogue, especially in the shape of a Platonic exchange of question and answer. Understanding a text involves letting the text speak and present its subject matter. Only an intensive dialogue between text and interpreter can lead to the paradigm shift where the text suddenly starts asking the questions and the interpreter sees himself as the one being questioned. Gadamer continually emphasises the importance of language for the process of understanding. Being that can be understood is language. Every interpreter must be aware that his language and thus his entire worldview is embedded in a long process of tradition. Interpretation can only reach below the surface, if it is aware of the history of effect (*Wirkungsgeschichte*), if it considers the power of non-rational prejudice.

Two hermeneutical models were created in opposition to approaches focusing on the conscious intention of the author. Karl Marx (1818-1883) proposed a theory in opposition to Hegel's Idealism according to which personal intention is determined by materialistic circumstance. Economic conditions determine intellectual and spiritual production. Philosophy, religion and art are merely ideological 'superstructures' of economic realities. Understanding requires a critical description of the *material* interests articulated by a text. The determinative factor for any intellectual production is its function in the ideological stabilising of an existing system of ownership, government and labour conditions. This function must be subjected to rigorous ideological criticism in order to bring these material interests to light. Even though the ideology to which he is bound may not be clear to the author himself, historic–materialistic interpretation is capable of unpacking the economical roots of various statements in the text. Understanding the text is not just a matter of analysis; understanding involves societal and economic change. In the eleventh of his *Theses on Feuerbach* Marx states: 'Philosophers have only interpreted the world in different ways. The primary task is to change it.' In this view, the Bible may not remain the 'opium of the people'. Interpretation must shed light on its ideological function. In extension of the theories proposed by Marx and Engels, Ernst Bloch (1885-1977) emphasised that the Bible contains many impulses for changing the world.[45] The light of the Exodus that began to shine for the people of Israel still shines in order to lead us out of all forms of slavery and oppression. In the end it will even lead us out of God. Changing the world according to the vision in the Bible, especially the Old Testament, is a central element of his 'principle of hope' (*Das Prinzip Hoffnung*).

---

[45] *Das Prinzip Hoffnung*, Frankfurt 1959; *Atheismus im Christentum*, Frankfurt 1973.

Sigmund Freud (1856-1939) opposed the conscious intention of an author from a very different angle. He argued that a plethora of unconscious motives are part of both the production as well as the interpretation of texts. According to Freud, the basic problem confronting every human being is a tragic subjection to fear. Adult experience is preconditioned by subconscious experiences in earliest childhood. Already at birth, human beings are confronted with life-threatening experiences and the fear of death. Freud structures our personality into three aspects: the *superego* (comparable to our conscience), the *ego* (our conscious self), and the *id* (our unconscious drives and chaotic desires). This polarisation of the person is the unavoidable source of fear. Permanent frustration is caused by the limitations placed upon the *id* by the *superego*, especially in the area of sexual desire. This permanent conflict and the frustration it causes produces fear that is met by a series of defensive mechanisms such as dreams,[46] daily pathologies (e.g. thumb-sucking, bed-wetting, or obsessive washing), or sublimation by culturally recognized accomplishments (such as writing books). Other defences against fear are humour, repression, personality splitting, transfer of desires onto others, or regression. Freud believes that every text contains traces of these defensive mechanisms. For him, understanding thus (a) uncovers those elements within a text that lead to or increase fear; (b) recognises sexual implications of a text; (c) analyses the elements of earliest childhood experience in the text.[47] Freud uses this approach also for the Bible, which he examines according to its subconscious influences and its dealings with the libido and with fear.

The sociological contribution by Marx and the psychoanalytical contribution by Freud are combined in the so-called 'Frankfurter Schule'. The main representatives of its 'critical theory' are Max Horkheimer (1895-1973), Theodor W. Adorno (1903-1969), Herbert Marcuse (1898-1979), and Jürgen Habermas (b.1929). The 'critical theory' profiles itself in its harsh criticism of all authority. Society as a whole is seen as a kind of macro-soul. Just as the individual must deal with frustration and fear generated by the conflict of the *id* and the *superego*, society must deal with the problem of conflicting interest-groups. The societal *superego* is

---

[46] Dreams play a central role in psychoanalysis. As the 'via regia', they show most clearly the true desires of the subconscious. Most dreams are coded and much work is necessary to decipher the various symbols in order to decode what seems chaotic on the surface.

[47] Freud distinguishes three developmental stages from the ages 1-6 according to the organ that guarantees the highest amount of satisfaction: the oral phase (1st year), during which the mouth through sucking and eating conveys the most pleasure; the anal phase, during which the intentional closure of the sphincter, the holding back or the letting go of faces controls pleasure; finally, the phallic phase, during which the primary sexual organs, the penis and the vagina, move to the centre of pleasure. Experiences during these first six years determine much of the remaining life span. The decisive moments for human thinking feeling are thus located at a time during which the individual has no control over them. Every growing human being is more tragic victim that intentional actor.

represented by intellectuals, judges, or various church representatives. They clash with members of the societal *id*, embodied in rock groups or avant-garde artists. The average citizen represents the societal *ego*, which must mediate between the demands of these two groups. These groups are separated by communicational barriers and defensive mechanisms that are structurally analogous to those described by Freud for the individual. The dialectical goal must be the creation of a society in which all groups are led to an open dialogue without authoritative demands of one group upon another. This goal implies radical ideological critique, but also sexual liberation. Interpreting the Bible within the parameters of the 'Frankfurter Schule' would mean a study of the personal and social context of biblical authors as well as the ideological use to which the Bible is put in contemporary society. The goal of this study would be the elimination of barriers created by the Bible that inhibit the possibility of open dialogue.

The hermeneutical approaches discussed so far have been concerned with understanding the text by understanding factors *behind* the text (the psychology of the author, the economic circumstances, the prejudices and traditions of its time, etc.). A different approach arose during the mid 1950s that was concerned primarily with understanding the *text as text*. Rooted in French structuralism as well as German work-immanent approaches, the opinion arose that true and intersubjectively communicable understanding could only be possible through total immersion in the world designed by the text. Within this paradigm, it was a mistake to leave the world of the text in order to examine the world of the author, the reader, or even the subject matter, especially as these approaches are always burdened by a high degree of subjective speculation. Every text designs its own world, or – according to the late work of Ludwig Wittgenstein (1889-1951) – its own language game. Understanding must limit itself to the discovery of textual structure and the recognition of its linguistic rules and retrace the details of the world designed by the text, instead of creating highly speculative hypotheses with questionable legitimacy. The central position of the 'text and its world' is found within linguistics, structuralism, semiotics, new literary criticism or rhetorical criticism.

Another important hermeneutical approach has developed in the past 30 years. Recipient-oriented literary studies have redirected the focus of hermeneutical discussion. Whereas earlier hermeneutic tendencies focused primarily on the *intentio auctoris* or the *intentio operis*, this new approach emphasises the importance of the *reader* for the process of understanding. Some see in this paradigm shift a movement from literary studies to a science of communication.[48] A main representative of this movement is Umberto Eco (b. 1932) in his two books *The open text* (1962) and *Lector in fabula* (1987). He observes the text-pragmatic

---

[48] Dohmen, Ch. (1996), *Hermeneutik der Jüdischen Bibel und des christlichen Alten Testaments*, Stuttgart, p. 193.

fact that each text is necessarily filled with gaps that must be filled.[49] Each statement contains semantic obscurities, grey areas and ambiguities that must be 'fixed' by the reader. Eco speaks of dis-ambiguing ambiguity as the task of every reader. He shows this ambiguity with a host of wonderful examples: 'Carlo has intercourse twice a week with his wife. So does Luigi.'[50] As soon as an author has produced a text, this text leads a quasi independent existence. The author has no control over the exact degree to which his statements are clear or ambiguous, leaving room for the role of the reader. Every text reaches a point, where the cooperation of the reader is no longer guided by text. Interpretation, instead, *must* become a free adventure.[51] In the postscript to his book *The Name of the Rose*, Eco states:

> Nothing pleases an author more than discovering readings that he had never considered himself, but which were communicated to him by his readers. When I wrote theoretical works I reacted towards critics as a judge: I examined whether the critic had understood me and judged accordingly. Things are quite different with a novel. An author of a novel can indeed encounter readings which he finds odd, but he must remain silent and leave it to others to refute such readings by means of the text. The vast majority of readings, however, reveal new and exciting connections that were never thought of while writing the work. What does this mean? ... It is unimportant what I say after writing the text, the text itself exists and produces its own meanings ... The author should have the grace to pass away after writing the book, so that he would not disturb the momentum contained in the text.[52]

'A narrator may not interpret his own work. If he does, he has not written a novel. A novel is a machine for the production of interpretations.'[53] Here we find a certain correspondence between Eco and Augustine: The intention of the author is no longer of primary interest; a richness of interpretative possibility is built into the text and intended by it.

The resulting plurality and the divergence of possible understandings (also in regard to biblical texts) is reflected philosophically within so-called postmodern thinking. Basic to postmodern hermeneutics is the conviction that a single text *must* produce different meanings in different discursive settings without the possibility of determining the correct meaning. Jean-François Lyotard (b. 1924): 'A debate (French: *différend*), in contrast to a legal argument ... would be a conflict between two or more parties that could not be decided, as there is no common criteria by which to assess both sides of the debate legitimately. If one applies the same criteria to both, turning the debate into a legal argument, one does injustice to at least one of the parties ... This injustice results from the difference between the

---

[49] Eco, U. (1987), *Lector in fabula*, München, p. 63.

[50] Ibid., p. 110.

[51] Ibid., p. 71.

[52] Postscript to *The name of the Rose* (1984), Münech, pp. 11-14.

[53] Ibid., p.10.

rules of discourse which one uses to judge and the rules of discourse of that which is judged. The title of this book [*The debate*, M.O.] implies that we do not have criteria of judgement that apply to different types of discourse.'[54] A hermeneutics influenced by a recipient-oriented approach must live with the absence of universal criteria of right and wrong in a postmodern setting. In the extreme, we end up in a situation where the world of interpretation dissolves into many different worlds that are no longer able to communicate with each other. As with Leibniz, individuals are seen as windowless monads; however, the pre-stabilised harmony that Leibniz still guaranteed is lost and replaced by radical pluralism. The correct interpretation no longer exists. Never-ending interpretation and limitless semiotics arise in its place.[55]

An analysis of our contemporary situation based on this brief sketch of philosophical hermeneutics reveals three main tendencies:

■   A growing plurality of methods: many different hermeneutical concepts exist side by side. The history of hermeneutics has not led to a final resolution. Every old theory *mutatis mutandis* still has adherents and defendants. Various methods face off with strong antagonism; the representatives of each method view each other as members of enemy camps and find it difficult to communicate with each other. This pluralistic state of affairs can be understood according to the hermeneutical square as isolated emphasis on one of the four corners: author, text, reader, or subject matter. Any combination of these four aspects occurs as well. The consequences of cementing this plurality in 'schools' cannot be underestimated.

■   A growing plurality of meanings: the medieval teaching of a four-fold meaning of Scripture was reduced to meaning as historical meaning; the modern era, however, has returned to multiple meanings far in excess of the number four. Postmodern thinking is in agreement on the theory of a never-ending semiotics. The existence of numerous and highly varied models confronts us today not with a fullness of meaning but with a flood of meanings.[56]

■   The loss of the objective: hermeneutics began by claiming to make correct statements about objects (Aristotle). In contrast, the contemporary discussion seems to question more and more the mere existence of such

---

[54] Lyotard, J.-F. (1989), *Der Widerstreit*, München, p. 9.

[55] Eco finds it difficult to limit this arbitrariness, which appears as a result of his theory. He attempts it more by humour and irony than by methodologically clear argument (Eco, U. (1992), 'Unbergrenzte Semiose und Abdrift', in U. Eco, *Die Grenzen der Interpretation*, München and Wien, pp. 425-441).

[56] This flood of meanings has truly biblical proportions. The German word 'Sinnflut' ('flood of meanings') is also the proper term for the biblical Flood described in Gen 6-8 (J.F.V.).

correct statements. Objective interpretation and the precise meaning of a certain statement are becoming more and more ghosts of the past. Subjective interpretation is credited with ever more truth-content; the concept of the *one* truth as a regulating guideline for studies in the humanities is losing ground quickly. In its place, pluralistic models of truth and understanding appear along with their 'language games' and a plurality of discursive possibilities.

Biblical hermeneutics is closely tied to this general intellectual development; movements within philosophical hermeneutics influence biblical hermeneutics more or less directly. One of the tasks of theology is the explication of biblical statements to contemporary readers. Theology must therefore take these contemporary intellectual precedents into consideration. With the help of the hermeneutical square, we can classify and present the plethora of approaches to the Bible.

PART II:
The Plurality of Current Approaches to the Bible

Chapter 4

Methods Focused on Authors and their Worlds

a) The Historical–Critical Method

A) The historical–critical method of interpreting the Bible is one of the prime achievements of academic theology. In its century-long history, is has been differentiated into many sub-groups and individual approaches. The historical–critical method is the academic standard which every student of theology in an academic setting must learn. Academic interpretation of the Bible is almost synonymous with historical–critical interpretation. This book cannot do justice to the complexity of this approach; however, a brief sketch of its various tools can give a good impression of its goals and its character.

The tools of biblical exegesis result from a combination of different impulses: Humanism, Renaissance and Pietism sound the call: *Ad fontes*! Back to the sources, i.e. back to the Bible in its original languages and manuscripts. Systematic studies of the many manuscripts revealed important variations of content; grammatical philology uncovered important differences between the historical meaning of the text and church dogma. The Reformation was made possible partially due to these discoveries. Rationalism and Enlightenment contribute a critical scepticism towards miracles and the doctrine of inspiration; from their time on, the Bible could no longer be seen as a work of God, fallen from heaven, but rather as a very earthly product of human creativity. Romanticism gave us the admiration of the individual genius, as well as a fascination with beginnings, with the original and the unspoiled. Scientific discussion in the field of historicism provided biblical interpretation with a high ideal of objectivity: the interpreter must distance himself from any personal judgement, must humbly draw close to the strange world of the author. The interpreter must become the advocate of the author and defend his 'otherness', his difference and non-identity with the present. Before entering the deep well of the past, the readers must rid themselves of all things that define their contemporary existence; dogmatic or moral attitudes only discolour and prevent the comprehension of historical truth. Biblical and historical events must be respected in their uniqueness and the interpreter may not draw any direct conclusions from the past for the present. The abyss of history must be accepted as a fact. Interpreters must not only be critical of easy applications of the text; they must also inquire critically whether the text itself reports historical facts correctly. Exegesis is required to maintain close ties to historical disciplines such as historical science, sociology, comparative religious studies and archaeology.

A synthesis of these elements within the discipline of theology (Protestant theology at first, Catholic theology also from the 20th century on) had the paradoxical effect of creating a critical distance to one of the foundations of theology, namely the Bible. This methodological approach thus produces a host of dogmatic problems.[57]

B) The goal of this method is the recovery of the *original* meaning each text had at the time when it was written. To understand the Bible is to understand the intention of the human author within his own world, using tools common to academic disciplines outside of theology. In order to reach this goal, the historical-critical method has developed several procedures in the last 200 years, many of which were taken from other historical–philological disciplines.[58]

B1) Like all other texts prior to the invention of the printing press, the Bible in antiquity was copied by hand. A vast number of handwritten manuscripts exist from the 4th to the 5th century A.D. (prior to this time, the manuscripts are largely fragmentary and concentrated in the Qumran findings). This textual tradition is not uniform, not even for central passages. The various translations of the biblical texts from their original languages into the respective *lingua franca* (Aramaic, Greek, Syriac, Latin etc.) are highly divergent, leading to the speculation that the translations were based on differing Hebrew or Greek originals. It is the task of *textual criticism* to sift through all the variants in order to determine the oldest text upon which all others are based.[59] Critical editions of the biblical text gather the main textual variants in a so-called critical apparatus. Modern translations used in church and liturgy can thus be checked against their textual basis.

C1) Examples: The vast majority of variants concern minor details. They are the result of errors in reading, hearing, or writing caused by similar letters at the

---

[57] Compare the works of Ebeling, G. (1963) and Söding, Th. (1995) listed in the bibliography.

[58] The following overview is based on Steck, O.H. (1993), *Exegese des Alten Testaments. Leitfaden der Methodik*, Neukirchen-Vluyn; for other summaries of this method see bibliography.

[59] The exact purpose of textual criticism is meanwhile a matter of debate: is the goal of textual criticism the text that was declared sacred and canonical by church and synagogue between 300 B.C. and A.D. 300? (Compare Childs, B.S. (1985), *The Old Testament as Scripture*, London, pp. 84-106, and Tov, E. (1997), *Der Text der Hebräischen Bibel. Handbuch der Textkritik*, Stuttgart, pp. 239-242. Both authors attempt to reconstruct the *one* text that stands at the end of the creative process and at the beginning of textual tradition.) Or should each case be decided individually by determining which variant most probably gave rise to all others? (For the majority of exegetes, compare Würthwein, E. (1988), *Der Text des Alten Testaments*, Stuttgart, pp. 116-118.

beginning or the end of words, the influence of parallel passages, or incorrect separation of syllables. Several variants, however, signal difficulties with the content of the text that may have provoked a deliberate change. In Exod 3:14, the God of Israel reveals himself according to the masoretic text with the name: 'I am who I am'. The Greek version of this passage in the Septuagint (abbr. LXX) reads 'I am THE BEING', the Aramaic tradition reads: 'I am the God, who created heaven and earth.' According to two basic rules of textual criticism, *lectio brevior probabilior* and *lectio difficilior probabilior* (the shorter and the more difficult text is the more probable text), the more difficult, even enigmatic, Hebrew text must take precedence. The Greek translation connects the God in the burning bush to ontological questions in an attempt to make him more attractive to Greek readers. The Aramaic translation simplifies the text, placing the universal creator-God in the desert bush.

In 1 Cor 15:51, important textual witnesses read: 'Listen, I will tell you a mystery! We *all* will *not* die, but we will all be changed.' Other major witnesses read: 'We will *not all* die, but we will all be changed' or 'We all will die, but we all will be changed', and finally, 'We all will die, but *not all* will be changed.'[60] What was the mystery that Paul conveyed to the Corinthians? The most difficult version is the statement that no one will die because the coming of Christ is part of the immediate future. Everyone will be changed into a new form of being with Christ's coming. Many interpreters believe this general statement to be difficult and thus impossible for all times. They instead propose that Paul counted on personally witnessing Christ's coming (compare 1 Thess 4:17). This expectation was proven incorrect with the death of Paul. In order to counteract this mistake, later scribes changed the text by omitting the negation (all not, not all) before 'die'. The second part of the statement was then changed by inserting the negation before the number of people who will participate in the eschatological transformation that will occur after the resurrection of the dead (all, not all, all of us Christians). These examples can also show that and why text critical judgements cannot be made with final certainty. Formal arguments are almost always combined with arguments based on the prior theological judgements made by respective interpreters. A famous opus magnum of *textual criticism* thus proceeded by gathering a team of specialists and simply voting on the most probable variant.[61]

B2) As soon as the text-critical decisions have been made (this is already an important part of academic work), we continue with the questions directed at the text by *literary criticism*: the text is examined according to its structure, its inner consistency and logical coherence in order to determine whether the text is a

---

[60] A listing and a discussion of these variants appears in Conzelmann, H. (1969), *Der erste Brief an die Kornither*, KEK V, Göttingen, p. 344 note 1.

[61] Barthélemy, D. (1982ff), *Critique Textuelle de l'Ancien Testament*, OBO 50/1-4, Fribourg.

literary unit or a composite of different redactional layers. The last 150 years of textual exegesis have shown that many biblical texts are not written by one author, but are rather put together by several authors; the Bible is more the product of tradition than the product of an author. The current dissection of the text into its primary layer and its successive expansions reaches into individual verses and even single words. Based on the results of literary criticism, texts are dated and connected to specific authors or author-groups. The final result of this work is a detailed picture of the history of biblical literature from its beginnings to its final form. These are then presented in 'Introductions' to the Old and New Testaments. There is a high degree of debate and argument concerning this history, from the exact dissection of individual texts to their final chronological constellation. Conservative authors believe that most of the biblical material is old and the product of the authors identified by the texts. In contrast, more critical scholars believe that large parts of the text are secondary material introduced by anonymous authors at a later stage. Yet the work of even the most critical scholars can result in texts that are old and authentic; the distinction between conservative and critical should be subordinated to the arguments made in each particular case.

C2) The flood narrative in Gen 6:5-8:22 contains several doublings, some of which contradict each other (according to Gen 6:19 the animals number one pair, according to 7:2 seven pairs; the flood itself lasts 40 days and nights according to 7:12, yet 150 days according to 7:24 along with other examples). The text also uses different names for God (Yahweh and Elohim). The coincidence of the change in divine name with a change in style, worldview and theology has led to the hypothesis that two originally independent sources with their own unique recognisable features have been combined by one or several redactors.[62]

Literary criticism has further argued that different layers exist not only in the Pentateuch, but also in almost every biblical book.[63] The prophetic books are thus not the product of the prophets identified by name in the title. These prophets contributed only the basic layer to these books. The rest, which some scholars consider to be the majority of the text, was added by many different redactors over several centuries. The wisdom books – such as Job – show that old texts were continually combined with new ideas. Even the Psalms show traces of later additions. The same is true for the New Testament. The gospels are the result of a combination of sources, i.e. the 'Sayings-Source' Q that collected the sayings of

---

[62] A source analysis showing the individual strands and their own inner coherence is found, for example, in Schmid, H.H. (1970), *Die Steine und das Wort*, Zürich, pp. 50-57.

[63] A helpful introduction to these studies is found in Schwager, H. (1968; 1970), *Die Schriften der Bibel literaturgeschichtlich geordnet. Vol. I: Vom Thronfolgebuch bis zur Priesterschrift; Vol. II: Von der Denkschrift Nehemias bis zu den Pastoralbriefen*, Stuttgart and München; or Smend, R. (1967), *Biblische Zeugnisse. Literatur des alten Israel*, Frankfurt.

the historical Jesus, or the 'Signs-Source' which gathered the miracles of Jesus as a basis for the Gospel according to John. These sources were combined with Marcan material and passages unique to each gospel. The book of Acts is also not a literary unit. Even the Pauline epistles show traces of combining several letters.[64] The various hypotheses postulating various models of textual growth differ greatly from each other, which should come as no surprise considering the style of the biblical texts.

In 1 Cor 14:32-35 we find embedded in the context of exhortations to peace and harmony a sharply worded attack against women:

> And the spirits of prophets are subject to the prophets,
> for God is a God not of disorder but of peace. As in all the churches of the saints,
> women should be silent in the churches. For they are not permitted to speak, but should be subordinate, as the law also says.
> If there is anything they desire to know, let them ask their husbands at home. For it is shameful for a woman to speak in church.

The passage stands without parallel in the context of Pauline thinking. In 1 Cor 11:2-16, Paul obviously allows women to pray and prophesy publicly (11:5); he only requires them to cover their heads. And in Gal 3:28 he clearly states:

> There is no longer Jew or Greek, there is no longer slave or free, there is no longer male and female; for all of you are one in Christ Jesus.

We can thus speculate that the passage in 1 Cor 14 is an interpolation which uses the authority of Paul to promote sexist attitudes. Or should we assume that this passage is an original Pauline text – after all, it fits the flow of the context very well – in which Paul fails to consistently uphold his revolutionary theology in the face of external pressures (perhaps an agitation within the congregation initiated by certain militant Corinthian women), falling back into patriarchal structures of thinking? Or was Paul merely overtired and in a bad mood?

B3) Once literary criticism has separated the individual strands of a text, these literary units may still contain elements of tension. In these cases we can assume that these literary units themselves show traces of their own prior history. The *history of oral transmission* (*Überlieferungsgeschichte*) tries to explain tensions within literary units by referring back to the prior oral history of the text. Hypotheses taking this element into consideration can be of great assistance in explaining certain elements in the text.

---

[64] Compare Schmithals, W. (1996), 'Methodische Erwägungen zur Literarkritik der Paulusbriefe', in *ZNW* 87, pp. 51-82.

C3) The Elijah traditions in 1 Kings 17 to 2 Kings 2 show a strange alternation in the identification of Elijah's opponents. He is attacked by the king, the entire people, the prophets of Baal, or Queen Jezebel. It would be possible to separate the text on a literary level and postulate written texts to be dated in different eras.[65] It is also possible look for an answer to this question in the history of oral transmission[66] which reflect changing external circumstances in the 9th century, in which the oldest Elijah traditions originated: During his reign (ca. 874-853), king Ahab was Elijah's 'enemy' (1 Kings 21:19). Following the brief reign of Ahaziah (ca. 853-852), Queen Jezebel ruled in the role of the king's mother (ca. 852-842); now the 'enemy' shifts onto this foreign protector of the Baal cult. In the end, the people of Israel as a whole become Elijah's enemy, reflecting the failure of the Elijah movement during the reign of Joram (ca. 848-845). The development of history thus has a formative influence on the creation and oral transmission of the Elijah material.

B4) Redaction criticism builds on literary ciriticism and the history of oral transmission. It pursues the question of the theological and historical relation between the various textual layers of a book or between different books and asks whether different expansions of the text can be credited to the same redactional group or school (such as the wisdom or deuteronomistic movement). Literary criticism focuses on the dissection of texts, redaction criticism focuses on the combination of texts and analyses their linguistic and theological profiles.

C4) The book of Jeremiah shows close ties to Deuteronomy, especially in its prose speeches. These ties led earlier scholars to believe that Jeremiah was involved in the authorship of Deuteronomy. W. Thiel has shown, instead, that a deuteronomistic redaction can be seen in all of Jeremiah as well as in other prophetic books.[67] Whereas, for example, the authentic Jeremiah preaches the impossibility of repentance and the irreversibility of divine judgement over Judah (13:23; 4:22; 6:10), the deuteronomic redactor re-interpreted this radical divine judgement as a pedagogical tool to shake up and wake up Israel: 'At one moment I may declare concerning a nation or a kingdom, that I will pluck up and break down and destroy it' (Jer 18:7; compare 26:3; 36:3).[68] In this manner, the intention of Jeremiah is changed dramatically.

---

[65] See Würthwein, E. (1984), *Das Buch der Könige*, ATD 11,2, Göttingen.

[66] See Steck, O.H. (1968), *Überlieferung und Zeitgeschehen in den Elia-Erzählungen*, WMANT 26, Neukirchen, Oeming, M. (1906), 'Naboth, der Jesreeliter. Untersuchungen zu den theologischen Motiven der Überlieferungsgeschichte von 1 Reg 21', in *ZAW* 98, pp. 362-382.

[67] See also Schmidt, W.H. (1965), 'Die deuteronomistische Redaktion des Amos-Buches. Zu den theologischen Unterschieden zwischen dem Prophetenwort und seinem Sammler', *ZAW* 77, pp. 168-193.

[68] Compare Graupner, A. (1993) '*sub* (repent)', in *ThWAT* VII, pp. 1147-1151.

The Gospel of John stands for an eschatology based not in the future, but seen in the present where true life exists and judgement has already occurred.[69] As a consequence, the sacraments play a subordinate role. The synoptic narration of the Lord's supper is replaced by a foot-washing (John 13) and a long farewell speech (14-17). In contrast, other passages in John retain a futuristic eschatology with divine judgement at the end of time (5:28f.), as well as a 'normal' presentation of the sacraments (6:51-58). This tension within the Gospel of John is best explained by assuming different textual layers with varying theologies: the basic layer of the gospel taught the meaning and importance of the present decision for, and acceptance of the faith. A later ecclesiastical redaction[70] expanded the text by elevating the importance of the sacraments for the future and thus made the book acceptable for the canon.

B5) From the middle of the 20th century, sociology sharpened our focus for the concrete social context into which texts must be placed. By examining the institutions and situations in which a certain social group would have used a text (the so-called '*Sitz im Leben*' of a text), the real-life function of a text becomes an aid in our understanding of the interaction between linguistic shape and social meaning. *Form history* is thus concerned with the contextualisation of texts within specific social settings.

C5) Understanding the Psalms, for example, involves the reconstruction of various liturgical settings[71] in which a certain prayer or song may have been used: the enthronement of a king (Psalm 2), services of lament during the exile (Psalm 137), thanksgiving services at night under an open sky (Psalm 8), devotional services at a sickbed far from the temple, administered by special religious leaders (Psalm 22), political evening services attended by members of the lower class as protest against the establishment (Psalm 12; 14) and many others. The unique genre of the gospels was also explained by the special needs of early Christian mission work. A hypothesis sees them as a collection of ideas or sketches for sermons, which specific missionaries would have to flesh out according to the particular needs of a congregation.[72]

B6) Tradition history concentrates on ideas and thematic networks in the Bible, examining their theological content and interaction. In this case, understanding is networking.

---

[69] 'Very truly, I tell you, anyone who hears my word and believes him who sent me has eternal life, and does not come under judgement, but has passed from death to life' (John 5:24; compare 3:16–18).

[70] See Bultmann, R. (1986), *Das Evangelium des Johannes*, KEK II, Göttingen, Index p. 560, *sub verbo*: Redaktion, kirchliche.

[71] Mowinckel, S. (1992), *Psalms in Israel's worship*, ND Sheffield.

[72] Dibelius, M. (1919), *Die Formgeschichte des Evangeliums*, Tübingen.

C6) Lev 16 describes the ritual for a great day of reconciliation. Two male goats become the object of a ritual of atonement. By placing his hand on one of the goats, the priest confesses Israel's sin. The goat is then cast out, metaphorically carrying Israel's sin into the desert (Lev 16:21). The other goat and the young bull are sacrificed, their blood cleansing Israel from sin. There is no consensus on the exact interpretation of this ritual. Perhaps the point is the substitutionary giving of life: in the ritual laying on of hands, the animal is identified with the individuals enacting the sacrifice. The people who had lost their life because of their sin are allowed to live again without sin because of the sacrifice. By means of this atonement, the grace of God granted salvation so that human beings could live again despite sin and transgression. This complex theology of sacrifice and atonement is transferred in Isaiah 53 to the suffering of a human being: 'Surely he has borne our infirmities and carried our deseases; yet we accounted him stricken, struck down by God, and afflicted. But he was wounded for our transgressions, crushed for our iniquities; upon him was the punishment that made us whole, and by his bruises we are healed ... Yet it was the will of the LORD to crush him with pain. When you make his life an offering for sin, he shall prolong his days; through him the will of the LORD shall prosper.' (Isa 53:4f.10). This basic idea, as a growing tradition, is then used in the New Testament to interpret the suffering and resurrection of Christ as well as the Eucharist (i.e. Matt 8:17; 26:28; 27:12,38; Rom 4:25; 1 Pet 2:21-25).[73]

B7) Through intensive study of semantic fields, supported in recent years by computer software, individual *word studies* have become ever more precise and refined. The semantic clarity of biblical languages is growing.

C7) Exegesis of the Old and the New Testaments is supported today by several large theological dictionaries that unpack the specifics of biblical languages.[74] Similar terms often show specific differences despite their similarity in meaning. 'Justice' in the Old Testament, for example, is not a virtue that allows every person to receive what he or she deserves (*iustitia distributiva*), but rather a communal code of conduct. Justice thus does not refer to an individual insistence on rights and privileges, but rather to the establishment of a common good. The protection of the weak and the needy is of special importance, as these groups have no means of ensuring their own rights. Justice is thus strongly connected to terms such as 'solidarity', 'helpfulness', or 'compassion'. Theologically speaking, divine justice can mean exactly the opposite of *iustitia distributiva*. God grants the gift of salvation *(iustitia salutifera)* to those who can expect nothing but punishment for

---

[73] See Janowski, B.B. (1993), *Gottes Gegenwart in Israel*, Neukirchen.

[74] *Theologisches Wörterbuch zum AT*, ed. Botterweck, Fabry and Ringgren (1970ff.); *Theologisches Handwörterbuch zum AT*, ed. Jenni and Westermann (1971); *Theologisches Wörterbuch zum NT*, ed. Kittel and Friederich (1933ff); *Exegetisches Wörterbuch zum NT*, ed. Balz (1978ff).

their sins. This is the gospel of Jesus' sacrificial death for our sins, 'For in it the righteousness of God is revealed through faith for faith; as it is written, "The one who is righteous will live by faith"' (Rom 1:17). 'If, because of the one man's trespass, death exercised dominion through that one, much more surely will those who receive the abundance of grace and the free gift of righteousness exercise dominion in life through the one man, Jesus Christ' (Rom 5:17).

B8) Due to intensive research on the history of Palestine and the historical environment of the Bible, we are capable of describing the *historical context* of the texts in detail, even if certain time periods remain largely in the dark (this is especially true for the early monarchy and the Persian era). In this context, we must clearly distinguish the context of the original text and the changing contexts of various textual redactions and expansions. The historical context does not refer to the historical location of the desk on which the text was written; it refers instead to the collection of every historical fact that is relevant for understanding the text. This includes archaeological data as well as insights from the history of religion.

C8) The importance of the respective historical context for understanding any text is so obvious and evident that I will refrain from giving any examples at this point and refer instead to the varied and rich literature produced by biblical scholarship in this area.[75]

B9) A concluding *interpretative summary* gathers the results of the individual approaches described above. Methods asking questions beyond the immediate structure of the text are now compiled in such a manner as to illuminate the intention of the text, the *intentio recta*. An attempt is made to read the text with the eyes of the author(s) as well as those of the (changing) readers.

C9) What was Paul's intention in writing his epistle to the Romans? This text was definitely not produced to provide us with an object on which to perform exercises in textual criticism, style analysis, or literary criticism. The main goal is not the determination of its *Sitz im Leben*, various elements of tradition and theological context, the historical context of the Apostle or the exact semantics of individual words. We are called instead to proclaim the gospel of justification by faith and to draw the consequences from this gospel. The individual methods help us to better understand the details of this Pauline gospel; the interpretative summary, however, must clearly articulate Paul's main concern in writing the epistle.

D) The historical–critical methods have uncovered a wealth of new information about the Bible. We can now work with an amazing insight into the authors' worlds. These scholarly achievements deserve our highest respect. This scientific approach to the biblical texts meets the needs of a modern, rationalistic age. Free from dogmatic constraints, these methods examine the Bible with an array of

---

[75] See Gunneweg, A.H.J. (1989), *Geschichte Israels. Von den Anfängen bis Bar Kochba und von Theodor Herzl bis zur Gegenwart*, Stuttgart, and many others.

scholarly tools. By interpreting the Bible *etsi deus non daretur*, these methods comply with the modern autonomy of reason. They are involved in a discourse with an atheistic world on the basis of history. In the face of a global rejection of the Bible as fairytale, lie, illusion or priestly propaganda, they differentiate between historical certainty and probability, between fact and creed. They also remove from the texts the burden of being something they were never intended to be: factual reports. The Bible is kerygma, a profession of faith written by human beings in different historical situations. The historical–critical method has opened our eyes to the fact that the texts of the Old and the New Testaments have been shaped by a long process of growth and tradition. Understanding this process is of great help in understanding the texts. The high intellectual sincerity of the historical-critical methods as well its continuing courage to ask questions have rooted the biblical texts in honest exegesis. A precise analysis of varying theological concepts within the Bible protects its texts from dogmatic simplification and reinforces the breadth and the depth of the Word of God. The historical–critical method especially protects the Bible from being monopolised by fundamentalism.

On the other hand, these indisputable achievements have paid a high price by introducing a host of new dangers. The confusing array of different methodological tendencies and an avalanche of secondary literature on almost every detail of the Bible have created a highly ambivalent state of affairs. No single person can truly stay on top of what has been and is being written. The entire academic enterprise leads to a high degree of insecurity. Theologians not specializing in biblical exegesis are afraid to deal with biblical texts directly, not to mention the laity. Experts in specific fields are only partial experts, driven to ever higher degrees of specialisation, leading to the development of special-specialists. Viewed from the outside, it often seems as if we all are merely 'counting peas'. Historical–critical scholarship as an elitist, highly specialised literary science remains largely at the fringes of theology. It is a highly demanding field (one merely needs to consider learning the languages required for biblical scholarship) and at the same time a field quite distant from any practical application. It is next to impossible to communicate the highly theoretical results of this scholarship on a congregational level. Instead, it produces frustration and confused paralysis. The academic enterprise also witnesses to a further internal problem. The system of qualifying oneself through 'original' and 'progressive' dissertations and publications forces the creation of ever more outlandish games of interpretation with questionable argumentative support. The flood of hypotheses is almost too vast to be taken in; interpretative truth becomes a regional phenomenon: the current interpretative trend in one university is considered to be completely ludicrous only a few hundred kilometres away. From the outside (and not only from there), this divisiveness and discord turns academic scholarship itself into a barrier between the text and its readers, instead of becoming a means by which such barriers are lifted. By differentiating between various layers within the text, academic discussion closes itself off from the lay observer, especially as the debate on the extent and nature of these layers leads not to agreement but to a 'typical chaos'.[76] It can also be observed that more and more 'biblical' studies are far removed from biblical texts, focusing instead on the Ancient Near East, on Hellenism, or on rabbinical Judaism. These studies deal with aspects that only touch upon the Bible peripherally in isolation from any current discourse on issues related to faith. The call for objectivity and neutrality makes biblical exegesis politically neutral and potentially subject to various ideologies. The basic postulate of interpreting the Bible as if God did not exist, i.e. as if the Bible were a product of human interest, need and psychological necessity, is viewed by some students of theology as the most sublime form of religious criticism, an elegant form of corrosive atheism. The Word of God falls apart into many different text-critical, literary-critical, form-critical, tradition-critical and historical hypotheses with more or less questionable authority. What does the basic Reformational principle: *sola scriptura* mean in the face of all these theories? In actual academic exegesis, historical and theological judgements often go hand in hand. The later strata of a text are qualified as inferior (or vice versa). The dissection of the texts and the 'humanising' of the circumstances of their production threaten the very centre of the Bible and drive out its spirit. By giving up the premise of the existence and efficacy of God, agnostic research finds only what it has brought to the text in the first place. Does the Word of God not lose its special status?

> If you are not willing to respect the one into whose sphere you enter, if the Bible does not take you by the hand, then you will certainly not be able to understand what matters in the Bible. You will break it apart and separate it into many, many small pieces like a clock, you will study and examine these pieces in detail, but you will not be able to put it back together. The clock-work – its particular way of chiming the hours – will be destroyed. It is not important that we study the individual pieces in isolation, but rather understand how the pieces interact with each other, producing movement that keeps everything else going. Every interpretation of Holy Scripture should take us into this movement, a movement that stretches from the departure of the people of God to their God-appointed goal.[77]

This misguided development has led to widespread dissatisfaction and criticism of the historical–critical method. Historical–critical exegesis, the pride of Protestant theology, is facing a severe crisis. Ways out of this crisis go in several directions: there are some who believe that diligent progress along the same lines will open new possibilities; historical–critical scholarship will overcome this period of confusion and find new consensus. In their eyes, any talk about crisis is just talk.

---

[76] Stated with refreshing honesty by Merkel, H. (1996), 'Das Gesetz im lukanischen Doppelwerk', in *Schrift und Tradition* (FS J. Ernst), Paderborn, p. 121.

[77] Iwand, H.J. (1962), 'Glauben und Wissen', in *Nachgelassene Werke I*, München, p. 272.

Others – myself included – hope to lead exegesis back into the centre of theological interest by combining it intensively with current theological issues and honest hermeneutical reflection. Historical–critical research must give up its 'splendid isolation' and seek a dialogue with systematic and practical theology as well as with contemporary atheistic or agnostic trends in society.

A third group fears or propagates the end of the historical–critical method and turns to alternative ways of approaching the Bible. This tendency is especially prevalent among theologians 'in the field'. In various seminars for professional education, I have encountered a frightening lack of interest and expectation in regard to the historical-critical method in combination with a high level of interest in alternative approaches to the Bible.

Despite these observations, this method is in fact connected intimately to a modern critical spirit, to the Protestant principle '*sola scriptura*', and the Catholic premise of orienting one's teaching around the witness of the saints and apostles. For this reason, the historical–critical approach will continue to be of basic importance. It cannot be omitted or substituted; however, we must deal with the dissatisfactions produced by this method. A large part of the hermeneutical debate over the last thirty years is based on a discomfort with the results of this approach. Historical–critical scholars must deal with the richness of alternatives and examine them in relation to how they contribute to our understanding of the Bible.

Before we approach this task, I will present three disciplines that belong to the same paradigm discussed so far, but examine the world of the authors with tools not yet discussed.

b) Historical Sociology

A) The writings of Karl Marx and Friedrich Engels[78] provide the philosophical foundation for historical sociology. This foundation works with the premise that the production of texts is always influenced by economic circumstance and that texts themselves influence the political and economic situation either by stabilising or challenging the status quo. In this view, authors are never neutral, even if they claim to be. They are instead the advocates of a certain class. Even when an member of a class decides to change sides and advocate the needs of a different class (as in the case of Engels himself), his statements are structurally bound to his societal circumstances. Interpretation must be turned upside down; a materialistic reading always takes precedence over any idealistic reading that remains in the sphere of abstract speculation and spiritualising theory.

---

[78] See for example Marx, K. and Engels, F. (1958), 'Die deutsche Ideologie (1845/46)', in *Werkausgabe* 3, Berlin/DDR.

B) We must understand the social circumstances of the biblical world(s) in order to fully understand biblical authors in their world. Sociological exegesis applies its questions (what is the structure of the society? How does it deal with its fringes and foreigners? How were production and trade organised? How were profits distributed? What type of tax system existed?) to biblical texts. The question: *'cui bono?'* or 'Who stands to benefit politically and economically from the biblical texts?' is a legitimate question. Any contemporary history of religion must include sociological elements.[79] We thus widen our perception: biblical texts have a political dimension. Religion can function ideologically by either stabilising the status quo or by promoting revolutionary ideas. Exegetes must also perform ideological criticism. They must show that the theology promoted by a certain biblical author is 'relative' because of its ties to certain societal interests. Various theologies can be understood as the result of a societal discourse on how certain historical developments are to be interpreted from God's point of view and what consequences this interpretation carries.

C) Certain texts reveal indirectly which social class an author belongs to and what interests he may pursue. The preacher in Ecclesiastes is obviously a member of the rich ruling class. His wealth and his conservative stance prevent him from fighting for a more just society.[80] His resignation in the face of a seemingly unchanging reality and his scepticism towards optimistic statements in older wisdom literature are not the result of an overall cultural trend, but are rather connected to the particular sociological circumstances of his time. The older wisdom literature in Israel was based on the clear and transparent social structures of a society with little economic and political differentiation. In this 'small' world, the immediate causal connection between action and consequence worked almost as predictably as a natural law. When the state of Israel vanished and the people of Israel were incorporated into the huge Persian empire, life became increasingly complex. Every individual became a mere cog in a machine that could no longer be understood. The rise of a monetary system, the loss of civil autonomy and any formative group identity, and the rise of individual hedonism changed theological thinking drastically. Ecclesiastes speaks not about something universally human, but rather about the consequences of a certain societal development and the interests of a specific social group in the face of this development. In a time when traditional faith and ethics clash with empirical reality, his writings are influenced by money and the interests of a certain class, interests that clash with the needs of the oppressed. These oppressed classes, gathered mainly in rural areas and holding

---

[79] Compare Albertz, R. (1992), *Religionsgeschichte Israels in alttestamentlicher Zeit*, ATD.E 8,1+2, Göttingen, p. 31.

[80] See Crüsemann, F. (1979), 'Die unveränderbare Welt. Überlegungen zur "Krisis der Weisheit" beim Prediger (Kohelet)', in W. Schottroff and W. Stegemann (eds), *Der Gott der kleinen Leute. Sozialgeschichtliche Bibelauslegungen*, München, pp. 80-104.

on to traditional concepts of prophecy, temple and law, instigated the Maccabean revolt only decades after Ecclesiastes, proving that his unchanging world could indeed be changed dramatically.

A number of late Old Testament prayers show a significant accumulation of terminology referring to the poor ('poor, afflicted, needy, lowly' Ps 9/10; 12; 14; 109). This poverty does not refer to spiritual poverty in the presence of God,[81] it refers to actual economic poverty increasingly present in the lower classes during Persian rule. This poverty led to a particular 'piety of the poor'.[82] We can assume the existence of specific cultic systems with prophets and rituals far removed from the Jerusalem temple cult that followed its own goal of reclaiming dignity and hope for victims of social oppression. These people did not succumb to their hopeless circumstances. They voiced their weakness and their anger, accusing the structures and carriers of injustice while establishing their own self-awareness and self-confidence. There were those among the oppressed who were not content with their situation on the fringes of society, where they were recognisable only as the recipients of good will and as receivers of alms. Their poverty was not a sign that God had forgotten and deserted them, as proclaimed by mainstream theology. Yahweh as a liberating God was especially close to the poor (Ps 35:10; 140:13).

D) Historical sociology adds an important component to our understanding of the author's world. This is its positive contribution to exegesis. Form criticism's emphasis on *Sitz im Leben* is expanded by including information on the political and the economic world. This expansion enriches and enlivens the biblical message, while uncovering a long-forgotten aspect of the Bible: its intention to shape societal structures. The biblical message is politically explosive! The focus on daily human life is found not only in the Old Testament. The ethical instructions as well as the narrative examples (e.g. the parable of the Good Samaritan or the christological hymn in Philem 2:5-11) of the New Testament intend to change the world through human action. A sociological focus prevents the Bible from becoming a spiritualised book of comfort for private devotionals focused on the after-life. The Bible is not opium *of* the people, written as self-made salvation; the Bible is also not opium *for* the people, produced by priests to maintain social stability. The Bible is a material force capable of changing the world. By uncovering the particular social circumstances in which texts were produced, we see how God enters the reality of this world. This 'humanity' of God leads to a 'humanising' of our reality.[83]

---

[81] See Lohfink, N. (1986), 'Von der "Anawim-Partei" zur "Kirche der Armen". Die bibelwissenschaftliche Ahnentafel eines Hauptbegriffs der "Theologie der Befreiung"', in *Bibl.* 67, pp. 153-175.

[82] See Albertz, R. (1992), *Religionsgeschichte Israels*, pp. 569-576.

[83] Schottroff, W. and Stegemann, W. (eds) (1979), *Der Gott der kleinen Leute. Sozialgeschichtliche Bibelaulegungen*, München, p. 10.

Nevertheless, there are several theological problems with this approach. How do we draw a systematic line between historical materialism and faith in an active God? Are the preacher's observations – that injustice rules instead of justice with brutal consistency, that death falls upon everyone without difference, or that one's success in life is not dependent on ethical behaviour – truly an expression of a certain social class, or, as I am inclined to believe, are they not basic anthropological truths?[84] Kohelet's exhortation to find joy in the midst of suffering and to enjoy what God has given us (food, drink, love, life) in proper measure speaks to every human being no matter what class he or she may belong to. I would also question whether the following statement does justice to the piety of the poor in the book of Psalms: 'The fact that oppressed social groups existed in the religious life of Israel that were able to use their personal piety as means for liberating self-expression shows once again on a small scale how the concept of liberation was basic to Israel's religion.'[85] Does this approach not underestimate the power of true religious experiences, classifying them instead as expressions of special interest groups?

Sociological exegesis is also in danger of succumbing to certain ideological trends. Many of its representatives work with a one-sided emphasis on the poor and the oppressed while negating or discrediting statements to the opposite. This can easily lead to a selective view of the Bible, turning the Bible into a party platform. This 'option for the poor' in the Old Testament is often not more – but also not less! – than a call for the rich to remember their social responsibility towards the poor. The Old Testament does not condemn wealth in and of itself (see Job 31). A one-sided focus on the poor is reductionistic. A God defined solely as a 'God of the poor' does not do justice to the biblical witness. Most biblical heroes that stood under special divine protection were relatively wealthy (e.g. Abraham, David, Solomon, Job, and others), or belonged at least to the middle class of tradesmen and artisans (such as Jesus the carpenter). Ideological reductionism also definitely occurs when the Bible is used to support and stabilise unjust systems of wealth and power. When either the political left or the political right tries to monopolise the Bible, certain biblical authors are always devalued as literature of the 'class enemy' that 'unfortunately' made it into the biblical canon. A further important point of criticism is the problematic connection of sociological exegesis to religious criticism. This has not been fully analysed to date: how can one bathe in Marxism without getting soaked in religious criticism? Does the acceptance of Marxist theories not lead necessarily to the conclusion that biblical religion is only an ideological superstructure?

---

[84] Compare Zimmerli, W. (1983), '"Unveränderbare Welt" oder "Gott ist Gott"? Ein Plädoyer für die Unaufgebbarkeit des Predigerbuches in der Bibel', in *Wenn nicht jetzt, wann dann?* (FS H.-J. Kraus), Neukirchen, pp. 103-114.

[85] Albertz, R. (1992), *Religionsgeschichte Israels*, p. 567.

c) Historical Psychology

A) In the 20th century, psychological analysis of the author had become a standard tool of literary science. The hermeneutics of empathy, proposed by Schleiermacher and Dilthey, provide the philosophical foundation for this approach; its theoretical foundation is found in Freud's psychoanalysis. Whereas depth psychology attempts to discover overarching principles not limited to a certain time or a certain person, historical psychology tries to understand a certain historical person with his/her own unique features, especially in contrast to present norms and categories. Abnormalities and aberrations, as Freud describes them in his pathologies of daily life, are especially interesting for historical psychology. According to this approach, texts invite readers to read them as a means of reconstructing the psychological profile (and neuroses) of the author.

B) The tools used in the psychological analysis of biblical authors are no different from tools used in regard to non-biblical authors. The goal of this approach is the creation of the author's psychological profile. In biblical exegesis, historical psychology faces the basic problem that much of biblical literature is not author-produced literature but tradition-produced literature going back to several anonymous authors. The composition of the individual layers of the text is a secondary element of text production. If anything, we can only postulate a single author for short literary units. Based on such sources, psychological criticism has little to work with, especially as the subtle hints regarding an author's psychology must be filtered out of a relatively large amount of material that provides insight into the author's psyche. The only material that meets these criteria are the prophetic books in the Old Testament and the Pauline letters in the New Testament.

C) The Heidelberg psychiatrist and philosopher Karl Jaspers was one scholar who approached the texts by the prophet Ezekiel from a medical point of view, in order to determine the psychology of the prophet.[86] Jaspers diagnoses visions (especially of Jerusalem), abnormal states of mind such as long periods of staring into space, sudden influences by outside voices, moments of awakening, cataleptic seizures followed by states of paralysis and lack of speech, abrupt and direct comments on sexuality, strange and ever-changing symbolic rituals, as well as frequent alternation between cold, pedantic and abstract rationalism and coarse displays of unashamed emotion. The psychiatrist comes to the conclusion that he is dealing with a hysterical schizophrenic. The theology created by this psychotic author stands at a turning point in the history of Judaism: 'The priestly, hierarchic

---

[86] Jaspers, K. (1947), 'Der Prophet Ezechiel. Eine pathographische Studie', in *Arbeiten zur Psychiatrie, Neurologie und ihren Grenzgebieten* (FS Kurt Schneider), Heidelberg, pp. 77-85.

way of thinking loses itself in details, in the obsession with small and momentary things. Piety and God seem to be lost in a never-ending host of regulations.'[87]

The Heidelberg psychiatrist H. Tellenbach draws a much more cautious conclusion.[88] Every interpreter must take the nature of prophetic experience seriously without immediately applying pathological categories to it! Prophetic experience is completely a-biographical. Nothing from the life of a prophet can foreshadow this specific calling, not even in retrospect. The a-historical nature of prophetic experience results from its completely involuntary nature. During a prophetic experience one breathes the 'air of a different planet'[89] while encountering the divine in sight and hearing.

The personal history of Paul, seen through the eyes of historical psychology,[90] looks like this: Saul of Tarsus grew up at home in subjugation to a dominant, authoritative father, as well as an authoritative 'super-father', the Torah. His rabbinic education under Rabbi Gamaliel as a substitute father figure reinforced his tendency toward blind, perfect obedience to the law as a means of self-identification. The appearance of Christianity called these very ideals into question. Paul escaped his self-doubts by fanatically persecuting and eradicating his opponents (see Acts 7:58). These actions, however, could not resolve his inner crisis, which he finally overcame in a radical conversion experience on the road to Damascus. This encounter led him to identify himself with a new 'super-father', Jesus (Acts 9). He now propagates his new authority with the same fanaticism as before. As a new convert, Paul was initially rejected by both sides. This rejection inflicted deep narcissistic wounds. Nobody accepted him as the perfect disciple as he would have expected. Individuals with narcissistic aberrations are easily insulted, turn to anger, and can even develop suicidal tendencies. Paul's incessant attempt to be recognised by the Christian community on the same level as the other apostles reaches hysterical levels when which he tries to force respect on the basis of his experience on the road to Damascus (see especially 2 Corinthians). The sickness that Paul describes, his 'thorn in the flesh' (2 Cor 12:17), is not a psychotic ailment, nor epilepsy, but rather a somatic neurosis connected to his conversion. Paul's theories on justification by faith help him to overcome his inner immaturity. He leaves his anal rituals behind and finds freedom from the law. God's liberating word frees him to move from identification to identity. Grace, joy

---

[87] For a discussion of latent anti-Judaism within psychological exegesis, see Oeming, M. (1995), 'Altes Testament und Tiefenpsychologie. Aufklärung oder Freudsche Fehlleistung', in *ThLZ* 120, pp. 107-120.

[88] Tellenbach, H. (1987), 'Ezechiel: Wetterleuchten einer "Schizophrenie" (Jaspers) oder prophetische Erfahrung des Ganz-Anderen', in *Daseinsanalyse* 4, pp. 227-236.

[89] Ibid., p. 235.

[90] See Thilo, H.-J. (1985), 'Paulus – Die Geschichte einer Entwicklung psychoanalytisch gesehen', in *WzM* 37, pp. 2-14.

and love (agape) are the elements that overcome his narcissism and establish a healthy sense of self. In Gal 3:28 he voices the joyful experience of being accepted: there are no differences based on value or achievement, nothing that separates Jew and Greek, slave or free, male or female. In Christ's love all are unified and equal. The psychological approach tries to show that Paul's journey is a journey from Oedipal identification to mature identity. Paul's authoritative 'super-father' is replaced by a healthy sense of self. Narcissism is replaced by the experience of full acceptance. In theological terms we can say that Paul moves from law to freedom. In psychological terms we can say that Paul replaces defensive mechanisms with self-acceptance. Where this occurs, religion can be a path to self-recovery and an important therapeutic tool. Certain questions about Paul's psychology are still debated: how much of Paul's vengeful and immature narcissism remains in his mature ethical statements?[91] Must we suspect relapses into old patterns of thought and action in the midst of his statements on Christian freedom and autonomy? What do we do with highly moralistic passages, with simplistic black and white thinking, with intolerant attacks against opponents (see Phil 3), or with strange images of foreign domination (see Gal 2:20)? Are his teachings on justification by faith and his concept that the weak are strong (2 Cor 12:10) not psychological aids similar to those erected by countless 'helpless helpers'? Ulonska voices this fear:[92] 'With this sentence, Paul left us a burdensome legacy. By using sickness as a weapon against his missionary opponents in Corinth who boasted of good health and vitality as signs of God's affection, this statement becomes a source of depression if taken out of context and promoted as exemplary behaviour.'

D) The advantages of historical psychology are obvious. By entering the psyche of biblical authors, the reader is able to get very close to the material while, at the same time, finding a stance from which to critically evaluate psychological aspects of his present situation. Paul basically suffered through the same problems of self-discovery that many of us are faced with today. This interpretation of Paul suggests that we must relativise Paul's theology – with its grand concepts of Gospel and law, death and new life – as ambivalences in Paul's personality. On the other hand, it is an attempt to reconcile Paul's theological demands with human experience. Ezekiel, like many patients in psychiatric wards today, is burdened with many strange and frightening 'gifts' that signal the special status of religious experience within human psychology.

The tendency towards relativising the theological concepts proposed by biblical authors as well as the pathologising of religious experience show clearly that we

---

[91] See Klessmann, M. (1989), 'Zum Problem der Identität des Paulus. Pychologische Aspekte zu theologischen und biographischen Fragen', in *WzM* 41, pp. 156-172, p. 171.

[92] Ulonska, H. (1989), 'Die Krankheit des Paulus und die ritualisierte christliche Demut', in *WzM* 41, pp. 355-367.

must make a careful distinction between historical psychology and psychological criticism of religion. By definition, faith borders on the exceptional, the irrational, or the paradoxical. This does not imply that faith itself is lost beyond this border. Even where expressions of faith are interpreted as infantile regression of psychosis, this estimation only says something about its function in the psychology of an individual but nothing about its truth content. The fact that 1 plus 1 equals 2 is true whether stated by a normal or by an 'abnormal' person. God's justification of the sinner for Christ's sake is still the basis of our faith, even if this truth were proclaimed by a psychopath. With these statements, however, we have entered a field that goes far beyond our current discussion.

d) New Archaeology

A) The beginnings of modern archaeology are now seen more as a 'treasure hunt'. From the mid 19th century on this treasure hunt was replaced by the scientific gathering of artefacts from different locations, by the systematic description of wide surface areas (surveys), and by systematic excavations.[93] Older archaeology in Israel described itself programmatically as 'biblical archaeology'; its prime motivation was tracing signs of Israelite and early Christian culture from their origins to the present. The highest success was seen in finding artefacts that could be directly connected to a particular biblical story. This work was latently driven by the hope that the work of shovel and spade might prove the Bible to be correct after all (a further driving force was the need to support Israel's political claim to the land by revealing its long-standing history in the land).[94] After World War II, this attitude changed. The intensive archaeological work in Israel had uncovered a vast amount of material that bore witness to all eras of human history. Yet only a very small portion of these findings could be connected directly to biblical texts. Exegetical work on the texts and excavational work of the archaeologist had to be evaluated separately as two different methodological approaches.[95] The cultural

---

[93] For the history of this research see Ben-Arieh, Y. (1979), *The Rediscovery of the Holy Land in the Nineteenth Century*, Jerusalem and Detroit; Daniel, G. (1982), *Geschichte der Archäologie*, Bergisch Gladbach; Silberman, N.A. (1982), *Digging for God and Country. Exploration, Archaeology, and the Secret Struggle for the Holy Land 1798-1917*, New York; Fritz, V. (1993), *Einführung in die Biblische Archäologie*, Darmstadt, pp. 29-48.

[94] For the political implications of archaeology, see Silberman, N.A. (1990), *Between Past and Present. Archaeology, Ideology, and Nationalism in the Modern Middle East*, New York.

[95] Noth, M. (1938), 'Grundsätzliches zur geschichtlichen Bedeutung archäologischer Befunde auf dem Boden Palästinas', in *PJB* 34, pp. 7-22; Schmid, H.H. (1975), *Die Steine und das Wort. Fug und Unfug Biblischer Archäology*, Zürich.

and temporal framework for the exploration of the Holy Land also had to be expanded. Biblical archaeology became the archaeology of Palestine. The biblical era, as well as Israelite and Christian culture, became a small part of a much wider spectrum.

B) The development of natural sciences enabled a continual improvement of archaeological tools.[96] Material considered useless in prior excavations such as the decayed remnants of waste depots or decomposed animal bones were now important. The technique of carbon-dating was able to determine the age of these waste products, archaeo-botany could analyse and determine the plants present in a certain excavation, archaeo-zoology and the determination of ancient animal bones could determine which pets were held as food sources. These insights painted a picture of everyday life in biblical times.[97] Studies on local characteristics were able to determine cultural differences between various regional areas.[98] In analogy with sociological developments, the interest of archaeology moved from palaces and treasures (of which there were only a few anyway) to the daily life of 'normal' people, the culture of the powerless who did not have the ability to read and write. Archaeology also worked and works toward a systematic collection of inscriptions (epigraphy) and pictures (iconography), found primarily on seals, stamps, or coins. The systematic study of the visual world of the Ancient Near East has made large contributions to understanding life in biblical times.[99] Inspired by the work of

---

[96] See Hachmann, R. (ed.) (1969), *Vademecum der Grabung Kamid el-Lodz,* Saarbrücker Beiträge zur Altertumskunde 5, Bonn; Joukowsky, M. (1980), *A Complete Manual of Field Archaeology: Tools and Techniques of Field Work for Archaeologists,* Prentice Hall; Riederer, J. (1981), *Kunstwerke chemisch betrachtet – Materialien, Analysen, Altersbestimmung,* Berlin/ Heidelberg/New York; Fritz, V. (1993), *Einführung,* pp. 49-68.

[97] See Paul, S.M. and Dever, W.G. (eds) (1973), *Biblical Archaeology: Library of Jewish Knowledge,* Jerusalem; Weippert, H. (1988), *Palästina in vorhellenistischer Zeit,* Handbuch der Altertumswissenschaft, München; a recent comprehensive summary of daily life in biblical times is not yet available. It is possible to create a synthesis based on many partial studies: see Galling, K. (ed.) (1977), *Biblisches Reallexikon,* Tübingen; Keel, O., Küchler, M. and Uehlinger, Ch. (1984), *Orte und Landschaften der Bibel, Ein Handbuch und Studienreiseführer zum Heiligen Land, Vol. 1: Geographisch-geschichtliche Landeskunde,* Zürich and Göttingen; Fritz, V. (1987), *Kleines Lexikon der Biblischen Archäologie,* Konstanz; Fritz, V. (1990), *Die Stadt im alten Israel,* München; Negev, A. (ed.) (1991), *Archäologisches Bibellexicon,* Neuhausen Stuttgart; Avi Yona, M.. and Stern, E. (ed.) (1993), *Encyclopedia of Archaeological Excavations of the Holy Land,* 4 vols, Jerusalem.

[98] See Theißen, G. (1992), *Lokalkolorit und Zeitgeschehen in den Evangelien. Ein Beitrag zur Geschichte der synoptischen Tradition,* Göttingen.

[99] See Keel, O. and Uehlinger, Ch. (1996), *Altorientalische Miniaturkunst. Die ältesten visuellen Massenkommunikationsmittel,* Mainz; Keel, O. (1995), *Corpus der*

cultural anthropology, new archaeology strives to reconstruct cultural processes and transformations; moving away from static catalogues and dates for individual artefacts, it aims to create a picture of Israel's history without the use of biblical texts.

**Figure 2   A cylinder seal from Beth-Shean (8th/7th century B.C.):
An anthology of gods and numinous creatures**[100]

C) The exegesis of Old Testament texts has much to gain from the input of new archaeology. Striking examples of this are seen in the interpretation of the Psalms,[101] the Song of Songs,[102] and of the Book of Job.[103] O. Keel and Ch.

Stempelsiegel-Amulette aus Palästina/Israel. Von den Anfängen bis zur Perserzeit, OBO. Series Archaeologica 10, Fribourg and Göttingen.

[100] By courtesy of Verlag Herder, taken from Keel, O. and Uehlinger, Ch. (1992), *Göttinnen, Götter und Gottessymbole. Neue Erkenntnisse zur Religionsgeschichte Kanaans und Israels aufgrund bislang unerschlossener ikonographischer Quellen*, QD 134, Freiburg, p. 359.

[101] Keel, O. (1972), *Die Welt der altorientalischen Bildsymbolik und das Alte Testament. Am Beispiel der Psalmen*, Zürich and Neukirchen-Vluyn (Göttingen 1996).

[102] Keel, O. (1986), *Das Hohelied*, ZBK 18, Zürich.

[103] Keel, O. (1978), *Jahwes Antwort an Ijob*, FRLANT 121, Göttingen.

Uehlinger have even attempted to reconstruct the religious history of Palestine based solely on the visual imagery found in Palestine/Israel.[104] This visual material suggests the following historical process. During the Middle Bronze Age, male and female gods (with strong anthropomorphic features) existed in an equal balance of power. The anthropomorphic imagery was displaced by symbolic animals, the moon, and even trees towards the late Bronze Age. The Iron Age IIB (925-720) repressed goddesses in favour of a male god depicted with with solar images (see Isa 6). The goddess experienced a renaissance during Iron Age IIC (720-587). This period is also interesting for its increase in non-visual signatures and seals, perhaps reflecting the consequences of a Deuteronomic theology. The post-exilic era shows

evidence for a wide network of inter-cultural contacts. The divine images are once again separated into male imagery for a warlike, heroic father-god and a nurturing, protecting mother-god. These divine images had a strong influence on emerging Christian imagery. Orthodox Judaism at this time was completely closed off to the idea of feminine divinity.

This example shows briefly how iconography can lead to hypotheses on large religious developments. A further example shows how new archaeology can aid us in understanding individual biblical passages. In Matt 11:7 Jesus speaks to the crowds who have followed the Baptist into the desert:

> As they went away, Jesus began to speak to the crowds about John: 'What did you go out into the wilderness to look at? A reed shaken by the wind?'

This is a difficult passage: Jesus is either speaking of certain aspects of his immediate natural surrounding, or he is implicitly criticising John the Baptist for not creating a lasting legacy. Both interpretations are un-

Figure 3   A so-called 'pillar figurine' of a woman presenting her breasts (Jerusalem 7th century B.C.): One of a multitude of illustrations of goddesses of fertility[105]

---

[104]   Keel, O. and Uehlinger, Ch. (1992), *Göttinnen, Götter und Gottessymbole*.
[105]   By courtesy of Verlag Herder, ibid., p. 372.

satisfactory, especially in the light of the literary context of this passage. The metaphors in the Old Testament using the image of a reed refer to the concept of divine judgement; in Greek fables the same image stands for a clever person who can adapt to changing political 'winds'. Neither of these interpretations fits John the Baptist. An 'emblematic' interpretation based on coins struck by Herod Antipas celebrating his new capital, Tiberias, helps us beyond this impasse.[106] Based on these coins, it is quite possible to associate Herod Antipas with reeds, because reeds appear on these coins where Herod's head would be expected. The legend around the reed symbol states: 'This coin belongs to Antipas'. Tradition plays with this image of Herod, using it to ridicule the king who swayed between Roman rule and orthodox Judaism. Luke 13:32 describes him as a 'clever fox'. The paradoxical passage in Matt 11:7-9 (how do reed and desert belong together?) is determined by the opposition between Antipas and John, between a life of luxury in the palace and a life of critical asceticism in the desert. Knowing when exactly these coins were struck enables us to date this passage during the life of John and locate it somewhere in the area of Tiberias. This logion can thus be placed exactly in Jesus' time and sphere of action, making it highly probable that this statement was indeed uttered by Jesus.

D) Archaeology makes an intergral contribution to understanding the Bible. Without explicitly promising to do so, it adds a completely new dimension to the biblical texts by working out concrete details of the daily life of biblical authors. Archaeology is highly important, even when its findings cannot be connected directly to the world described in the biblical texts.

Dangers lurking from a one-sided emphasis on archaeology arise primarily because of the mistaken assumption that, in contrast to biblical exegesis, extra-biblical images, inscriptions and stones are 'objective', presenting us with a reliable foundation on which to construct the 'real' biblical world. A one-sided reduction of historical reality through a focus on 'external evidence' does not do justice to the subject matter.[107] Archaelogical artefacts and ancient oriental images

---

[106] See Theißen, G. (1985), 'Das "schwankende Rohr" in Mt 11,7 und die Gründungsmünzen von Tiberias. Ein Beitrag zur Lokalkoloritforschung in den synoptischen Evangelien', *ZDPV* 101, pp. 43-55.

[107] An example of such an approach is found in Lemche, N.P. (1996), *Die Vorgeschichte Israels. Von den Anfängen bis zum Ausgang des 13. Jahrhunderts v. Chr.*, Biblische Enzyklopädie 1, Stuttgart. A critical response to this form of 'hyper-criticism' is found in Herrmann, S. (1990), 'Die Abwertung des Alten Testaments als Geschichtsquelle. Bemerkungen zu einem geistesgeschichtlichen Problem', in H.H. Schmid and J. Mehlhausen (eds), *Sola Scriptura. Das reformatorische Schriftprinzip in der säkularen Welt*, Gütersloh, pp. 156-165.

are themselves not without ambiguity and in need of interpretation.[108] The fact that a picture 'says more than a thousand words' emphasises its problematic usefulness for biblical exegesis.

> Only very few anthropomorphic depictions are identified clearly by their context as divine entities, male or female. The situation is even more difficult with theriomorphic or zoomorphic images ... Religious content can only be derived from archaeological findings within narrow limits. Lunar standards can refer to a divinity with lunar characteristics, perhaps even to a moon-god. They say nothing, however, about the religous ideas that were connected to this god. The intensity of worship and cult can hardly be derived from the archaeological data. A description of religious horizons based solely on archaeological material must remain a mere sketch. Topics such as ethics, cosmology, creation, anthropology, eschatology, historicity, problems of suffering, theodicy, priestly office, sacrificial beliefs, sin, atonement, etc. can hardly be derived from non-literary archaeological data. These limitations show clearly ... how little can be said about religious beliefs based on the interpretation of artefacts and how much the interpretation of archaeological findings depends on a priori judgements about religious phenomenology that are informed by literary traditions.[109]

The reconstruction of the author's world cannot be successful in isolation from literary texts!

---

[108] See Frevel, C. (1989), '"Dies ist der Ort, von dem geschrieben steht ..." Zum Verhältnis von Bibelwissenschaft und Palästinaarchäologie', in *BN* 47, pp. 35-89.

[109] Frevel, C. (1995), *Aschera und der Ausschließlichkeitsanspruch YHWHs*, BBB 94,1+2, Weinheim, pp. 746f.

Chapter 5

Methods Focused on Texts and their Worlds

The methods described thus far were primarily concerned with authors and their worlds. The methods that will be described in the following emphasise a very different aspect, even if elements of authorship and historical-critical exegesis are present here as well. The basic creed of text-oriented methods states: a text is a cosmos, a world, closed and complete in itself, a quasi a-temporal autonomous entity, a whole dependent only on itself.[110] A text must exist on its own as a linguistic world, a world of language. The interpreter should not lose himself in an obscure reconstruction of history, nor in an author's inner life only guessed at, nor in the chaos of personal subjectivity. Only the concentration on the text itself brings security and objectivity. We can take home only what exists black on white. Positivism and a certain pragmatism are a part of all text-centred methods. Linguistics, narratology, the canonocial approach (with limitations), and the 'new hermeneutics' proposed by Ernst Fuchs and his followers all separate written language strictly from anything non-linguistic.

a) Linguistic–Structuralist Methods

A) The following statement is true for many of the methods described in this chapter:

> The strong emphasis on the text itself leads to a reduction of the subjective element of intepretation: The analysing self is eliminated to a large degree from the process of analysis ... It also leads to a reduction of the objective element: the referential function of language – language always refers to something outside itself – is left aside. Newer linguistic approaches no longer operate with referential semantics but rather with system-immanent semantics. The cessation of the relation between signifier and signified implies the cessation of any question concerning the truth content of a linguistic statement ... In order to guarantee the consistency of its results, linguistics does not allow its object to change. It removes all historical (diachronic) dimensions in

---

[110] See Stenger, W. (1977), 'In Texten zu Hause', in *KatBl* 102, pp. 705-714 for a further exploration of this concept.

favour of synchronic cross-sections. The literary object, in other words, must be a static object ... The results of linguistic analysis are subject to the highest criteria of universality, review, and reliability ... The vocabulary of everyday language is often burdened by subjective, historically conditioned, and referential contexts and is thus not suited for description without ambiguity. For this reason, modern linguistics frequently utilises non-verbal (mathematical, logical) symbols. The language of the object studied and the language used for its description belong to two different semantic systems of communication.'[111]

The focus of such study is a precise, formal analysis of composition, of the 'blueprint', and the logical network of connections within a text. Who wrote a text, and for whom a text was written are questions that recede into the background completely. This far-reaching departure from diachronic, historical questions and the radical affirmation of the synchronic work results in a high increase of objectivity. Understanding a text is now a matter of uncovering the elements that constitute a particular work and finding the meaning contained in the structure of the text. This 'work-immanent' interpretation goes hand in hand with philological precision and inner coherence. Its results can be refreshingly uniform in comparison to the widespread disagreement on historical layers and texual growth.[112] There are several philosophical roots for this highly formalised treatment of biblical texts.[113] L. Wittgenstein (1889-1951) was an important pioneer of this approach. His attempt at designing an ideal, logical language in *Tractatus Logico-Philosophicus* (1921) was especially important, as well as his posthumous work *Philosophische Untersuchungen* (1953), which examines how various different 'language games' with their own respective rules overlap each other in daily life. Other impulses come from French philosophy, in which

---

[111] Plett, H.F. (1974), 'Möglichkeiten und Grenzen einer linguistischen Literaturwissenschaft', *Zeitschrift für Literaturwissenschaft und Linguistik* 4, pp. 15-29, pp.16f.

[112] At times linguistics and historical approaches are placed in irreconcilable opposition. The actual use of these methods is not entreched so dramatically.

[113] See summary presentations such as Erlich, V. (1964), *Russischer Formalismus*, München; Vachek, I. (1966), *The Linguistic School of Prague*, Bloomington and London; Schiwy, G. (1969), *Der französische Strukturalismus. Mode, Methode, Ideologie*, RDE 310/311, Reinbek; ibid. (1971), *Neue Aspekte des Strukturalismus*, München; Heerschen, C. (1972), *Grundfragen der Linguistik*, Urban TB 156, Stuttgart; Todorov, T. (1972), *Poetik der Prosa*, Frankfurt; Eco, U. (1991), *Einführung in die Semiotik*, UTB 105, München (1972); Hund, W.D. (ed.) (1973), *Strukturalismus. Ideologie und Dogmengeschichte*, Darmstadt and Neuwied; Dietrich, R., Kanngießer, S. and Sinemus, V. (eds) (1974), *Sprachwissenschaft*, Grundzüge der Literatur- und Sprachwissenschaft, Vol. 2: DTV.WR 4227, München.

structuralism[114] reached a high point after 1960, promoted by authors such as F. de Saussure (1857-1913), R. Jakobson (1896-1982), C. Lévi-Strauss (b. 1908), R. Barthes (1915-1980), M. Foucault (1926-1984), or J. Derrida (1930-2004). Linguistics is further enriched by influences from generative Grammar (N. Chomsky, b. 1928), Russian formalism and the Prague school, as well as the analytic philosophy of R. Carnap (1891-1970), W.V.O. Quine (b.1908), A.J Ayer (1910-1989), and J.L. Austin (1911-1960). Positivist ideas from the realm of natural science made further contributions. The growing application of computers has refined stylistic analysis to a high degree.[115] It was discovered, for example, that the average length of a sentence in Rilke's *Cornet* was 12.5 syllables, in Goethe's *Italienische Reise* 38.6 syllables, in Marx's *Das Kapital* 65.4, and in an article of a 1968 issue of *BILD*[116] 20.5 syllables.[117] The clear separation of linguistics from everyday language led to the creation of a host of tools (which are difficult to learn) as well as a large body of highly inaccessible terminology. [118] This special vocabulary makes the reading of linguistic studies a very difficult enterprise.

B) General introductory textbooks enable a first step into the world of linguistics.[119] Textbooks dealing specifically with the structural analysis of the Bible have been written by W. Richter[120] and H. Schweizer.[121] The periodical *Biblia Linguistica* (edited since 1971 by E. Güttgemanns) is devoted to this

---

[114] Structuralism is a very inprecise term with several meanings: (a) a method of analysing language with emphasis on its structural elements, (b) a platform from which to analyse society, (c) a basic philosophical approach to understanding reality in terms of primal structures of human thinking.

[115] See Schmidt, F. (1972), 'Numerische Textkritik: Goethes und Schillers Anteil an der Abfassung des Aufsatzes "Der Piccolomini"', in *Zeitschrift für Literaturwissenschaft und Linguistik* 2, pp. 59-70.

[116] Germany's leading tabloid newspaper (J.F.V.).

[117] Thiele, J. (1978), 'Statistische Methoden', in M. Maren-Griesbach, *Methoden der Literaturwissenschaft*, UTB 121, München, p. 98.

[118] A word is called a lexeme or a term, a syllable is a morpheme, 'everyone' is an *allquantor* whereas 'it is' is a *existencequantor*. Words with several meanings are polysemous, the subject of a sentence is a Signifikat, whereas the predicate is referred to as Signifikant. Reducing sentences with multiple meanings to a single meaning is referred to the removal of ambiguity from polysemic structures, etc. Sometimes I wonder whether all this is really necessary or merely a lot of verbal 'hot air'.

[119] See for example Titzmann, M. (1993), *Strukturale Textanalyse. Theorie und Praxis der Interpretation*, UTB 582, München.

[120] Richter, W. (1971), *Exegese als Literaturwissenschaft. Entwurf einer alttestamentlichen Literaturtheorie und Methodologie*, Göttingen.

[121] Schweizer, H. (1986), *Biblische Texte verstehen. Arbeitsbuch zur Hermeneutik und Methodik der Bibelinterpretation*, Stuttgart.

approach. A good summary of the so-called Kampen School is found in J. Kim, *The Structure of the Samson Cycle*.[122] Detailed stylistic analysis is possible with the help of several computer programs with concordances, modern translations and search engines.[123]

C) As a small example of this approach, we will look at H. Schweizer's analysis of Job 16:18-22. His first step is the presentation of a translation structured into small segments:

> 18*a*   'O earth, *b* do not cover my blood,
> *c*   and without resting place shall be my cry for help!
> 19*a*   But now, *b* look, *c* my witness is in the sky
> *d*   he that vouches for me is on high.
> 20*a*   Because my friends ridicule me
> *b*   my eye pours out tears to God my eye
> 21*a*   May he achieve justice for man before God
> *b*   and between person and person.
> 22*a*   For but a few more years will come
> *b*   and I will wander down the path, *c* from which one does
>   not return.'[124]

He then proceeds to analyse the types of words and their effect in the text:

(1) Types of words/pragmatic
The text contains 18 nouns. It creates the semantic impression impression that 18 substantive items are presented to the outside world. – When verifying this impression pragmatically, one discovers layers in the degree of abstraction:

a. *true concrete terms* (first order): earth, blood, sky, witness, he who vouches, friends, eye, man, person (2×), path = 11.

b. *second order entities*: resting place (this is not merely a place, but a place used for a specific purpose, call for help, year = 3.

c. *greatest abstraction* (third order): God (2× – 'God' can appear in the text without doubt as a very concrete and personal entity. In this critical analysis, we must take into consideration that he cannot be localised. His reality is of a different nature than than of the other concrete entities), justice, on high = 4.

After Schweizer has gathered the word-types with mathematical precision, he analyses the nouns in relation to verbs, adverbs and prepositions:

---

[122] Kim, J. (1993), *The Structure of the Samson Cycle*, Kampen, pp. 118-134.

[123] Three programs worth mentioning for the Old Testament are Compucord (developed in Maredsou, Belgium), Quest (developed in Amsterdam/Bielefeld/Greifswald) and the user-friendly BibleWorks (developed in the USA).

[124] Schweizer, H. (1986), *Biblische Texte*, p. 93.

– The words: 'sky, man, path' each refer to conecte, observable phenomena in the outside world. They could each stand on their own (static-qualitative). The word 'God' (2×) is also a term for an autonomous single entity.

– In contrast, 'blood, eye' specify and describe elements of the outside world that can only be thought of in connection with a larger whole. This whole is indicated by the pronoun ('my'), so that this gap is filled. The text refers to the blood and the eye of the speaker.

– A statement of identity, used as a proper name, is found with 'earth' in 18a.

– 'person' is a group designation.

– 'friends' belongs to a separate noun. The classification of the friends is accomplished with pronouns.

– 'resting-place', 'high places' are localities.

– 'years' is a temporal statement.

– the nouns 'cry for help, witness, he who vouches, justice' refer not only to an activity (dynamic-initiating); they belong closely to the codes. The 'cry for help' is more than a vocalised exclamation; it describes an exhortation (speech-act: INITIATION; code: INITIATIVE). "Witness" and 'he who vouches' aim at reporting and evaluating a state of affairs (Code: epistemology and axiology). 'Achieving justice' means in this case the process of reversing prior incorrect evaluations (AXIOLOGY) and proclaiming this reversal (EPISTEMOLOGY). The inner structure of these words creates the need for further information (who is supposed to act? how?), a need only partially filled by the context: the question of who is supposed to 'witness' is clarified – God himself. What he is supposed to witness about, in which temporal-spatial context, is a question left open by the text.

Evaluation: It is noticeable that only a few of the nouns (5) describe independent phenomena. In most cases (9) the noun itself, even without the pronoun, implies a relation of some kind. This is striking linguistic support for the basic theological theme which also deals with a problem of relation (Job–God).'

In conclusion of this section – there are of course many more possibilties for detailed studies – Schweizer analyses the way in which language is used figuratively:

18a (vocative) and 18b (imperative) show that earth is personified. In combination with the metonymic understanding of 'blood' as 'life', the text creates the picture of earth as a gravedigger. In absence of the metaphor, 18a.b state: 'I do not want to die'. This also reveals the advantage of the use of metaphor: a dramatic flair is added through the unusual addressee as well as through the briefly appearing funeral scene ... 20b is also metaphoric: it describes a space in which inner desire can be portrayed. 'God', who is now addressed directly (in contrast: 19c.d) is not only the goal of the movement, but also a cipher for hope, help, and strength. In a visual and mythic manner, this sentence and the following project objectively into the outside world what is at home subjectively within the speaker ... After the path has found its way through many metaphors from fear to a positive vision, the passage ends simply and clearly: 22a is to be understood literally, 22b.c contain metaphors that were most likely in common use. Death is described euphemistically as a final act undertaken in free will ('wander' = dynamic-initiative); a path is mentioned described by a specific attribute (22c): this specific attribute is mentioned only on the side. The main emphasis on 'path' describes it first and foremost as a general path comparable to many others.[125]

D) The advantages of this approach are clear: this method forces us to look at the text in great detail and observe its texture closely; the compositional structure of the text can be analysed down to its smallest components.

The limitations of this method lie in the danger of exaggerating the analysis of details and gathering a host of information that may be correct but completely irrelevant for understanding the text. What help is it really to know how many nouns are in a text? Determining types of words, counting and classifying words, creating statistical charts, etc. can easily turn into dull, shallow formalism. The specific terminology in some publications is simply overdone; the graphical presentations can hardly be de-coded and contribute little or nothing that is really new. In any case, the vision of complete objectivity, in analogy with mathematics, cannot be realised: the hermeneutical square clearly shows that certain elements involved in the process of understanding can never be objective. The more objective an insight is (e.g. the number of suffixes in a given text), the more they are in danger of being irrelevant. The large amount of work thus stands in inverse to the amount of insight gained.[126] We must also ask if language can refer only to itself. Is the removal of any historic reality or the reality of the recipient not a problem in and of itself? Pure linguistics, i.e. an analysis of language without any reference to the historical reality of the authors or the recipients can be an aid to understanding, but not understanding itself.

b) New Literary Criticism

A) Whereas most of French structuralism had mostly worked on the level of words, sentences and small units, a group of scholars emerged within structuralism who also worked with a text-immanent approach, but without this focus on micro-

---

[125] Ibid., p. 15.

[126] Examples: After a long and difficult analysis of 1 King 21 by Bohlen, R. (1978), *Der Fall Nabot. Form, Hintergrund und Werdegang einer alttestamentlichen Erzählung*, TThSt 35, Trier, the author comes to the conclusion that the King is interested in Naboth's vineyard. This insight is shared by every reader who has barely glanced at the text. In the worthwhile book by Fuchs, O. (1982), *Die Klage als Gebet. Eine theologische Besinnung am Beispiel des Psalms 22*, München, nothing is gained by adding the complex structural lists pp. 77-81; 104-107; 124-126 or the depth models pp. 99; 116f; 135f.

structures. They tried instead to uncover the communicative design of entire passages by studying the logic of a narrative, its narrative 'grammar' as well as its intertextuality: each text can be understood as a transformation of already existing texts.[127]

A trend emerged also within general literary studies towards the late 1930s in the USA that developed analytic procedures concerned solely with the text itself. This 'New Criticism' was highly influential and developed quickly into many sub-branches.[128]

B) New Literary Criticism was mainly developed in the USA,[129] Great Britain,[130] the Netherlands[131] and Israel. This view of the Bible as literature has produced several books with very similar sounding titles (see bibliography), differing from each other in several methodological details. This survey is only able to give a general overview of this approach.

1. Many of its representatives are not institutionally bound to particular denominational theological faculties, but consider themselves a general part of humanities. Their approach to the Bible is necessarily more liberal. The Bible has to compete in a free market against all other masterworks of literature, be it Homer, Goethe, or Shakespeare. The interaction of general literary studies with biblical studies has proved very productive for the interpretation of the Bible.

2. New Literary Criticism deliberately seeks to communicate with a non-theological community. Its representative is not tied to denominational structures, but wish to contribute to a general discussion of literature (see 1.)

3. New Literary Criticism deliberately uses everyday language. This choice distinguishes it clearly from structuralist research with its 'art-language'.

4. New Literary Criticism thrives on its critique of the historical-critical method, especially as developed within the German tradition: tearing apart an organic literary work of art in the attempt to reconstruct prior layers of textual development is criticised as something typically German. The historical-critical methods lose themselves in details without the their ability

---

[127] See Todorov, T. (1973), 'Poetik', in F. Wahl (ed.), *Einführung in den Strukturalismus*, stw 10, Frankfurt, pp. 43ff.

[128] Titles used in this context are 'New (Literary) Criticism', 'Literary Approach', 'close reading', 'synchronical approach', 'narratology', or 'narrative criticism'. Some of these scholars refer to themselves as 'poeticians'.

[129] Caroll, R.P. (1993), 'The Hebrew Bible as Literature – a Misprison', in *StTh* 47, pp. 77-90 speaks of 'the Indiana Voice', referring to the 'Indiana Studies in Biblical Literature' published by H. Marks and R. Polzin.

[130] See the series 'Bible and Literature', published by Sheffield University Press.

[131] See work of the so-called 'Amsterdam School' and 'Kampen School'.

to see the whole. Their way of dealing with the text is 'excavative'.[132]
Narratology focuses on the final text and tries to understand and appreciate
the functional structure of the whole (of chapters, groups of chapters, books,
and even groups of books).

5.   New Literary Criticism is concerned with discovering the aesthetics of the
       Bible and the artistry of the biblical authors in their depiction of both the
       beautiful and the ugly.

6.   New Literary Criticism focuses primarily on narrative texts, although the
       methodological principles can be applied to other genres as well.

C) Erich Auerbach has presented an exemplary literary analysis of Genesis 22
in his book *Mimesis: the representation of reality in western literature.* His
remarkable analysis of different depictions of reality in western literature opens
with an essay on ancient literature. In his first chapter, 'The scar of Odysseus's
Auerbach compares the epic prose of Homer's *Ulysses* with the minimalist
depiction of the sacrifice of Isaac in Genesis 22. He comes to the conclusion that
the Old Testament narrative is particularly striking because of what it does *not* say.

Luther translates the beginning as follows: After these things, God tried Abraham and
said to him: Abraham! And he answered: Here I am! – Coming from Homer, this
beginning already gives us reason to pause. Where are the two partners in dialogue
located? This is not stated. Yet the reader does know that the two are not always present
at the same earthly location, that one of the two, God, must arrive from somewhere, must
break into the earthly sphere from some height or depth in order to speak to Abraham.
Where does he come from, from where does he turn to Abraham? Nothing of this is said.
He does not arrive like Zeus or Poseidon from the Ethiopias, where he has enjoyed a
sacrificial meal. Nothing is said of the reasons that motivated him to try Abraham in such
a horrible manner. He did not, like Zeus, discuss these with other gods in a divine
assembly; even his own deliberations inside his own heart are not communicated to the
reader; without warning and mysteriously he breaks into the scene from unknown heights
or depths and calls: Abraham! We can quickly say that this derives from a particular
Jewish view of God, which was so different from its Greek counterpart. This is correct,
but it is not an argument. For how can we explain the particular Jewish view of God?
Already their desert god was a lonely god, not determined according to shape and
dwelling place; his shapelessness, placelessness and loneliness not only stood its own in
competition with the much more picturesque gods of the ancient orient; it was even able
to sharpen its profile. The Jewish view of God is not so much the reason for, but rather a
symptom of, a Jewish way of understanding and portrayal ... Here God appears without
form (and yet he 'appears'), coming from somewhere; we hear only his voice and this
voice calls nothing but a name: without adjective, without descriptive modification of the
person addressed, as we find with every Homeric address. Abraham is accompanied by

---

[132] Alter, R. (1981), *The Art of Biblical Narrative*, London and New York, p. 13.

no tangible attribute, except for the words with which he replies to God: Hinne-ni,[133] here see me – a reply that does suggest a very impressive gesture, expressing obedience and readiness – words that are left to the reader to be further explicated. Both partners in dialogue do not become tangible in any way, but these short, unprepared words following each other in harsh succession; at the most we have a gesture of supplication; all else remains dark.[134]

This technique of minimalist narration leaves lots of room for the reader to become active. It can be found throughout the Old and the New Testament.

A second example is found in Moshe Greenberg's interpretation of the book of Job.[135] The book of Job has been a favourite candidate for diachronic dissection because of its complex structure and its compositional tensions. Traditionally, the prose frame (chs 1-2 + 42:6ff.) is separated from the poetic dialogue. The fragmentary third section of the dialogue, contradictions within Job's speeches, the repetitive arguments of the friends, and other aspects have led to several theories on the original form of these speeches. The hymn to wisdom (ch. 28), Job's final monologue (chs 29-31), and especially the Elihu-speeches are widely considered to be secondary additions. The theophany and God's final speech, which does not seem to answer Job at all, are seen as complex extensions of the original text. Historical-critical analysis separates all these elements from the text and reconstructs the (supposed) original text.[136] None of the historical-critical theories are able to answer the all-important question of the intention and the compositional structure of the final text. And this is where the synchronic, poetic approach demands 'an awareness of the complexities of interplay among the elements of the book'.[137] Greenberg tries to show 'the artistry in the narrative'[138] based on all elements within the book. A synchronic approach to Job aims to understand the final composition of the book, something historical criticism can never accomplish because it destroys that very structure. The pious Job, full of patience, and the rebellious Job in the poetic section are not two textual layers but two sides of a person of faith who has been pushed into suffering. The fragmentary nature of the third dialogue is not a result of textual corruption, but a signal that all debate must fall silent without final conclusion. The end must occur in Job's monologue in

---

[133] Hebrew for: 'Here I am'.

[134] Auerbach, E. (1946), *Mimesis. Dargestellte Wirklichkeit in der abendländischen Literatur* (4th edition 1967), p. 10f.

[135] Greenberg, Mosche (1987), 'Job', in R. Alter and F. Kermode (eds), *The Literary Guide to the Bible*, Glasgow (London 1989), pp. 283-304.

[136] Witte, M. (1994), *Vom Leiden zur Lehre*, BZAW 230, Berlin/New York, presents a recent summary of 73 different historical-critical analyses and then presents his suggestion as #74!

[137] Greenberg, 'Job', p. 283f.

[138] Ibid., p. 285.

which he cries out to God. Elihu's speeches with their focus on suffering as a pedagogical tool are the only possible answer to the question of the meaning of suffering; they must be valued highly. God's speeches protect the mystery of God by refusing to give Job a clear answer, teaching Job that God's horizon is much too wide for him to understand. Greenberg comes to the convincing conclusion that the abrupt stylistic changes between psalmic, wisdom, and juridical theology as well as the inner tensions are stylistically and theologically intentional: 'With its ironies and surprises, its claims and arguments in unresolved tension, the book of Job remains the classic expression in world literature of the irrepressible yearning for divine order, baffled but never stifled by the disarray of reality' (301). The final form of the book has a sensible structure despite its literary tensions. These tensions make it possible to portray the broken texture of reality and the non-systematic nature of God.

D) The advantages of a synchronic–literary approach result from the way in which the Bible is analysed as literature, unburdened by the constraints of academic tradition. This approach is driven by pure enjoyment of the literary beauty of biblical texts. And it is astonishing how many biblical passages, which at first sight seem simple and somewhat dull, turn out to be complex and compositionally dense works of art.[139] Despite detailed analyses of the texts, the results of this approach can very often be easily understood even by non-theologians; this method can also contribute a great deal on a congregational level. Perhaps one can even say that this method revives the reformational call *sola scriptura* in the form of a call for *solus textus*.

We should also not overlook the weaknesses of this approach: several textual problems cannot be solved by synchronic interpretation such as striking contradictions within a text. In Jeremiah, Nebuchadnezzar is both called 'my [=Yahweh's] servant' (25:9; 27:6) and attacked as a hungry, ugly 'dragon' (51:34). These conflicting titles can hardly go back to one and the same author. It is quite sensible, if not necessary, to assume a changing appreciation of Nebuchadnezzar that occurred over time.[140] Unless one assumes that everything in the biblical text makes sense, the textual structure of the Bible forces the scholar to consider diachronic arguments from time to time. New Literary Criticism often underestimates the explanatory power of the historical–critical methods. Many of its observations have already been made by classic representatives of historical criticism and can still be made within this method. A further criticism voiced against synchronic approaches is that they are an expression of a certain middle-class political attitude that deliberately renounces any form of change, showing a

---

[139] See Koenen, K. (1997), 'Prolepsen in alttestamentlichen Erzählungen: Eine Skizze', *VT* 47, pp. 456-477.

[140] This still does not eliminate the task of understanding these two designations as they appear alongside each other in the final text.

lack of ideological awareness.[141] I find this argument hard to follow. The content of the biblical texts is often enough explosively political, even in the final text. The political nature of the biblical text can also to be uncovered by tracing its diachronic growth.

c) Canonical Interpretation of Scripture

A) The philosophical background here is quite similar to that of New Literary Criticism. Once again, an important motivation behind the development of canonical interpretation is a critical stance towards the historical–critical method.[142] In particular, it criticises the constant questioning of the state of affairs behind the final form of the text, and the reconstruction of supposed earlier stages of the current text leads to a confusing jungle of hypotheses. Instead of engaging in a highly speculative search for the original and the genuine (e.g. the *ipsissima vox* of Jesus), canonical interpretation limits itself to the existing final form. The final form is the text to be interpreted. In the concentration on what exists beyond doubt in written form, we encounter true American pragmatism and positivism. Any differentiation between genuine prophetic words and secondary additions, or between the original words of Jesus and later supplementation by the believing community, cannot be the *goal* of the exegetical effort. The later additions themselves are theologically highly important; Gadamer's theory of the filtering function of time and his optimistic belief that only the true and the good are able to persist and find new proponents cultivates a deep trust in the biblical tradition. Its capacity to survive over time is already proof of its quality. The ecclesiastical–confessional character of canonical interpretation can be seen, for example, in the fact that it attributes revelatory qualities to the very process that creates tradition within the believing community. In other words, it 'confesses' the actual development of the history of tradition to be the work of the Holy Spirit. Within the *gratia spiritus applicatrix* (the grace which the Holy Spirit grants each individual personally) tradition made the distinction between that which was necessary, fruitful and enlightening for the life of the believing community and that which obscured or falsified the truth. For this reason, the process of supplementing the text may not be reversed. It should, instead, be accepted in gratitude as a normative guide, created under the auspices of the Holy Spirit. The historical–critical method simply cannot appreciate the fact that *the Bible occupies a special status* within world literature: it is Holy Scripture for two communities of faith (synagogue and church). Its development is thus inseparably connected to this

---

[141] See Caroll, 'The Hebrew Bible'.

[142] See the programmatic monograph by Childs, B.S. (1970), *Bibilical Theology in Crisis*, Philadelphia, which traces the failure of the Biblical Theology movement in the States in the 1940s and 50s.

'ecclesiological' dimension. For this reason, the Bible makes the claim of validity and normativity throughout all generations. In the face of hermeneutical approaches which segment the text and balance its different points of view according to date of origin, place and provenance, canonical interpretation – in analogy to text-immanent literary approaches, as well as Jewish midrashic exegesis and the pre-critical interpretation of the church fathers – focuses on the connectedness and organic unity of the whole Bible. The design of canonical criticism is thus oriented towards a pan-biblical, or – as it says of itself – a holistic approach. Canonical interpretation is not interested in isolated individual texts, but in groups of texts and even entire books. Beyond this, it strives to illuminate the structuring principles of groups of books and even the canon as a whole, always working under the reformational motto: *sacra scriptura sui ipsius interpres* ('sacred scripture is its own best interpreter'). Last, but not least, canonical interpretation aims to show the validity of Scripture in relation to contemporary modes of thinking. By transcending the boundaries between theological disciplines, it seeks a dialogue with systematic and practical theology and a renewal of the importance of Scripture for all of theology.

B) Even though this approach is not much more than 20 years old, it has – as was to be expected – developed in various directions.

B.S. Childs is probably its most important representative. He has written a number of books in which he clearly develops his exegetical programme: an introduction to the Old and an introduction to the New Testament as canonical (!) writings, a theology of the Old Testament on its own, and a theology of the whole Bible. The defining feature of his writings is the constant emphasis on the final form of the text. A close proximity to the theology of Karl Barth allows him to understand the Bible as the Word of God with its centre in Jesus Christ. The biblical text is fixed as the result of the canonical process. It has attained, as it were, a congealed, irreversible dignity and truth which are unique and absolutely normative.

J.A. Sanders, on the other hand, tends to understand the canon as process; truth, in his view, is dynamic, changing and adaptive according to ever new circumstances. He emphasises the processes of transformation within the canonical process. According to Sanders, the development of the canon witnesses to the continual adaptation of the traditions of faith within their respective surroundings. Just as the pupil of an eye accommodates itself to different degrees of light, biblical traditions adjust themselves to their inner biblical context. When studying these processes of adaptation, the contemporary believer – by structural analogy – is able to bring his life in line with the traditions of faith.

In Germany, through scholars such as F.L. Hossfeld, K. Koenen, N. Lohfink, O.H. Steck, and E. Zenger, to name but a few, canonical interpretation is especially understood as the highest level of redaction criticism and form criticism. The aim of these scholars is an analysis of the networks in which texts are placed by their authors that aims to uncover the macrostructures and compositional techniques of biblical books. The object of exegesis, for example, is no longer a single psalm as an individual work of art, but rather as a part of a group of psalms or a book of psalms, which itself is also connected to other psalm books, which again is part of the large structure of the Old Testament canon. Canonical interpretation can also mean the detailed search for traces of the process of canonisation within the Old Testament. In this, the emphasis can lie with canonisation as a step towards fundamentalism (Barr, Barton), or, quite to the contrary, with canonisation as the documentation of an intense theological discourse in which different conflicting positions are represented (Oeming).

C) 1. An instructive example of the intention of the biblical macrostructure is found in the comparison between the Hebrew canon and the Greek canon of the Septuagint.[143] The three-fold Masoretic canon signals a theological evaluation: God's revelation in creation, history (especially the exodus from Egypt) and law (giving of the law at Sinai) stands at the beginning and forms the foundation for the whole. The subsequent prophets and writings are explanations and applications of the Torah. The cornerstones of the various building blocks are explicitly connected to the Torah (Jos 1, Mal 3, Ps 1). At the centre of the Torah stands Lev 16 with its theology of holiness and cultic atonement at Yom Kippur. The ending of the Biblia Hebraica in 2 Chr 32:22ff is programmatic: 'Whoever is among you of all his people, may the LORD his God be with him! Let him go up [to Jerusalem]!' The point of this ending is the description of a new Israelite exodus from exile and movement back to the spiritual centre. In contrast, the Greek canon has a very different centre of meaning. The individual books are arranged in a strikingly different order, in accordance with a unique historical–theological blueprint. In its first section, the past of the people of God is portrayed chronologically; this chronological guideline determines the order of the books. Its second section contains wisdom teachings that are aimed at the present and are meant to provide guidance for a life in accordance with God. Its final section – its main goal and focus – contains the prophets as those who bear witness to the future. The Hebrew book of law becomes a Greek book of expectation; the Jewish focus of the Tenach on the Torah becomes – and this is basic to the Christian Church – orientation towards and hope for the future. The programmatic ending of the LXX is found in Mal 3:23f: 'Lo, I will send you the prophet Elijah before the great and terrible day of the LORD comes. He will turn the hearts of parents to their children and the hearts of children to their parents, so that I will not come and strike the land with a curse.'

---

[143] See Zenger, E. (1991), *Das Erste Testament*, Düsseldorf, pp. 162-184 as well as the critical comments by Mosis, R. (1997), 'Canonical Approach und Vielfalt des Kanons. Zu einer neuen Einleitung in das Alte Testament', in *TThZ* 106, pp. 39-59 and Budde, A. (1997), 'Der Abschluß des alttestamentlichen Kanons und seine Bedeutung für die kanonische Schriftauslegung', in *BN* 87, pp. 39-55.

2. The example of 1 Kings 18 and 19 shows that seemingly contradictory passages can be placed together in a way that makes sense.[144] After Elijah's triumphant success against the prophets of Baal the mood of the narrative changes drastically. Jezebel vows revenge and Elijah flees into the desert. Historical criticism has traditionally assumed two separate sources for these two chapters.[145] In contrast, Childs has shown how the juxtaposition of this material is intentional and makes a theological statement on a narrative level. Faith has two sides: a battle facing outward and a battle facing inward, a public and a private dimension. By placing these chapters side by side the redactor shows the close relationship between faith and temptation, success and despair. Faith is not just a success story; experiences of adversity and rejection – theologically speaking: the experience of the cross – are integral to it. Tearing apart the final form of the Elijah narratives destroys these insights.

3. Canonical exegesis wants to show how the meaning of a particular passage is also determined by its precise position in the canon. A very nice example of this is Psalm 1. In traditional exegesis, Psalm 1 is seen as a difficult piece of poetry, highly influenced by wisdom literature. It constructs the picture of a dual path: the righteous are saved (= the tree, planted by flowing waters); the unrighteous face damnation (= chaff, blow away by the wind). This interpretation is expanded considerably by taking the canonical placement into account. The immediate context is Mal 3 and Psalm 2. Both these texts emphasise the scope of the coming judgement. Where Psalm 1 focuses on the individual, Psalm 2 speaks of the nations. A common term combining both is the phrase of 'descending into the abyss' (Ps 1:5; Ps 2:11). Psalm 1 thus connects the Psalter to the prophetic works, a situation highlighted by the quote from Jer 17:8 in verse 3 as well. A further question posed by Psalm 1 is the exact meaning of *Torah* (teaching). God's Torah, the Pentateuch, comes to mind. On the other hand, it is reminiscent of the repeated 'his teaching' in Deut 17:19, where the king is called to read the law all the days of his life. In addition, the verse is almost identical to Jos 1:8. In this manner, the Psalter is intimately connected to the Torah and its continuing importance in Israel's history. Psalm 1 and Psalm 41 frame the the first book of the Psalter. Psalm 41 also begins with a beatitude. It calls the one blessed, who takes care of the weak (Ps 41:2). Whereas Ps 1 starts with a negative statement ('Blessed is who does *not* follow, *not* walk, *not* sit'), Psalm 41 starts with a positive statement ('He who takes care of the weak is spared from judgement'). And with Psalm 150, Psalm 1 frames the entire Psalter. Psalm 1 is the opening door with a focus on judgement, Psalm 150 ends with all the instruments in jubilant praise of Yahweh. We can thus see that the entire book of Psalms moves from lament to praise. The strong interconnectedness of Psalm 1 shows its key position in the entire Old Testament. The

---

[144] See Childs, B.S. (1980), 'On Reading the Elijah Narratives', in *Interpr* 34, pp. 128-137.

[145] See e.g. Würthwein, E. (1984), *Die Bücher der Könige*, ATD 11,2, Göttingen, pp. 205-232.

'ugly duckling' (when seen in isolation) becomes a stately swan when read canonically.

4. I will present one final example of how theological discussion exists within the Bible around a certain passage. This discussion does not resolve the issue; it instead takes the reader into the discussion. Gen 15:1-6 tells of Abraham who believed in an heir from his own seed despite the evidence of his old and frail body.[146] Neh 9:7 interprets this to mean that God made a covenant with him, because he found him faithful. This explains Abraham's importance for Israel. It does not become quite clear whether Neh 9:7 refers to Gen 15:17 or rather to Gen 22 (the sacrifice of Isaac). In 1 Macc 2:51-52, Abraham is seen by the leader of the rebellion, Mattathias, as an example for his own current situation: 'Remember the deeds of the ancestors, which they did in their generations; and you will receive great honour and an everlasting name. Was not Abraham found faithful when tested, and it was reckoned to him as righteousness?' The text here refers clearly to Gen 22. Paul responds to Abraham in a different manner again. He sees Abraham's faith as defined by believing the impossible promise of a son. In contrast, James 2 explicitly makes the point that faith without works is dead. Just as Abraham's faith was seen in his action of sacrificing Isaac, our faith should show itself in our actions. The canon contains a discussion on the correct balance between faith and works. It is not our task to resolve this discussion, but rather to take part in it. This shows clearly that the formation of the canon is not an early form of fundamentalism, as J. Barton believes, but rather the institutionalising of a continual theological discourse. The wisdom of the canon consists in the preservation of different statements on one and the same topic. It prevents the mutation of faith into ideology, ensuring honest insight is kept alive by permanent discourse.

D) Canonical interpretation in all its forms makes important contributions to the enterprise of understanding biblical texts. By taking large compositional structures seriously, even across different books, it highlights an aspect which is as important as small, detailed analysis. By reading biblical texts (from the Old and New Testaments) in combination, an old tradition of the Church is revived. Its dismissal of historical criticism makes it possible for the theological laity to follow its arguments and insights: connections between theological texts are not only made by theological professionals. A further important achievement is the reminder that the Bible is Holy Scripture for a community of faith (in the case of the Old Testament, even two communities) and can never be dealt with adequately by scholarly exegesis alone. Canonical exegesis can be an important bridge between exegesis and dogmatics, two disciplines that have been drifting apart for some time.

---

[146] See Oeming, M. (1998), 'Der Glaube Abrahams. Zur Rezeptionsgeschichte von Gen 15,6 in der Zeit des zweiten Tempels', in *ZAW* 110. pp. 16-33.

Among all these strengths, we should not overlook certain deficits and dangers. The overly critical attitude towards historical criticism is unfortunate. This can lead to the creation of false oppositions which only futher the cause of fundamentalism. An analysis of the macro-structure of the Bible can be combined without problems with the historical–critical method. This combination can also serve as a critical control of these macro-analyses. The canonical approach does not overcome the confusing plethora of historical–ciritical hypotheses, it merely adds to them. It is also in constant danger of over-interpreting apparent thematic connections. Finally, it remains an open question which canon should be used as a framework for interpretation and why.

d) Exegesis as Speech-Act and Word-Act

A) Martin Heidegger's late work is obscure in many ways, especially in regard to his philosophy of language. In conversation with language, which itself speaks not just as an entity among other entities ('Vorhandenes unter Vorhandenem'), human beings enter into a relationship with being itself, in which they receive a 'message from being' ('Botschaft des Seins') calling them to 'say what has to be said'.[147] Poetry, that is artistic language, is thus of special importance: 'Poetry and thought are each in their own unique way the true nature of speech.'[148] In language, being comes into being. Language is the 'house of being'.[149] H.-G. Gadamer makes a similar statement: 'All being that can be understood is language.'[150] As the house of being, language is of utmost importance. Far from just naming something that exists independently, language forges the path for being itself, which only exists in language. Language is thus elevated to almost sacramental status. Being, transcendence, and immanence occur in, with and under language.

Language is understood in completely different terms than in the organon model of K. Bühler.[151] According to this view, language is a tool that can accomplish three basic functions: presentation of the outside world, expression of the inside world, and exhortation. These tasks of statement, revelation and initiation of action are seen by Heidegger as derived modes of language; he takes a much more fundamental and original view of language. Language does not refer to something outside itself; it does not aim to initiate action or speak about the future. Language is not a function of 'I', 'you', 'he', 'she', 'it'. Being itself reveals itself in language.

---

[147] Heidegger, M. (1959), *Unterwegs zur Sprache*, Pfullingen, pp. 125.136.150.

[148] Heidegger, M. (1954), *Was heißt denken?*, Tübingen, p. 87.

[149] See Anz, W. (1967), 'Die Stellung der Sprache bei Heidegger', in H.-G. Gadamer (ed.), *Das Problem der Sprache*, München, pp. 469-482; Jäger, H. (1971), *Heidegger und die Sprache*, Bern; Kockelmans, J.J. (ed.) (1972), *On Heidegger and Language*, Evanston.

[150] Gadamer, H.-G. (1960), *Wahrheit und Methode*, Tübingen, p. 450.

[151] Bühler, K. (1934), *Sprachtheorie. Die Darstellungsfunktion der Sprache*, Jena.

The important word here is *in*; only *in* language does being come into being. The development of this theory, which has its critics, of course, cannot be understood without referring to the theory of the biblical logos and to christology. Being only exists because of God's creative Word. We cannot speak about this Word objectively. It is an event that is performed at every moment.

B) Heidegger's view of language is applied to biblical texts, or better, biblical thinking, in E. Fuchs' (1903-1983) 'language of faith'[152] and G. Ebeling's (b. 1912) teachings on the word of God as 'word-act'.[153] As a new hermeneutical approach, these theories were discussed widely in the 1960s.[154] On the one hand they appear quite complicated and abstract; on the other hand they are very concrete. If the Word has such importance and power, then an emphasis on the *viva vox evangelii*, the word proclaimed and preached as kerygma, is a necessary consequence.[155] Heidegger's philosophy enables a theoretical justification of the primacy of Christian proclamation, of the preached Word (see Romans 10:14-17!). Reading E. Fuchs, one feels the the power of the living Word of Jesus Christ, the 'hot breath' of the Word of God. God said 'yes' in Jesus Christ, 'yes' to the world, 'yes' to human beings despite their sins, 'yes' to the future. This saving Word of God is the sacramental word. It occurs again and again, new every moment.

C) An example of the application of this approach to the Bible is the concept of holistic biblical interpretation proposed by A.H.J. Gunneweg (1922-1990), which I have described as a 'model of language history'.[156]

> The Old Testament as transported into the ecumenical Greek language presents us with the linguistic means for the proclamation of the Christ-event. Stated differently: Christian proclamation creates a new language for itself, worthy of the eschatological novelty of the Christ-event, but it creates this language by referring back to the language of the Old Testament. This referral is necessary: the historical contingency of the Christ-

---

[152] Fuchs, E. (1963), *Hermeneutik*, Bad Cannstatt, pp. 101f. Fuchs is concerned with the portrayal of the history of being as a language of being (see also: (1960), *Zur Frage nach dem historischen Jesus*, Tübingen, p. 429). He states: 'Being grows out of language when language teaches us about the space in which our existence is determined ... the theological teaching of the the the word of God is the question of existence within the horizon of biblical language' ((1959), *Zum hermeneutischen Problem in der Theologie*, Tübingen, p. 115).

[153] See Ebeling, G. (1959), 'Wort Gottes und Hermeneutik', in *ZThK* 56, pp. 224-251, as well as many different essays gathered in 3 volumes with the title *Wort und Glaube*.

[154] See Robinson, J.M. and Cobb, J.B. (eds) (1965), *Die neue Hermeneutik*, Neuland in der Theologie 2, Zürich/Stuttgart.

[155] Ebeling, 'Wort Gottes'. Robinson and Cobb *Die neue Hermeneutik*: 'Where the word happens in truth, existence is illuminated' (139). 'Proclamation that has occurred should become proclamation that is occurring' (142).

[156] Oeming, M. (1987), *Gesamtbiblische Theologien der Gegenwart*, Stuttgart, pp. 165-181.

event, of the paradox of Eschaton who 'once and for all' entered history, the Word that became flesh, correlates to the contingency of this – and of no other – language of the beginning. The fact that the initial proclamation of Jesus Christ goes back to this language and immerses itself in this language, lays the foundation for the necessity and the canonicity of Old Testament texts. If the Christ-event is primarily a proclaimed event that must continually be proclaimed anew, if it thus is necessarily dependent on language, and if language is different and more than the verbal wrapping and an interchangeable medium for communicative content, then we can recognize the central and contextual interconnectedness between the message of the New Testament and the language of the Old Testament. Language as such is always an interpretation of the world and of existence – which can only be questioned critically by means of a meta-language. This is even more true for a language which claims to contains the statement: Thus says JHWH, and which cements the claim of a faith in God beyond all other gods in language. This language articulates an understanding of existence and the world, which – despite all cross references, dependencies, and analogies to religions and cultures of the surrounding peoples – remains recognizably different. This understanding of existence is the same as that of the New Testament, the same as the Christian in the face of the Greek, the humanistic, or the idealistic understanding of existence ... The New Testament does not only presuppose the monotheism of the Old Testament and proclaim the Christ-event as the act of the one creator God and Lord. This proclamation can only grow out of – and only exist within – the sphere of creation, earth, humanity, history of the peoples and of Israel, of blessing, fruitfulness, and wisdom, and also of the desire for the immortal, of sin, curse, distance from God, despair, misguidance, and rejection which the the Old Testament uncovers with its language. All these 'topics', which are almost as numerous as the aspects and facets, contents and figures of human life, are presupposed by the New Testament and continued through affirmation, rejection, shaping, and correction. As the New Testament itself concentrates on one aspect, on Christ and his salvation, it needs not reiterate all this again and again. This context itself resounds through the linguistic connection to the Old Testament. The a priori interpretation of world and existence through the language of the Old Testament envelops the proclamation of Christ; this proclamation enters this pre-interpretation: the Word becomes – as well – *this flesh* ... Scripture becomes this testimony to Christ, by presenting this language and the contents directly connected to this language which is now used to express this witness to Christ. For this very reason, Christ is born of a virgin, is born in Bethlehem, and has to flee to Egypt, so that the prophecy may be fulfilled that God has called his son out of Egypt (Matt 1:23; 2:1; Luke 2; Matt 2:15,18; and Isa 7:14; Mi 5:1; Hos 11:1; Jer 31:15): Christ himself proclaims in his first sermon in Nazareth that Scripture has been fulfilled in him (Luke 4:16-21). For his great and formative sermon he climbs a mountain, like Moses whose law he fulfils and supersedes (Matt 5:1). Christ's passion story, especially, is full of Old Testament quotes and allusions. Jesus enters Jerusalem according to Zech 9:9 – even on two animals because the prophet is understood to have proclaimed it thus. Judas betrays him for 30 silver shekels, because this amount is found in Zech 11:9f (Mt 21:5; 25:15; 27:3-9). In other aspects the description follow the details in Ps 22. This description aims to show that

Scripture has been fulfilled in its very details. Scripture has prophesied and this prophecy has been fulfilled in Christ ... We only have to imagine a church cleansed of the Old Testament with a New Testament equally free of the Old Testament, with clean agendas and a cleaned out hymnal, without "Macht hoch die Tür", without the manger in Bethlehem, without ox and ass, without the Cananite-Israelite festivals that have determined the high days of our church year! Without the language of the Old Testament, the church would lose its language altogether and it would fail to find words to proclaim its witness of Christ.[157]

H. Weders presents us with an example for the New Testament. In his view, language not only has the power of depiction, but also the power of creation. Language is 'not just mimesis, but also poesis'.[158] He sees the parables as metaphors[159] containing creative speech able to draw something from the past, to let something come to life, something that cannot exist other than in language. The parables are a correspondence of the past with the present. In the parables, the reign of God becomes reality. The parables of Jesus cannot be separated from the person of Jesus and understood as general truths. The reason for the speech and action of Jesus was to let the reign of God become reality for those who encountered him. How much closer could a person get to the reign of God than by experiencing it in himself? God's presence comes into language in the parables and thus into being! We must understand the miracles of God in the same manner: they draw the future of God into the present[160] and are thus of universal eschatological, not apocalyptical importance.

D) By making the text a necessary and unavoidable medium for the presence of God and thus elevating language to a sacramental level, this model values language like no other. It is highly important when biblical proclamation becomes God-in-language and thus the location of his presence. Reformational thoughts on Scripture and the basic beliefs of dialectic theology appear here from a new perspective.

The criticism addressed to this approach from many sides says with Goethe's Faust: 'I cannot elevate language to these heights!'[161] There is a poster in a centre for professional education, established by the Lutheran church close to Rengsdorf. The picture displays the head of a minister. His mouth is wide open and the word 'words' flows hundredfold out of it. Words, words, words, all across his face, all across the entire picture. The painter, certainly no friend of a Word-of-God theology, is obviously trying to say: words, nothing but words, everything is empty

---

[157] Gunneweg, A.H.J. (1988), *Vom Verstehen des Alten Testaments. Eine Hermeneutik*, GAT 1, Göttingen, pp. 187f.192.197f.

[158] Weder, H. (1986), *Neutestamentliche Hermeneutik*, Zürich, pp. 155-203, pp.168f.

[159] Weder, H. (1990), *Die Gleichnisse Jesu als Metaphern*, FRLANT 120 Göttingen.

[160] See Weder, H. (1984), 'Wunder Jesu und Wundergeschichten', in *VuF* 29, pp. 25-49.

[161] Goethe, J.W. (1821), *Faust. Der Tragödie erster Teil*, Weimar, line 1226.

drivel and nothing but hot air. There have been enough words, let us see some action. This is a painful statement, especially in a centre for the training of ministers, but it clearly speaks to a fatal misunderstanding of biblical preaching in the mind of many ministers. It is a mistake to believe that a focus on language, on a quasi-sacramental biblical 'performance' is lofty, abstract and non-political, that a 'normal' person wants to understand the Bible along the lines of Bühler's theory as a depiction of God's nature, his actions, the experiences of believers, or the call for personal action. The hermeneutical approach of E. Fuch and those close to him[162] make the important point that God's salvation occurs primarily in believing in his words of promise and forgiveness. One thing must be said in all this: the persuasive power of this model is closely connected to the personal charisma and the rhetorical power of its representatives. This may be true with all hermeneutical models, it is especially obvious here. One could say with a poem by J. Eichendorff

A song asleep in all things
dreaming on and on,
and the world begins to sing,
if the magic word is found.[163]

Finding this 'magic word' in order to proclaim the spirit of Scripture anew, to unleash the power of the Bible for the contemporary world, is something that transcends any method.

---

[162] Such as G. Ebeling, J. Fangmeier, A.H.J. Gunneweg, E. Jüngel, D. Lange, Ch. Möller, D. Nestle, M. Trowitzsch, and H. Weder.

[163] 'Schläft ein Lied in allen Dingen / die da träumen fort und fort, / und die Welt beginnt zu singen, / triffst du nur das Zauberwort.'

Chapter 6

Methods Focused on Readers and their Worlds

In the search for the meaning of a particular text it becomes quickly apparent that meaning is not objective, but is rather constructed by the individual reader and interpreter.[164] This insight into the productivity of the reader leads us to an altogether different area of the hermeneutical square: not the intention of the productive author, nor the aesthetics of the text itself, but the reception of the reader will now be our focus.[165] It is no longer important what kind of message is sent out. Instead, the focus shifts to how the message is received and who receives it. This paradigm shift has increased the importance of the reader in modern literary criticism immensely. The poet Martin Walser sums it up: 'Reading is not like listening to music, but rather like making music. The reader himself is the instrument.'[166] Interpretation no longer draws meaning out of the text; interpretation places meaning into the text. Interpretation is construction, production, re-reading. The political, social and cultural contexts of respective readers determine to a much greater degree what happens in the act of interpretation than the Bible itself. The climax of this reader-oriented criticism is deconstructionism.[167] Rebelling against and critically mocking any objective interpretation, be it author-centred or work-centred, deconstructionism aims to show that every interpretation is part of a highly subjective game of meaning-making. A spoken word is already a personal re-actualisation of written language. A text's claim to reality is secondary to this intra-subjective activity; language refers to language. The manifold connections of a text to its intertextual context can never be fully described and analysed by any method. In this vein, Derrida

---

[164] See Dohmen, Ch. and Stemberger, G. (1996), *Hermeneutik der jüdischen Bibel und des Alten Testaments*, Stuttgart, p. 193.

[165] Warning, R. (1979), 'Rezeptionsästhetik als literaturwissenschaftliche Pragmatik', in idem (ed.), *Rezeptionsästhetik. Theorie und Praxis*, München, p. 9.

[166] Walser, M. (1993), *Des Lesers Selbstverständnis*, Eggingen, p. 12.

[167] See Derrida, J. (1988), *Grammatologie*, Frankfurt, 2nd edition; overviews: Culler, J. (1988), *Derrida und die poststrukturalistische Literaturtheorie*, Reinbeck; Rorty, R. (1993), *Eine Kultur ohne Zentrum*, Stuttgart.

refers to his approach as anti-hermeneutics.[168] The deconstruction of biblical texts enables many possibilities for free association,[169] even a certain interpretational anarchism. It encourages word plays as well as wild improvisations in the mother-tongue of the interpreter, no matter what the original language of the text may be.

An example as brilliant as it is blatant is presented by Moore in his essay *The Gospel of the Look*[170] ... His ideas about Luke–Acts cannot be presented or understood in any language but English. In Luke–Acts the narrating 'I' (cf. Luke 1:3; Acts 1:1) turns to be an Eye: that of a roving-eye or at-the-scene-reporter (174). The gospel of Luke displays Jesus as the 'Son/Sun of God'. By applying deconstructive 'differing/deferring' in respect to Luke 9:45, Moore moves from Luke to Lacan: 'the phallus can play its role only when veiled' (171) – the Lacanian phallus is not the penis; rather, it is the signifier, that (unconscious) lack in every subject that feeds desire while keeping it insatiable. It is 'the signifier which has no signified' ... Thus, the following is true (or not): 'Luke, Look, lack, Lacan' ... Even if exegesis turns into a free fall of ideas, one aspect of deconstructive criticism of biblical texts seems to be important: the discovery of deconstructive, myth-critical, non-fundamentalist movements *within the texts themselves*, urge us to demythologise the texts and take a critical look at our exegetical methods.[171]

This increasingly radical focus on an analysis of what happens in readers when they interact with text is probably the most important theoretical shift within the last 25 years as compared to older hermeneutical trends.

---

[168] Forget, Ph. (ed.) (1984), *Text und Interpretation. Gadamer–Derrida-Debatte*, München; Michelfelder, D.P. and Palmer, R.E. (ed.) (1989), *The Gadamer–Derrida Encounter*, New York.

[169] See Gumbrecht, H.U. (1986), 'Déconstruction Deconstructed. Transformationen französischer Logozentrismus-Kritik in der amerikanischen Literaturtheorie', in *PhR* 33, pp. 1-35; Hunter, J.H. (1991), 'Deconstruction and the Old Testament. An Evaluation of "Context" with Reference to 1 Samuel 9,2', in *OTE* 4, pp. 249-259; idem (1994), 'Interpretationstheorie in postmoderner Zeit. Suche nach Interpretationsmöglichkeiten anhand von Psalm 144', in K. Seybold and E. Zenger (eds), *Neue Wege der Psalmenforschung*, HBSt 1, Freiburg, pp. 45-62; Hayner, S.R. and McKenzie, S.L. (eds) (1993), *To Each Its Own Meaning. An Introduction to Biblical Criticisms and their Application*, Louisville.

[170] Jobling, D. and Moore, S.D. (eds) (1992), *Poststructuralism as Exegesis*, Semeia 54, Atlanta.

[171] Schunack, G. (1996), 'Neuere literaturkritische Interpretationsverfahren in der anglo-amerikanischen Exegese', in *VuF* 41, pp. 28-55, 55; however, I fail to understand the origin of Schunack's urge for self-critical demythologising.

It must be stated, however, that this approach is not nearly as new and modern as it claims to be. The passages on hermeneutics by Augustine have shown that one text carries several meanings that enable different readers at different times to draw different aspects from the text. Deconstructive reading stands in a long, long tradition, despite its tendency to act as the wild new kid on the block. Free association was part of the interpretation of Scripture from rabbinical hermeneutics and Christian allegory right up to contemporary homiletic techniques. A 'deconstructive' reading of the Bible (allowing the texts to inspire a free flow of thoughts and pictures) is probably the most common way of dealing with the Bible. The only new aspect is the conscious affirmation and reflection upon this fact.

a) The History of Effect (Wirkungsgeschichtliche Exegese)

A) H.-G. Gadamer has been a strong voice calling for the recovery of an awareness of a text's particular history of influence.[172] He understands this history as the melting of our contemporary horizons with the horizons of previous times. All understanding of traditional material cannot be immediate understanding. The interpreter always stands (mostly subconsciously) within a tradition that strongly influences his personal horizon. Exegesis without preconditions is not possible. This unchangeable hermeneutical situation must be methodologically reflected. Instead of approaching a text directly as a blank slate, interpreters must become aware that all understanding is determined by prior understanding (='prejudices'). The hermeneutical and the historical are thus inevitably connected.

A further philosophical precondition is the postmodern insight that all understanding is contextual and that truth is in part necessarily situational, perhaps even in total.[173] The meaning of a work can only be understood fully by focusing on the various meanings it has had in different historical and geographic contexts. Part of this focus is the place of a particular work within the large context of all literature. 'Theories that focus on the history of reception not only allow us to understand a work in its various situations, but also to place this work in its "literary order" in order to recognise its status within the experience of literature as

---

[172] See Gadamer, H.-G. (1960), *Wahrheit und Methode*, Tübingen, pp. 284-290.

[173] For theological consequences of this insight see Sundermeier, Th. and Usdorf, W. (eds) (1991), *Die Begegnung mit dem Anderen. Plädoyers für eine interkulturelle Hermeneutik*, Gütersloh; Sundermeier, Th. (1996), *Den Fremden verstehen. Eine praktische Hermeneutik*, Göttingen; Kunstmann, J. (1996), *Christentum in der Optionsgesellschaft. Postmoderne in Theologie und Kirche*, theol. diss., München, esp. pp. 224-227 where postmodernism is evaluated as a gain for theology.

such.'[174] The historical interaction between author and reader leads to a continual increase in the role of the reader, especially as the author who wrote for an actual audience could not have foreseen the varying audience his text would address in the future. 'Quidquid recipitur, recipitur ad modum recipientis.'[175] The history of the influence of a text (as seen from a postmodern view) is the history of the reader's victory over the author. For our approach to Scripture, these ideas open a vast field for study. In how many ways did the Bible, as one of the formative aspects of western culture, influence its readers?

B) The task of understanding is the study of the many ways in which a biblical text has been read. This task faces huge obstacles. Exegesis becomes intimately connected to church history, with the cultural history of the Judaeo-Christian world and its transformations in other cultures. Innumerable areas of art (painting, sculpting, architecture), music (from Gregorian chant to pop-music), media (from the Biblia Pauperum as picture-Bible for the illiterate and Bible illustrations and Bible comics to the Bible atlas on CD-ROM), literature (from the explicit reworking of biblical material to subtle allusions), daily language, advertisement, or highly abstract philosophical thinking – the influence of the Bible (be it only as critical rejection) can be discovered in virtually every area. G. Ebeling has called church history the history of interpreting the Bible.[176] In order to understand the Bible, one must work through the entire spectrum of re-reading within church history as well as the spectrum of influence of the Bible upon culture.[177] The scientific method is redefined on this premise as the comprehensive study of the history of interpretation and the discussion of the changes of understanding within this history.

For the Old Testament, the Jewish history of reception is of special importance.[178] A basic principle of rabbinic exegesis is 'narrative

---

[174] Jauss, H.R. (1970), 'Literaturgeschichte als Provokation der Literaturwissenschaft', in idem, *Literaturgeschichte als Provokation*, Frankfurt, p. 189.

[175] Jauss, H.R. (1979), 'Racine und Goethes Iphigenie – mit einem Nachwort über die Partialität der rezeptionsgeschichtlichen Methode', in R. Warning (ed.), *Rezeptionsästhetik*, p. 383.

[176] Ebeling, G. (1966), 'Kirchengeschichte als Geschichte der Auslegung der Heiligen Schrift', in idem, *Wort Gottes und Tradition. Studien zu einer Hermeneutik der Konfessionen*, Tübingen, pp. 9-27.

[177] See Sivan, G. (1973), *The Bible and Civilization*, Library of Jewish Knowledge, Jerusalem.

[178] See e.g. the vast collection of material gathered by Strack, H. and Billerbeck, P. (1965), *Kommentar zum Neuen Testament aus Talmud und Midrasch*, München; Gradwohl, R. (1986ff), *Bibelauslegung aus jüdischen Quellen*, Vos. 1-4, Stuttgart; Osten-Sacken, P. von der (1985), 'Vom Nutzen jüdischer Schriftauslegung für Christen', in idem (ed.), *Wie aktuell ist das Alte Testament? Beiträge aus Israel und Berlin*, Berlin, pp. 86-106;

amplification'.[179] Understanding a text involves the combination of two or more stories loosely associated by common terms. The creation of ever new collages leads to ever new situations in which new meanings are uncovered. The rabbis allow themselves many freedoms in their interpretation of texts. They are propelled by the conviction that the Torah has an inner unity without chronological order of before or after. The Torah contains everything; it just needs to be shaken in the right way. An 'interpretation' can consist of Gematria. Every letter of the Hebrew alphabet is associated with a number. The resulting numerical connections lead to new meanings in the text. Another approach is the use of a word as anagram.[180] According to the 32 hermeneutical rules of Rabbi Eliezer, we are even allowed to read words backwards, to introduce substitutionary alphabets or to separate a single word into several words. In this way, the rabbis combine very strict rules (especially in the interpretation of legal material) with a high degree of freedom reminiscent of dream interpretation in late antiquity.[181]

The study of the history of homiletical intepretation is also part of the history of textual influence, because it is a clear indication of the various ways meaning was introduced into biblical texts during various times and in various cultures. It is a well known fact that preachers of all times interpreted a text homiletically[182] and

---

idem (1991), 'Der Wille zur Erneuerung des christlich-jüdischen Verhältnisses in seiner Bedeutung für biblische Exegese und Theologie', in *JBTh* 6, pp. 243-267.

[179] Ebach, J. (1985), 'Die Schwester des Mose', in idem, *Hiobs Post. Gesammelte Aufsätze zum Hiobbuch, zu Themen biblischer Theologie und zur Methodik der Exegese*, Neukirchen, p. 135.

[180] The letters of a certain word are written vertically and form the initial letters for new words to be filled in. In this approach, also referred to as notaricon, a single word becomes the starting point for a crossword puzzle.

[181] See Stemberger, G. (1979), *Das klassische Judentum. Kultur und Geschichte der rabbinischen Zeit*, München, pp. 132-138.

[182] Commentaries used to exist that did not interpret the text according to the historical–critical method, but rather with the explicit focus on hermeneutical concerns. Examples are *Theologisch-homiletisches Bibelwerk. Die Heilige Schrift Alten und Neuen Testaments mit Rücksicht auf das theologisch-homiletische Bedürfniß des pastoralen Amtes in Verbindung mit namhaften evangelischen Theologen bearbeitet und herausgegeben von J.P. Lange* (Bielefeld and Leipzig 1870ff), or the homiletical commentary by A. Dächsel, which inserted homiletical explications directly into the biblical text 'und den zur weiteren Vertiefung nöthigsten Fingerzeigen, miest in Aussprüchen der bedeutendsten Gottesgelehrten aus allen Zeitaltern der Kirche. Nebst Holzschnitten und colorirten Karten. Zunächst für Schullehrer und Hausväter, doch mit steter Rücksicht auf das besondere Bedürfniß der Geistlichen und Theologie-Studirenden' (Leipzig 1874ff). Similar commentaries are still available in the 20th century: *Herders Bibelkommentar: Die Heilige Schrift für das Leben erklärt* (1940-

often focused not on the intention of the work or of the author, but used the text rather as a quarry or a springboard[183] for ideas that seemed and seem appropriate for a certain context.[184] Sermons are a true treasure for studying the history of textual influence!

C) The narrative of Abraham's sacrifice of Isaac has always faced its interpreters with a difficult task: how can we understand that God demands that a father slaughters his only,[185] his beloved son? The interpretation of Gen 22 takes on different shapes, from the rabbis and the church fathers through the Middle Ages, Reformation, and Enlightenment up to today.[186] From the perspective of the history of religion, the text shows the synthesis of an important development in human history, namely the rejection of human sacrifice. The climax of the text, in this view, is found in verse 13. Large parts of Judaism interpret the text *collectively*: Isaac represents the people of Israel which was sacrificed again and again (had to suffer from persecution) in the course of its history and still survived; this interpretation has gained a lot of ground since the Shoa. The Aqedah is a picture of atonement for Israel and for the world (see Rom 8:32). Alongside these interpretations are many *individualistic* interpretations: Christians and Jews alike voice their admiration for Abraham, who passed the final test after a series of difficult tests:[187] God himself made it hard for Abraham to believe in him; Abraham's faith showed itself in holding on to this deep, dark, obscure and even revolting God despite all temptation.[188] This is true faith! According to a different

---

1950). Even the scholarly series *Biblischer Kommentar* contains a section with the title 'Goal' in which the critical approach is abandoned in favour of homiletical suggestions. It is noticeable that these suggests are often not tied to the previous exegesis at all. Theological faculties still offered courses until the 1960s with such titles as: 'Genesis – interpreted for homiletical use'. It is unfortunate that this tradition has completely come to an end. A good commentary should always combine the past horizon of the text with the present horizon.

[183] See Möller, Ch. (1982), 'Anfechtung und Schriftauslegung auf dem Weg vom Text zur Predigt', in *ZThK* 79, pp. 374-390.

[184] See Wiedemann, H.-G. (1975), *Die Praxis der Predigtvorbereitung*, Predigtstudien Vol. 3, Stuttgart, pp. 113-123. Following E. Lange, he describes the preacher as the *advocate of his listeners*. The text merely creates an alienation effect, profiling and controlling the homiletical situation.

[185] His only son with his legitimate wife.

[186] See Lerch, D. (1950), *Isaaks Opferung christlich gedeutet*, Tübingen.

[187] Pirqe Avot V,4 speaks of 10 different tests, Jub 17,17 of 7. In each case, Abraham's love for God is tested.

[188] Zvi Koliz let the Jew Jossel Rackower in the Warsaw Ghetto speak the following words to God: While his house was already burning and he himself could die at any moment, he said: 'It will not be more than an hour and I will be reunited with my wife and children

interpretation, Abraham is supposed to learn a certain mode of being: nothing is certain, nothing can be possessed, everything is grace, everything can be taken away. An existential interpretation sees Abraham as the symbol for the state of complete isolation (Kierkegaard); a psychological approach highlights the path of Abraham as the path that everyone must take: Abraham as the prototypical human being has to learn to be himself, to exist as if his son did not exist. He must find himself, and this implies letting go of his son. This release is also basic to the psychological health of every child: 'Children can only find their own life when parents learn to live theirs.'[189] Other interpretations place Isaac in the centre of interest. He stands as the example of the completely obedient child, representing the ideal for the Israelite who accepts his suffering.[190] A Christian perspective sees Isaac as a prototype of Christ: like Isaac, Jesus carried the wood; like Isaac, Jesus was willing to submit himself to the will of the father to the point of death. Again other readings emphasise God's pedagogical purposes: 'The Eternal One tests the righteous. Rabbi Yona says: He is like flax. If he is good, he will get better, the more he is pounded. If he is bad, the pounding will split him in two. Rabbi Yehuda bar Shalom said: A potter will never knock on fragmented vessels. He will only knock on solid ones. Rabbi Eliesar added: If a person owns two cows – one strong, the other weak – on which one does he put the yoke? Is is not on the strong one?'[191]

Against all these readings we also find objections and harsh criticisms of the text: Abraham should have objected to God; his actions are misguided religious insanity! Isaac should have defended himself! Obedience unto death only benefits those in power. How can Isaac support such a system? What kind of horrific God expects inhuman acts from his followers? The Old Testament God is an immoral

---

and with millions of my people in a better world without doubt, where God reigns alone. I die in peace, but I am not content, I am struck down, but not desperate, I believe, but I don't pray, I love God, but I cannot blindly say Amen. I have followed him even when he pushed me away; I fulfilled his commandments even if he punished me for it; I loved him even when he pushed me into the dust, made me suffer unto death, and turned me into an object of ridicule and shame ... These are my final words to you, my angry God: you will not be successful! You have done everything to make me stop believing in you, that I despair in my faith in you. Yet I will die just as I lived, believing in you without fail!' (See Preuß, H.D. (1984), *Das Alte Testament in christlicher Predigt*, Stuttgart, p. 194.)

[189] Drewermann, E. (1994), *Ich lasse nicht, du segnest mich denn. Predigten zum 1. Buch Mose*, Düsseldorf, pp. 198-215, p. 213.

[190] See Josephus, *Jewish Antiquities*, I, 13, 3f.

[191] Tanhuma, wayera, 20.

God. Obeying this God is religious insanity and 'worship of the anus' (*'Afterdienst'*).[192]

An overview of the various approaches to Gen 22 does not result in a single basis for understanding the text as was promised at least by the historical–critical method. Instead, we end up walking over a sea of varying evaluations in which we threaten to drown. The history of reception destroys any seeming certainty about this text; whoever draws close to Abraham in the night on Mount Moriah is thrown back onto himself and the question: 'What does this text trigger in *me*?'

The history of interpreting the Sermon on the Mount (Matt 5-7) shows that a central New Testament text has also undergone a complex history of understanding:[193] from the perspective of reception history, the Sermon on the Mount does not have a single correct meaning, but rather a host of differing, even conflicting, meanings. Some of these are sketched below:

■ The early Church and the Church in the Middle Ages understood the Sermon on the Mount not as daily ethics for everyone, but as an *elitist ethics* for those who strived for perfection, such as monks.

■ Jesus lived believing that the end of time was close at hand; the Sermon on the Mount was intended as *interim ethics* for the short time remaining until the full disclosure of the reign of God (A. Schweizer, who also firmly states that Jesus was mistaken on this issue).

■ The Sermon on the Mount is meant as *private ethics*, only applicable to the circle of family and close friends. As a guideline for political responsibility, this ethical system would lead to chaos (as seen by the Lutheran teaching on *two kingdoms*, its political manifestation most clearly seen with Otto von Bismarck).

■ The high ethical standards of loving your enemy and complete control of desire can never be met by sinful human beings. They only exist to reveal each person's deep sinfulness and need for grace (Luther spoke of the *usus elenchticus legis*).

■ The Sermon on the Mount breaks through the spiral of violence with rigorous demands and strict basic principles. These demands and principles are part of a *utopian ethics*, which enable peace exactly by being utopian (F. Alt).

■ The harsh demands and violent threats of punishment contained in the Sermon on the Mount are a *regression into Jewish legalism*. These ethics

---

[192] Kant, I. (2003), *Die Religion innerhalb der Grenzen der bloßen Vernunft*, Frankfurt, Viertes Stück, Zweiter Teil, B 255. Similar interpretations are also heard in many contemporary sermons.

[193] Luz, U. (1985), 'Wirkungsgeschichtliche Exegese. Ein programmatischer Arbeitsbericht mit Beispielen aus der Bergpredigtexegese', in *BThZ* 2, pp. 18-32.

are particular to the gospel of Matthew and are only one trend within the complexity of emerging Christianity. Matthew represents a Jewish–Christian position that attempted to prevail against the synagogue by living an even higher level of piety. These ethics are theologically questionable as they promote a 'better way of life' deserving a higher reward (see U. Luz).

The reception history of the Sermon on the Mount is by and large a history of reduction: Jesus' new ethical guidelines are only relevant for a certain group, a certain time, or a certain social sphere, or merely a standard to show humanity their fallenness. This example shows how the study of the reception history of a text will relativise any given interpretation. Is being a Christian really defined by a highly moralistic way of life? Or is such moralism a symptom of a life that has not yet fully accepted the justification of the sinner by grace? Reception history once again removes supposed certainties about a text and forces me to face the urgent question of what this text means *for me today*.

The influence of the Bible is not only limited to the areas of academic study or the official church. Literature in general has time and again taken up ideas and impulses from biblical texts, treating these with a great deal of freedom. Poets and writers have a fine sense for peculiarities of biblical texts and biblical personas. K.-J. Kuschel, who has studied the influence of the Bible on modern literature, has summarised four ways in which literature responds to biblical material:[194] major protagonists in the Bible are presented in a contemporary setting, biblical protagonists are used as a tool for self-reflection, linguistic aspects of biblical texts are copied and expanded, and the present is analysed by comparison with the Biblical past. Artists have especially taken up the material from the book of Job, probably because of the basic human questions it raises: why must I suffer? How can God allow one of his creatures to suffer? A vast amount of high quality literature deals with this relation between God and suffering.[195] I cannot review this material here, but it is a very worthwhile field of study.[196]

---

[194] Kuschel, K.-J. (1989), 'Erzähle etwas anderes. Deine Bibel ist kalt. Die Bibel in der gegenwärtigen Literatur', in V. Hochgrebe and H. Meesmann (ed.), *Warum versteh ich meine Bibel nicht? Wege zu befreitem Leben*, Freiburg, pp. 17-36; Ibid. (1991), *'Vielleicht hält Gott sich eigene Dichter...' Literarisch-theologische Portraits*, Mainz.

[195] See the anthology by Glatzer, N.N. (1969), *The Dimensions of Job. A study and selected readings*, New York; Langenhorst, G. (1995), *Hiobs Schrei in die Gegenwart. Ein literarisches Lesebuch zur Frage nach Gott im Leid*, Mainz.

[196] See for example Grimm, G.E. and Bayerdörfer, H.P. (ed.) (1985), *Im Zeichen Hiobs. Jüdische Schriftsteller und deutsche Literatur im 20. Jahrhundert*, Königstein; Langenhorst, G. (1995), *Hiob unser Zeitgenosse. Die literarische Hiob-Rezeption im 20. Jahrhundert als theologische Herausforderung*, Mainz.

D) 'Whoever has studied Talmud and Mishnah will know that, from a Jewish perspective, every word of God in the Bible has 99 possible interpretations. Of these only the 100th is correct and only known by God. Christians could very well use some of this humility.'[197] An awareness of how understanding is conditioned by history leads to openness and tolerance over against different ways of understanding. Perhaps exegetes would be able to tone down some of their heated disputes by glancing through the centuries. The study of the reception history of a certain text should be a necessary part of scholarly work. A combination of exegesis and church history teaches us the continual lesson: we are not the first, not the only and definitely not the last readers to deal with this text. The Bible is comparable to a glistening diamond, which sparkles with new facets and surprising effects when held to the light of reception history. The fact that a text can be interpreted in so many ways is also a statement about the quality of the text.

There are also several highly problematic aspects to the history of textual influence. The belief in the one correct meaning of the text disappears quickly and is seen as hermeneutical self-deception. Even the (theoretical) belief in a possible single meaning vanishes. Every reading has its own contextual justification. The belief 'anything goes' is in danger of drifting into nowhere.[198] The theoretically and methodologically validated victory of the reader over the text leads to a full-blown 'anarchy of the reader'. In a certain sense the *ethos* of scholarship is at risk. Anyone who uses 'deconstruction' as a blank cheque for escaping the regulative power of the text in favour of a deregulated imagination sins against text and author. The unreflected accumulation of ever new re-reading is reminiscent of an old farmer in the Carpathian mountains who was 'made' a citizen of first the Austrian–Hungarian empire, then Hungary, then Czechoslovakia, then Slovakia, and finally the Soviet Union without ever having left his village or having changed himself. This situation must be corrected. The historical–critical method is of course only one way in which this correction can happen, but it is the method that has found its academic place among all other literary disciplines over the years. The differentiation between author, text and later interpretation is necessary and possible. Incorrect interpretations do exist! It is always surprising, how long some incorrect interpretations are able to stay alive. Job 19:25, for example, has long been understood within Christianity as an expression of the hope that Job will be met by the messiah Jesus Christ after his resurrection who will lead him into the presence of God. This is an exegetical error, despite Handel's beautiful aria. Job fully expects that a 'Redeemer' will come during his lifetime who will free him from the unjust sentence placed upon him by God. Nowhere does the book of Job indicate an awareness of post-mortal existence. Or Matt 16:18 where Jesus states

---

[197] Hartmann, K. (1997), 'Christen und Juden. Gedanken zu einem Gespräch, das nicht stattfindet', in *DtPfrBl* 97, p. 507.

[198] See Eco, U. (1992), *Die Grenzen der Interpretation*, München (Italian original 1990).

his intention to build his congregation on Peter as a foundation. The text refers to Peter's fundamental role in establishing early Christianity (in Acts 1-12 he gives 7 testimonial speeches). The text does not establish an eternal office in which *one* distinctive person holds all the authority for teaching and discipline in an unbroken *successio apostolica*.[199] But it has been this understanding that has been used as scriptural basis for the papacy.

b) Psychological Exegesis

A) The psychoanalytical theories of S. Freud (1856-1939) and C.G. Jung (1875-1961) form the theoretical foundation for this approach. The latter was faced with the problem of why his Swiss patients dreamed in pictures that corresponded closely to the myths and fairytales of different times in different ethnic groups. Geographical isolation and relative obscurity guaranteed that there could have been no cultural contact between these groups. Jung's answer to this strange phenomenon is expressed in his theory of the collective subconscious: the genetic material of every human being contains information that transcends the mere physical and includes a collection of primal picures and symbols that developed during human evolution because of their importance for the psychological health of the individual. These primal pictures can be separated into primarily rational, strict, logical male elements (Animus) and mainly emotional, irrational, nurturing female elements (Anima). The pictures produced in a dream are an important indication of the subject's psychological health. They lead the soul on a path of self-discovery (whereby 'self' is qualified as fully unified identity). Most of the time the self represses those elements that cannot be accepted into an area of hidden personality traits which Jung call the 'shadow'. A shadow that is not integrated into the self can cause the soul to become sick; the same is true for a unilateral reduction to either Animus or Anima. The results are neurotic disorders, aggressions, pathological projections of personal weaknesses onto others ('scape-goating'), and schizoid disorders ('Dr Jekyll and Mr Hyde'). Dream interpretation, the interpretation of pictures, fairytales and myths enable a recognition of the repressed traits and their integration into personal identity. The process culminates in a 'sacred wedding' in which the male, the female and the repressed elements are brought together in harmony, resulting in the creation of a mature self. This path, which Jung calls 'individuation', is difficult and painful because it forces the individual to honestly look at his or her ugly and repulsing traits in order to integrate them. In contrast to Freud, who was determined to reveal that every religion is illusion, Jung recognized that religions could lead to important

---

[199] Compare Matt 18:15-18, where the 'power to bind and to loose' is transferred over to the individual *congregations*.

experiences (gnosis, mysticism, meditation, myths, alchemy etc.). The Bible also relates to these basic mechanisms of the soul in many ways. Biblical religion can make an important contribution to the process of 'individuation' by replacing the fear of evil, sinful, dirty aspects with the promise of love and forgiveness.

B) The application of this method to biblical texts is as old as the method itself. Based on some early work by the Protestant theologian O. Pfister,[200] this method has been championed by the Catholic theologian E. Drewermann, who has presented a host of psychological interpretations of biblical texts.[201] According to Drewermann, exegesis is completly analogous to dream interpretation. The interpreter shows his art in his ability to carefully differentiate between the superficial layer of narration (the so-called 'objectal') and the encoded psychological problems revealed by this narration (the so-called 'subjectal'). A narration that at first sight reads as a report of the *outside* world turns out to be a cipher for the *inside* world. Anything external is a mere parable for a psychological process. A psychological reading is a reading in two layers: the surface of a narrative must be examined in order to decode the psychological conflict contained in it. Biblical texts, like all works of great literature, are concerned with problems of self-discovery and are of great help in this process. The healing power of the Bible is especially evident in its myths, legends, novels, and fables. The wisdom sayings, the legal texts or the prophets are of lesser importance.

C) An examination of the book of Tobit will give an example of a psychological interpretation.[202] Tobit is a law-abiding Jew who experiences the Assyrian conquest of the northern kingdom in 721 B.C. As a result, he is displaced and has to fight for survival in a strange land. His attempts to fulfil the commands of Torah in a pagan surrounding put his life in danger. In the end he becomes blind when birds drop their faces into his eyes while he is sleeping outside. Despite the king's prohibition, he had buried a fellow Jew and, cultically unclean, could not enter into his house. Blind Tobit has to be fed by his wife. Following a harsh argument between the two, Tobit despairs of his existence and asks God to kill him (Tobit 1-3:6). Drewermann[203] interprets the objectal narrative as a path into a subjectal dead end: a pious follower of Torah turns blind – he sees this as an expression of the psychological truth that strict legal obedience puts an end to all female elements;

---

[200] Pfister, O. (1944), *Das Christentum und die Angst*, Zürich.

[201] See his commentaries on the gospels of Mark and Matthew, several sermon collections (also on Old Testament texts), as well as interpretations of different ethnic fairytales. He presents the theoretical background for this approach in the two volumes idem. (1990), *Tiefenpsychologie und Exegese*, Olten.

[202] There are serious problems of textual tradition in regard to the book of Tobit, problems which will not be discussed further in this context.

[203] Drewermann, E. (1989), *Voller Erbarmen rettet er uns. Die Tobit-Legende tiefenpsychologisch gedeutet*, Freiburg.

the Anima is driven out and replaced by the domination of the restraining Animus. Tobit's constant obsession with dead Jews is an external expression of his inner death brought on by his extreme nomism. Tobit's unbalanced psychological profile makes him sick, his blindness is a cipher for the loss of his female side. Blind Tobit is the personification of the danger that lurks in an obsession with justification because it leads to inner hardness and hopeless rigidity.

Tobit's female counterpart, a young Jewess named Sara, is in a similar situation. She desires to fulfil the law, become a wife and bear children. She has been married seven times, but each time her husband died during the wedding night before the marriage could be consummated. Taunted by her maids, she too prays to God for her death (this occurs simultaneously to Tobit's prayer. The two are unaware of each other as hundreds of kilometres separate them; Tob 3:8ff). Drewermann see Sara's misfortune as the result of an immature relation to her father (and vice versa) and a fear of male sexuality as shameful and debasing lust. This inner tension turns her devotion to the law into a neurosis that prevents her from finding her way to true life. The 'demon' who kills all of her husbands is an expression of her dependence on her father and her strong rejection of any sexual contact.

God is the only one who can show a way out of this blindness. He sends an angel – disguised as a human being – to release both Sara and Tobit from their misery. Their path to salvation has several stages. The objectal narrative reports how Tobit suddenly remembers a treasure he left behind with a relative. His son Tobias (named after the father) must travel to Media to attain this treasure and is in need of a guide. He finds this guide in the angel Raphael. They have hardly started upon their way when Tobit is attacked by a large fish at the river Tigris who tries to eat him. Tobit is able to overcome the fish. Following the advice of the angel, Tobit takes out the innards and eats the rest. On a subjectal level, the fish is a phallic symbol representing Tobias' budding sexuality. Tobias is able to control this new situation. The heart, the liver and the gall-bladder are symbols for the best aspects of the libido. They are basic positive life-forces as long as they can be controlled and turned into love. After having mastered this process of maturation, Tobias meets Sara. This meeting is the turning point for both of their lives. The personal love between Tobias and Sara is consummated in their wedding night which symbolises the 'sacred wedding', the harmonious unification of reason and desire, conscious and subconscious, male and female. Tobias has passed beyond the level of purely external sexuality and becomes capable of sublime, controlled 'eroticism' and the complete acceptance of the other. This is depicted in the objectal narration as Tobias' burning of the fish's liver and the subsequent banishing of the demon (the Vulgate-text even speaks of the 'three nights of Tobias' in which the newly-weds refrain from intercourse in order to witness their love for each other).

Meanwhile, the father of the bride has dug a grave in his garden, fully expecting that Tobias, too, will die as the others have. He wants this death to pass by unnoticed. His actions on a subjectal level reveal a neurotic father–daughter relation: the father is not truly capable of letting his daughter go and leaving her with another man. Tobias' true love, however, overcomes this also, healing Sara's entire family. The parents can now release their daughter into independence.

With his return home, Tobias introduces the female element into the house of his father. The acceptance of this female element heals the father. This is narrated on the objectal level when Tobias anoints his father's eyes with the fish's gall-bladder and restores his sight to him. In the end, the angel reveals himself, and points to the fact that God controlled the events all along: he is the secret and unrecognised companion in the life of the faithful. The angel brings salvation to Sara by destroying her demon and granting her the insight that everything, all of existence is good and given by God and can be enjoyed in the presence of and in relationship with a loving partner. Tobit, the father, is also led to full identity and is enabled to see the positive again, in what had seemed to be only negative. From a psychological perspective the strange images of bird faces and fish livers, of demons and angels are brought together in a meaningful process of individuation. Every human being, no matter how broken they may be, can find peace in God beyond all fear if they remain faithful to him. Unseen and unrecognised, God works for our salvation even if we only recognise this in hindsight. There is no difference between finding oneself and believing, between faith and psychology; the one is rooted in the other.

This above summary is an example of how Drewermann and other psychological exegetes of the Bible are able to discover in most biblical narratives a journey from fear to liberation, from inner bondage and psychological illness to the creation of a strong, healthy personality able to integrate its dark sides.

D) The great strength of this approach lies in its ability to create the impression that biblical texts deal directly with the problems of readers; suddenly, the Bible no longer speaks of something distant, but of our deep initimate conflicts. This closeness is supported by de-emphasising reason in favour of emotion. 'Female' emotions and the non-rational world of dreams are the key to an adequate understanding of the Bible.

Such an emphasis on dreams and emotions can only be a correction of a one-sided rationalistic approach to the Bible but never a complete substitution for sober historical-critical work. Under the banner of dream interpretation, the Bible can be subject to general allegorising as the key hermeneutical concept. Must we truly assume that biblical authors were always concerned with the same pattern, i.e. moving out of emotional poverty and debilitating dependence? This reduction of the Bible and other literature to one basic pattern is highly questionable. Liberation from fear thus becomes the dominant theme in ancient Egyptian songs for the sun-god, the fairytales of the Grimm brothers, the *Little Prince* by Antoine de Saint-Exupéry, as well as every biblical narrative. This emphasis on the liberating God condemns *ex cathedra* any other biblical concept of God, such as God the law-giver, the judge, the avenger of the oppressed, the jealous Lord. The Bible is turned into a book of happiness and good feelings. This goes hand in hand with latent antijudaistic clichés. Fearful depiction of a violent, destructive God is found only in the Old Testament. Jesus is stylised as the great contrast who frees us from this heritage. In fact, many New Testament images are harsher and more threatening that those in the Old Testament.[204] The elimination of fear is a basic desire common to all human beings. But one of the central themes of the New Testament in all of its primary witnesses is the rejection of a large part of humanity: 'You knew, did you, that I was a harsh man, taking what I did not deposit and reaping what I did not sow?' (Luke 19:22). Psychological exegesis takes the Bible seriously only as a book of peace according to the needs of psychological therapy. This blind spot basically destroys any positive contribution psychological exegesis may make towards understanding the Bible.

c) Symbolic Exegesis

A) In contrast to the *discursive* symbols of mathematics and logic, a *representative* symbol has referential character. It cannot be defined as a precise term; it instead creates an analogy to something beyond empirical definition. Its philosophical importance is a matter of debate. As the expression of something that cannot be fully analysed or understood, something that goes beyond logical thinking, rationalistic philosophical thought treats such symbols with great suspicion. A high degree of caution is called for where the boundaries between sense and nonsense fade away. Yet, aside from philosophical theory, more pragmatic approaches show a high regard for representative symbols:

> Symbols are announcements. They focus on and emphasise something that needs to be recognised and respected; however, they leave this something partially in the dark - in a kind of limbo - so that they defy complete definition. Their meaning is composed of their referential meaning and the reflection upon themselves. They are a hybrid of the defined and the undefinable, of the concrete *this here! take a look!* and the aura of a life beyond. Something is mentioned which remains unmentionable at the same time. The boundaries of symbols are open and thus in principle undefinable. The depth of their meaning calls us to explore this depth while simultaneously denying full disclosure. A symbol can be explained, but it cannot be made fully transparent according to the standard of *pure* logic, *pure* reason, or *pure* theology. These tools are too rough, too broken for this to be possible. They lack clear lines ... symbols are the language of religion. The culture of symbols is the domain of religious culture. All religions at all times have used a semantics of signs that carry sacred depth. From the augurs who knew how to infer the appropriate moment for war or marriage from the flight of the birds to the soccer player who falls on his knees and makes the sign of the cross after scoring a

---

[204] See Oeming, M. (1994), Art. 'Gericht', in W. Bauer (ed.), *Bibeltheologisches Wörterbuch*, Graz, pp. 225-231.

goal so that his fans may know whom he thanks for his success: symbolic actions and symbolic signs are the life of religious piety.[205]

One of the prime functions of a symbol is the reference to the primal origin of being which cannot be thought of in the abstract, but must be experienced and understood in concrete living. A theory of symbols assumes a certain model of the human being as an entity striving to understand meaning. The symbol allows human beings to approach the absolute origin and fundamental meaning of all reality, even if understanding the symbol itself is not yet the same as the true presence of that reality. Symbols are not merely signs defined by convention (such as traffic signs) or abbreviated representations of a more complex phenomenon (such as the red cross). Religious symbols are signs pointing to the meaning of the whole, signs pointing to what surrounds us all,[206] ciphers for the transcendent.[207] 'The symbol gives us reason to think.'[208]

---

[205] Timm, H. (1993), *Wahr-Zeichen. Angebote zur Erneuerung religiöser Symbolkultur*, Stuttgart, pp. 136f. Timm develops a rational approach that is suited to the symbolic nature of religious thought: 'the principal of contemplation'. He defines contemplation as follows: 'A person in contemplation remains silently in one place, he stares at the floor lost in thought. He seems to be emerged in a flood of ideas, submerged in a primal sea of sensation: "I do not know what all this may mean" [the title of a well known German folk-song (J.F.V.)]. He does not have words to name what occupies his thoughts. Completely lacking are ways to pursue what he is thinking. Contemplation is less than knowledge and volition. It can only lay out the direction in which the search should proceed; a direction that emerges from affect and moves into awareness: this awareness becomes the confrontation between consciousness and reality, combining all of the bodily senses.' Timm uses his main term reflexively: 'Contemplate yourself! Wake up! Come to your senses! By adding the object (through contemplation), memory is activated and our primal senses are awakened, without which the present would have no reality.' He also uses it transitively: contemplate the other. Through contemplating the other 'the creative–poetic meaning of this principle becomes clear. Contemplating something means bestowing meaning upon something, so that we are moved to reflect upon the dual nature of existence and perception of the incarnated spirit. Perception is the passive acceptance of the other and the active naming of what confronts us. Both are two sides of the same coin' (158).

[206] See Tillich, P. (1964), 'Existentialanalyse und religiöse Symbole (1956)', in P. Tillich, *Gesammelte Werke*, Vol. 5, Stuttgart.

[207] See Jaspers, K. (1973), *Philosophy* (3 vols), Berlin, 4th edition, esp. Vol. 3.

[208] See Ricœur, P. (1974), *Interpretation. Ein Versuch über Freud*, stw 76, Frankfurt, p. 51. Ricœur uses this dialectical statement to describe the tension between listening attentively and analysing at a distance, between basic trust and critical reflexion.

B) The transition from this philosophical conception of symbols to the enterprise of theology[209] and biblical interpretation is easy. It is not difficult to understand the Bible as a reservoir of symbolic actions, symbolic stories, and symbolic characters all pointing individually and in connection with each other to what surrounds us all. The main task of interpretation lies in connecting concrete experience of the individual with these primal biblical symbols. Paul Tillich attempted this by his method of correlation: 'We must begin with the experience made by the individual in a certain situation here and now. We must deal with the questions grounded in this experience and related to it. Only then may we move on to the symbols claiming to contain the answer.'[210] It is not surprising in the face of the strong connection between symbol and concrete present experience that symbolic exegesis of the Bible has been promoted from the early 1980s on, primarily by certain branches of religious pedagogy, connected to such names as I. Baldermann, P. Biehl, A. Bucher, H. Halbfas, R. Sistermann, Y. Spiegel, N. Weideinger and D. Zilleßen (see also the bibliography). The individual systems may differ in detail, but all seem to be carried by the same basic assumption: even though we live in a visual age in which the individual is swamped by images, we have forgotten how to recognise 'true pictures' as manifestations of spiritual truth. We see much, but perceive little. We need a new 'alphabet of symbolic meaning', i.e. a renewed development of our ability to see the deeper truth pointed to by the phenomena we perceive. Modern secular human beings must re-learn that the aspects of this world are full of symbolic content pointing to the reality of God. We must re-learn the most elementary and fundamental facets of this truth. The anthology *Vorlesebuch Symbole. Geschichten zu biblischen Bildwörtern*[211] ('Anthology of Symbols. Stories about biblical word images') is an example of how this can be accomplished: different narratives aim to unlock the meaning of the sky and what comes from above (symbolic words: sun, moon, stars, rainbow, clouds, wind, lightning, fire), then what comes from the earth (earth, water, spring, well, stone, jewel), what is produced by the earth (tree, root, branch, seed, rose, vine), what lives on the earth (dove, egg, lamb, snake, caterpillar, fish), and also of many other seemingly neutral objects (house, door, key, path, garden, jug, bread, table, boat, anchor, treasure, ring, light, candle, cross). Psychoanalysis has shown how symbolic truth is hidden in dreams. The Bible, too, is an arsenal of elementary symbols that point in their simplicity to the final sacred truth.

---

[209] See besides Tillich Ricœur, P. (1972), *Symbolik des Bösen. Phänomenologie der Schuld II*, Freiburg/München; Ricœur, P. and Jüngel, E. (1974), 'Metapher', in *Sonderheft EvTh 34*; Jüngel, E. (1988), 'Gott – als Wort unserer Sprache', in E. Jüngel, *Unterwegs zur Sache*, München, 2nd edition, pp. 80-104.

[210] Tillich, P. (1964), 'Existentialanalyse', p. 236.

[211] Published by E. Domay (1989), Düsseldorf.

C) In contrast to depth psychology that focuses on the interpretation of complex actions and procedures, symbolic biblical exegesis tends to lift verses or half-verses from their context and deal with these in isolation. Just as a diamond is rotated in the light, basic biblical words, verses or short scenes are rotated between tradition, individual experience and future hope.

I. Baldermann, for example, worked with children on Psalms of lament. He wrote passages on the blackboard without telling the children that these were biblical statements:

THE WATER REACHES UP TO MY NECK
I AM SINKING INTO DEEP MIRE
WHERE THERE IS NO FOOTHOLD

The children thought about these words, talked about their own experiences, drew pictures, told stories from their past. It was surprising how easily they approached the text. It seems that the Psalms use a 'basic visual language depicting fear'[212] that releases primal emotions and incorporates them into a movement leading away from fear by developing a language against fear, even a language of praise that can be assimilated by children without any problem. H. Halbfas develops an approach to religious pedagogy that moves away from heady cognitive systems to emotional approaches to faith: 'We should not focus on conveying as much information about symbols as possible, but instead nurture a sense for symbols, so that individuals become able to communicate with symbols, to perceive symbols directly. This cannot happen without practice. Such practice involves continually dealing with symbols through observation, narration, listening, play, and action. What is important is not rational assessment, but emotional acceptance, the development of an intuition for the symbol, or – spoken symbolically – the development of a third eye.'[213] In dealing with this approach, Halbfas discovers the use of meditative pictures (mandalas), but also of myths, legends, fairytales and sacraments as symbolic actions. The Bible is used primarily through reference to its basic symbols such as light, heart, door, house, mountain, or path.[214]

---

[212] Baldermann, I. (1992), *Wer hört auf mein Weinen? Kinder entdecken sich selbst in den Psalmen*, Neukirchen-Vluyn 3rd edition, p. 15 note 1

[213] Halbfas, H. (1982), *Das Dritte Auge. Religionsdidaktische Anstöße*, Düsseldorf, p. 128.

[214] From 1982 to 1991, Halbfas developed a textbook for teaching religion in grades 1 through 10 which has given his concept a very concrete shape.

In strong dependence on P. Tillich and P. Ricœur, P. Biehl develops a 'critical introduction to symbols'.[215] Using various media (slides, overheads, textbook pictures, films etc.), biblical symbols are presented to the students. These symbols may be able to connect the daily experience of teenagers with the spheres of religion and the church, but they are also in danger of growing pale as they are commercialized in a secular market, or misused ideologically by politics. For this reason, Biehl demands that symbols must be connected to history; they must be rooted in the history of Israel (especially the exodus) and in the earthly life of Jesus. 'By thus anchoring symbols in history, the truth of these symbols becomes more concrete; they remain open to historical interpretation and are thus given the resilience of the historical.'[216] Critical assessment protects the symbols from inappropriate use and from ideological abuse.

D) Biblical stories have deeply influenced the symbolic world of Western civilisation. From sacred architecture to secular social organisations, from the language of poets to the way we decorate our homes (especially on feast days), the presence of biblical symbols is obvious. Many of us, however, no longer know the meaning of the symbols that surround us. An 'alphabet of symbols' is thus an important demand, especially in the context of our educational responsibilities in church and school. Because symbols have an easily understood surface that speaks immediatly to our senses and emotions, symbols can unlock a path to the world of faith. The basic comprehensibility of symbols speaks to us directly, yet they also enable a profound depth of religious feeling and searching. Uncovering the symbolic dimension of biblical narratives is also important as a missionary opportunity. The connection between biblical symbols and personal experience is a promising avenue of communication. A focus on individual verses and motives can be fruitful, as it enables a quick connection to the biblical text. A critical assessment of symbolic exegesis cannot overlook the danger of losing the specifically Christian aspects of reality. That stones point to eternity, light points to life, and darkness stands for the realm of the foreboding, that mandalas can be a wonderful form of relaxation is all true, but this truth remains on the surface of universal religious aesthetics. These thoughts are never clarified. The Bible can easily be mixed with the myths and fairytales of humanity to become a general religious pudding. For this reason, symbolic exegesis cannot stop at 'the symbolism of objects such as house, mountain, and path, but must move on to explain the most important symbols of the Christian faith ... This difficult task will necessitate de-emphasising the importance of experience and content itself with the

---

[215] See Biehl, P., Hinze, U. and Tammeus, R. (1991), *Symbole geben zu lernen. Einführung in die Symboldidaktik anhand der Symbole Hand, Haus und Weg*, WdL 6, Neukirchen, 2nd edition, esp. pp. 166-178.

[216] Biehl, P. (1987), 'Symbols', in W. Böcker (ed.), *Handbuch religiöser Erziehung 2*, Düsseldorf, pp. 484f.

realisation ... that symbols are not merely empty ciphers, but have *emotional* content.'[217] Symbolic understanding must also move beyond the isolated explanation of individual symbols and patiently lead into an understanding of the larger context of the Bible as a Christian system of symbols in order to avoid irrational mystification and theological superficiality. Symbolic learning must thus be complemented by rational theological education and historical–critical exegesis.

d) Bibliodrama

A) H.-G. Gadamer has analysed the philosophy of play.[218] He concludes that play is a serious matter: 'Whoever does not take play seriously, spoils the party'(97). Those who play become emotionally more and more involved with the game, the boundary between self and play becomes blurred until a significant shift takes place: the game becomes the subject; it plays with the players. The players immerse their whole existence into the game. Approaching the topic from a different side, the psychologist Jakob L. Moreno (1892-1974) arrived at similar conclusions. In his theories on 'psychodrama'[219] and their practical application as a part of group therapy, patients fall into a playful form of pretending to be someone else. The patient who acts out a situation with the group enters into a new space which he can fill with his own desires and ideas. It becomes apparent during the course of play that the roles are filled with personal experiences and emotions. At some point, the game turns around: the patient identifies himself with the role he is playing. This can lead to the eruption of deep-seated conflicts, requiring the constant presence of an experienced therapist. A group discussion then mirrors how the individual role-player was seen by the others. The group shoulders the primary hermeneutical responsibility. Periods of play and pretend alternate with periods of silence and meditation. Switching roles among the participants opens new horizons.

B) These insights from philosophy and psychotherapy have informed the development of bibliodrama. Bibliodrama is a method of understanding the Bible and also an approach to self-understanding and healing. Bibliodrama always occurs in a group. This group should be no larger than 8 participants who enter into a special relationship of trust and promise not to reveal anything from the sessions outside of the group. When putting a group together, prior relationships and

---

[217] Sistermann, R. (1996), 'Symbole, Mythen und Gefühle. Zur Theorie der Gefühle als Grundlage einer symboldidaktischen Glaubenslehre', in *EvErz* 48, pp. 69-85, p. 71. Sistermann emphasises especially the five basic symbols: creation, sin, cross, resurrection, and kingdom of God.

[218] Idem (1990), *Wahrheit und Methode*, Tübingen, pp. 97-127.

[219] Idem (1989), *Gruppenpsychotherapie und Psychodrama*, Stuttgart.

dependencies among the participants should be avoided. Every participant must abide by basic rules of group dynamics such as free speech, the right to be heard, mutual respect, acceptance of personal boundaries, etc. A smooth process is not as important as interruptions of the process, and each session must end with a time of reflection. A bibliodrama should be guided by an experienced group leader or therapist who is able to sense when boundaries are transgressed or when the play is in need of new impetus. A good bibliodrama needs time, several days is ideal, so that deeper issues can come to the surface. It will usually unfold something like this: the group starts with reading out loud of the biblical text to enter into the world of the text and gain a first impression of the various characters. The participants begin to identify with certain characters; this leads to an initial discussion: whom do I find agreeable, which character turns me off? The next step can consist of a scenic representation of the text similar to a Christmas pageant, followed by a period of reflection. A second possibility is true role playing, where participants take on a particular character and expand the biblical story while remaining in that character. The following discussion analyses the elements that were added to the biblical story. A third possibility uses strong alienation effects and moves far from the biblical text.

After participants have successfully identified themselves with certain characters and have come to understand their perspectives in the plot, the roles are switched and the participants are forced to approach the events from a completely new perspective. The group leader has the authority to break into the action, ask specific questions, stop a scene or make the participants play a certain section over again. The continued dramatic interaction with the text and subsequent periods of reflection do not lead away from the text – as one might expect – but quite the opposite: by allowing their personal biographies to interact with the text, the participants get to know the text very well.

C) The brief narrative in Luke 10:38-42[220] is carried by several interesting characters: Martha is the diligent, caring housewife, Mary is the quiet listener. Jesus fulfils the dual role of guest and teacher. After reading the text out loud several times, certain images emerge: a certain village in Israel, the travelling group of disciples who are not asked into the house ('we have to stay outside?'), Jesus, who seems to be permanently teaching – Why doesn't he help with setting the table?. Is Jesus bound by societal conventions? The group now divides the characters into roles. Every participant chooses a certain role and explains the reason for his or her choice. Personal information and personal experiences can already enter into the discussion at this stage. As preparation for the dramatic enaction, the group starts with a spatial constellation: Mary seats herself at the feet of Jesus: what kinds of emotions are triggered by this position? Now the scene is

---

[220] See the description of a bibliodrama using this text in: Kollmann, R. (1996), 'Bibliodrama in Praxis und Theorie', in *EvErz* 48, pp. 20-41.

played out. The participants take note of their impressions and the emotions that emerged during the play. The group experiences a high degree of dissatisfaction: none of the biblical characters acted the way they would have expected. The group starts to feel their distance from the biblical text. At the same time, they are curious about the meaning of the expression: 'choosing the better part'. There are also moments of aggression. Jesus, indirectly but harshly, disqualifies Martha's work. The sisters begin to argue. Martha disagrees with Jesus, she condemns Mary's lack of action. They debate what is more important: the *vita activa* or the *vita contemplativa*. 'Active members within any congregation will understand Luke's perspective. They know first-hand of the tension between those who count the number of participants at communion and those who meditate and do nothing, between those who organize large church events with diligence and great effort and those who revel in liturgy and trust in God. What situation did Luke face in his own congregation?'[221] After a while, the group leader suddenly intervenes and makes Mary and Martha switch their roles. The person of Jesus is irrelevant for the moment. The group must face the burning issue: which sister is better? The group divides into two groups who surround the individual sisters. These two camps now debate similar situations in which the same tension appears. This opens a new dimension: the individual participants contribute personal experiences and insights to the discussion. All of a sudden, they start talking about conflicts with their siblings. Jesus is compared to a mother-in-law who also did nothing but proclaim her wisdom and criticise the actions of others. – Recess – After a short recess the group deals with the question: what happens when others grade your performance 'from on high'? What emotions are produced by such actions? The individual contributions start to become highly personal and intimate. Participants start talking about their relationship to their spouse. What are the expectations that burden my life? The discussion intensifies, the feeling of aggression is now accompanied by a strong sense of vulnerability: no one has lived without the experience of failure. Some confess, in tears, to have always lived with the feeling that they did not choose the 'better part'. The group breaks for lunch. The afternoon opens with pantomimic exercises: 'express how you fight the fear of having chosen "the worse part"'. The wordless motions lead to outbursts of communal laughter. The group leader brings several Orff-instruments into the room; they are supposed to replace language in a renewed enaction of the plot. The leader interrupts the scene several times to insert periods of meditative silence. The actors remain in their expressive postures. The day comes to an end and the group retires for the night. The next day begins with the desire to learn more about the historical situation in which Luke wrote the text: what did he mean by 'better part'? The exegete is called for, but philology proves of little help. The group discuss how they understand this expression. The opinions drift apart but the group

---

[221] Ibid., p. 25.

agree that Mary did not spend her whole life merely listening and that the text describes a special situation: no one should miss the unique opportunity to experience the presence of Jesus; household work is of secondary importance when Christ passes by. This leads to a new topic: when does Jesus pass by? When do I have to stop and listen? The group discuss when this happens. They describe different situations. One participant contributes a story by Tolstoi: God promised a certain cobbler that Jesus would come and visit him. While he is working he waits expectantly for the coming of Christ. A few poor customers drop by, but not the one who was expected. At the end of the day he complains bitterly to God. He is told that Christ came to him in the form of the poor customers who walked through his shop (compare Matt 25). The essence of the story is captured in a statement by E. Levinas: the presence of God can be experienced in the close interaction with the other. The group expresses their feeling that the text has become clearer. The session closes with a long reflective summary of the past two days. The text triggered many emotions, positive and negative. In the end, the group could not fully identify with the text, but the intensive interaction with the text led to a deeper understanding of themselves, of each other as persons, and also of the richness and depth of the text. Their time together ends with the expressed desire to come together again for the purposes of bibliodrama with another text.

D) The advantages of this approach are clear: bibliodrama allows a first-hand connection to the text and the personal experiences of the participants! In a playful, spontaneous and intuitive manner it enables an emotionally deep, dramatic and realistic interaction with the text.[222] The rational exegetical perception is sharpened by a holistic approach that involves stomach, heart, eyes and ears, even if efficiency is sacrificed along the way. The text enters into the situations of faith and life that are particular to the individual participants. The disadvantages are also clear: a bibliodrama is very time-intensive; its success is highly dependent on the participants and the group leader. It can even become dangerous when processes break open that are beyond the control of an inexperienced but well-meaning leader. Bibliodrama is not a game for youth retreats but serious work involving intensive personal analysis. If successful, it can be a very positive experience, but success cannot be guaranteed. The often-voiced criticisms of psychologising or playfully distorting the Bible are in my opinion unfounded. The biblical narratives contain highly condensed experiences that believers have had with God; there is undoubtedly a wealth of psychological insight contained in the Bible and it will find its expression when played with seriously. In a multi-dimensional approach to the Bible, historical-criticism and bibliodrama do not have to oppose each other; they can also complement and enrich each other by mutual criticism. Bibliodrama is not merely a variant of psychodrama. There is a difference between enacting stories about humans and their problems, and a story in which the biblical God

---

[222] See ibid., p. 28.

plays a main role. With Jacob in Bethel, participants may say after taking part in a bibliodrama: 'Surely the LORD is in this place – and I did not know it!' (Gen 28:16).

e) Liberation Theology and Exegesis

A) Whereas the last three methods were concerned with the psychological inner aspects of the recipient, the two following methods deal with the recipient's external circumstances. Their goal is to analyse and especially *change* these circumstances with the help of the Bible: they are forms of *political* theology. In this view, theology should initiate and strengthen the emancipation of fringe groups in society (people in the third world, women) and lead them to victory.

These practical political intentions are combined with theoretical motives: the Judaeo-Christian faith can be sensibly maintained in a secular world only if it is interpreted as a programme for changing the world. The kingdom of God is a cipher for a classless society; the disciples as 'kingdom workers' are social politicians who fight for a just distribution of resources. The background to the approach is clearly found in the social analyses of K. Marx and F. Engels. Their declaration that the impoverishment of large masses is the direct result of a small upper class that steals the profits of their labour is very popular, especially when the upper class is replaced by multinational (primarily American) corporations in the first world. Their 'structural oppression' can only be opposed by the organised solidarity of the poor. In the absence of this solidarity, the rich create a world order in which the poor are pushed further in poverty and their opposition is defined as terrorism. Liberation theology articulates a continuing criticism of a western standard of living, which is defined by Coca-Cola, merciless competition, the exploitation of natural resources, pornography, prostitution, drugs, violence, and corruption despite all cultural, technical and medicinal advances. The symbol for this standard of life is the mega-city in which luxurious suburbs and pitiful slums exist immediately side by side. In comparison, the opposition between city and country seems to be a western contribution to liberation theology by those who side with the residents in rural areas, seen in analogy to the slums.

B) The hermeneutical approach that was created in the wake of liberation theology dates back to 1965-1970. From this time on, it has spread through Latin America, Africa and Asia, and has developed in several directions. It defines itself as a contextual hermeneutic with the goal of understanding Scripture from the perspective of people currently living, ethnic groups, or social classes (or also the female gender, see below), who experience oppression and exploitation. This hermeneutical approach combines theoretical and practical concerns. In a prophetic protest against the outrage of mass poverty, slavery, exploitation, oppression, as well as corruption, the approach aims to lead biblical scholarship back to its true task by liberating theology itself from the logic of capitalism or militarism. It criticises a bourgeois Christianity that has grown immune to the political force and the social power of the Bible by ignoring the cruel and catastrophic injustices that exist at the beginning of the 21st century. Interpreting the Bible must involve the radical change of existing injustices. The discovery that God is on the side of the poor has led to the (re)-interpretation of Jesus' actions as a political programme. At this point, liberation theology and sociological exegesis (see above, Part II, Chapter 4b) overlap. In the context of liberation theology, biblical exegesis is not an academic game, but an action that grows out of the concrete misery of biblical readers.[223] Liberation theology is theology 'from below', from the grass roots of society and church, from the mass of 'simple' people. Lay people, uneducated workers and farmers are of high importance for understanding the Bible. The hermeneutical emphasis lies firmly on application: How can I translate the biblical text into the societal reality so that the world is changed according to the vision of the text? The Bible can develop its liberating and healing powers especially in the depressing situations in South America, Africa and large parts of Asia. Ortho*praxy* is important not ortho*doxy*. Various groups in the congregation, led primarily by lay volunteers are called to interpret the Bible in accordance with their concrete situation in the belief that the gospel can only be experienced contextually. This type of political re-reading is informed by strong economic aspects; in the light of common misery, denominational differences are of little or no importance.

The basic a priori axiom that informs liberation hermeneutics is the belief that the liberation of the poor is the thematic centre of the Bible. The Bible belongs to the poor; it is written by the poor for the poor. Liberation theology claims to have the better approach to understanding the Bible. Readers in the third world live in economic situations that are much closer to the world of the Bible, which is the world of farmers, fishermen and artisans; biblical individuals are not westernised, i.e. individualistic, rationalistic and spiritually impoverished. Poverty thus is a preferential, if not necessary, precondition for adequately understanding Scripture.[224] This approach, as all other approaches, definitely has support among biblical texts: the exodus, the victory of the smaller Israelite force against the overpowering Philistine army (David against Goliath, 1 Sam 17), prophetic social criticism, Jeremiah's lonely battle against the religious traditions of his time, the special piety of the poor in the Psalms, the law protecting the defenceless in the Old Testament, the Sermon on the Mount, the Magnificat, and especially the actions of the historical Jesus and his solidarity with those who have failed – the rejected, the prostitutes and tax collectors.

---

[223] See Schoenborn, U. (ed.) (1994), *Hermeneutik in der Theologie der Befreiung*, Franziskaner Hefte 4, Mettingen; Pixley, J. (1997), 'Die Lektüre der Bibel in der Theologie der Befreiung', in P. Fornet-Betancourt (ed.), *Befreiungstheologie Kritischer Rückblick und Perspektiven für die Zukunft. Kritische Auswertung und neue Herausforderungen 2*, Mainz, pp. 161-183.

[224] Liberation theologians can even speak of the 'sacrament of poverty'.

C) We will look at an example from 'popular liberation theology'[225] taken from E. Cardenal's book: *The Gospel in Solentiname.*[226] Cardenal describes conversations that took place between Nicaraguan farmers, fishermen and himself during every Sunday service in place of a sermon. These conversations were a kind of 'Bible-sharing', a group process in which even difficult biblical texts were applied with surprising directness to the situation of the 'campesinos'. The beginning of the Gospel of John is one such example. One member reads the text after which each verse is discussed in succession:

In the beginning was the word and the word was with God, and the word was God.
A long silence

Then Felipe said: – Christ brought a message from God that was important for the whole people. This message was that he was the word. This was not just any word, it was a serious word, a word without deception. It is the word of God and because of this it is a true word. And this word came to the world and stayed with us human beings.

Alejandro, who like Felipe is one of the young men in the congregation, speaks up: I think that Christ is called 'the word' because God expresses himself through this person. God expresses himself to accuse oppression, to say: there is injustice, there is evil, there are poor and rich and the earth belongs to only a few. And to proclaim a new life, a new truth, with one word: social change. God liberates the people with this word.

I state that he is correct in saying this. In the entire Bible God accuses injustice and proclaims a just society: and this was the Word of God. The great news is that this proclamation appeared on earth in the person of Christ.

Leonel asks: – When it says 'in the beginning', does it mean the beginning of the world or the beginning of the life of Christ?

I say: – The beginning of the world. John starts his gospel with the same words used in the creation story ('In the beginning...'), as if he wanted to write a new creation story.

Leonel responds quickly: – Then this word is like a promise. God created human beings with the promise that he would send them a Messiah. Is this not right?

Now my friend Antidio Cabal, who is visiting us from Venezuela, speaks: – I believe that the expression 'the word' has several meanings, and we must look for the most important one before we deal with the others. I read: 'In the beginning the Word existed'. That which God tells us in Christ existed from the beginning in him. And the end of this prologue states 'None has seen God; It is God the only Son, who is close to the Father's

---

[225] This expression, as well as its counterpart 'professional liberation theology' is taken from Schmeller, Th. (1994), *Das Recht der Anderen. Befreiungstheologische Lektüre des Neuen Testaments in Lateinamerika*, NTA 27, Münster. Schmeller, referring to E. Dussel and E. Levinas, is especially concerned with emphasising that liberation hermeneutics stands in dysfunctional relation to western hermeneutics. Any interaction between the two is always an interaction between strangers.

[226] Cardenal, E. (1976-82), *The Gospel in Solentiname*, trans. by D.D. Walsh, Maryknoll.

heart, who has made him known'. So I believe that the first meaning of Christ as 'the word' lies in the fact that he wants to tell us who God is. Human beings do not know God, because they haven't seen him, and anything we haven't seen or touched we do not know. It is the purpose of the "word" to inform us who God is and how God is. And it informed us that God is justice and that he stands on the side of the poor. Christ declared this by his life and his actions; like a single word he worked until death, and the word is repeated over and over even after his death ... I don't know, I am afraid to speak here, the University has spoiled me ...

Antidio has stopped abruptly. There is silence. Then I affirm that his statement is true: word is about communication, we communicate with each other with words, just we are doing here. God wanted to communicate with us and he did this in the person of Jesus Christ. This is why Christ is the word of God, the connection between God and us.

Now Felix, a middle-aged farmer, speaks: – word is also teaching, just like when I show something to my children.

And Oscar, another young man: – The word of God is also his commandment that we should love each other.

And Julio, who is still very young: – I think the word the something that one person says to another and the other hears it. The word of God is there, so that we hear it and answer to it ...

Marcelino, Julio's father: – I read in the Bible that the word of God is like a mustard seed. Why? We sow the seeds and they multiply. And then they provide us with food. The word of God should multiply in us and produce food. And then we must share this food.[227]

'Professional liberation theology' is practised by individuals who have studied for an extended period in Europe or the USA or by residents of the 'first world' who have lived for an extended period in the third world. A few important names are Gustavo Gutierrey, Ernesto Cardenal, Leonardo Boff, J. Severino Croatto, Carlos Mesters, Milton Schwantes, Erhard Gerstenberger and Johann Baptist Metz. Their 'professional' hermeneutics is characterised by a fruitful interaction between historical–critical insights and impulses from liberation theology that lead to a new understanding of the text. The Exodus narrative, for example, becomes relevant in the present: God sees the misery of his people today as well, he hears their cry and takes sides. God gets involved in history. Even Pharaoh is given a new chance when Moses' sermons call him to repentance and when he experiences the power of God in the nine plagues. Pharaoh does not want to listen and keeps changing his mind. Only after the first-born in Egypt have died a violent death does Pharaoh release the people of Israel from their slavery. They journey to a promised land where they are given the task of building a society as a contrast to everything

---

[227] Cardenal, E. (1991), *Das Evangelium der Bauern von Solentiname. Gespräche über das Leben Jesu in Lateinamerika*, Wuppertal, pp. 13-15.

around them, a society in which, with the help of God, oppression, exploitation and misery do not exist. These political events are seen by definition as the salvific acts of God in history. The history we experience is a religious phenomenon. Faith and politics are not separate but coincidental. It is easy to see the analogies with modern-day society: the rural population in Nicaragua is exploited like slaves by multi-national corporations. The current pharaohs sit at the head of these corporations in the USA, Great Britain or Germany where they appropriate the profit achieved by the workers. 'Whoever fights against this situation of misery and exploitation and strives for a just society is part of the movement towards salvation, a movement that is still on its way to completion.'[228]

The liberation perspective also informs individual exegetical matters: when interpreting the prophets, it has always been seen as a problem that the blame is laid clearly at the feet of one group, namely the upperclass, but that the punishment falls on *all* of Israel, i.e. also on the poor. Liberation theology aims to show that the punishment foretold, for example, in Amos does not fall on everyone without difference, but is executed specifically upon the members of the ruling upper class.[229]

A defining characteristic of liberation exegesis is seen in the interpretation of miracle stories. In Mark 6:30-44 (the feeding of the 5000), the main emphasis is laid on the fact that the hungry organise themselves around tables in groups of 50 and 100 (v. 39). The primary point of the miracle story is thus not to show the power of Jesus, not to articulate a Christological creed, but rather to show that the masses are able to share the little they have if they organise themselves in a disciplined manner.[230]

---

[228] Gutierrez, G. (1992), *Theologie der Befreiung*, München, p. 148.

[229] See Zenger, E. (1988), 'Die eigentliche Botschaft des Amos', in *Mystik und Politik* (FS J.B. Metz), Mainz, pp. 394-406; Schwantes, M. (1991), *Das Land kann seine Worte nicht ertragen. Meditationen zu Amos*, Gütersloh; especially Reimer, H. (1992), *Richtet auf das Recht! Studien zur Botschaft des Amos*, SBS 149, Stuttgart. whether this particular goal of liberation theology can actually be met is questionable, especially in light of such statements as Am 6:6-11 according to which the entire city of Samaria, the large houses as well as the small, will be *completely* destroyed, or Amos 8:2 ('The end has come upon my people Israel').

[230] See Schmeller, Th. (1994), *Das Recht der Anderen*, pp. 245f; also Schmeller, T. (1996), 'Sünde und Befreiung von Sünde im NT – befreiungstheologisch gelesen', in H. Frankemölle (ed.), *Sünde und Erlösung im Neuen Testament*, QD 161, Freiburg, pp. 185-201, where sin is not primarily defined as a disruption of the relation God–human beings, but instead as a 'social reality' (189), the damaging of individuals (194); freedom from sin always implies the liberation from specific socially conditioned misery.

D) Liberation theology contributes a number of important impulses to the understanding of the Bible.[231] It demands a holistic understanding of the Bible. The Scriptures belong in the concrete reality of a world torn apart by social hardship. In the face of inhuman poverty in many countries we must revive the political dimension of the Bible! Biblical faith pushes us to fight hunger, poverty and mass unemployment (also in cooperation with secular humanitarian and social political movements), to do something about lacking medical facilities, to promote the education of women and children, to strive for the destruction of dictatorial systems of exploitation. These efforts must lead to a new just world economic order; perhaps the first world must grant the third world massive debt reduction. Theologians must fight about a one-sided emphasis on the transcendent and the reduction of faith to eschatology which denies any possibility of change in *this* life. This continual serious reminder of the responsibility of faith and church is the main contribution made by liberation theology.

Yet we must ask critically if partially true insights have not once again been turned into a hermeneutical master key. This criticism concerns mainly three aspects:

α) Biblical texts definitely have political potential, but they are not just political texts. Despite all criticism of a one-sided emphasis on the transcendent, we cannot ignore the transcendent dimensions of the text. The main content of these texts is about actions that can only be done by God; the function of Jesus Christ is not exhausted in his exemplary behaviour. Christ's pre-existence, his incarnation, cross and resurrection can only be reduced to moral exhortations when the texts are allegorised in a very questionable manner. According to the New Testament, the acts of God *also* concern salvation *after* death, after the current era. Even if liberation theology does not fully deny this, it strongly diminishes its importance.

β) Were the biblical authors truly poor? King David and King Solomon 'in all his glory' are traditionally seen authors of psalms and proverbs. Wealthy landowners such as Job, the patriarchs who were far from poor, Joseph as vice-regent in Egypt, queen Esther, top-level bureaucrats such as Ezra and Nehemia, middle-class plantation workers such as Amos or priestly sons like Isaiah cannot really be counted among the poor. Jesus the carpenter and Paul the tent-maker (with a rabbinic education!) are members of the middle class. Based on the social standing of its authors, the Bible is not the expression of the poor and the powerless. God's justice is also seen again and again in his interaction with power and the powerful, with wealth and the wealthy. And can we assume that the Bible was primarily intended for the poor? This, too, is unlikely. An examination of the implied reader of Job, Kohelet, or the Psalms shows a highly developed, artistic language. Chronicles especially requires a highly educated readership that is able

---

[231] See Crüsemann, F. (1990), 'Anstöße. Befreiungstheologische Hermeneutik und die Exegese in Deutschland', in *EvTh* 50, pp. 535-545.

to understand the many allusions and abbreviations contained in 1 Chr 1-9.[232] The gospel of John, the Pauline epistles and especially the letter to the Hebrews, but even the well-narrated books by Luke – often referred to as the gospel of the poor – are addressed to members of the upper classes.[233] Even the 'classic' example of the revolutionary message of the gospel, the early Christian 'communism of love', turns out to be characteristic proprium of the early church, but not in the least an example of the structure of every congregation to follow in the history of the church.[234] The authors and the addressees of the Bible were middle class and even wealthy members of society with a strongly developed social awareness. Biblical texts speak to individuals of good will who strive to be involved socially along the lines of Job 31. We can speak of God taking the side of the poor only in this context. God is not immediately on the side of the poor, no matter what their faith or their actions may be. Poverty in the Bible is a deplorable state of affairs that must be remedied. On the other hand, the blessings of God also include material blessings. The fact that the Bible describes situations in which a believer must experience the loss of property does not imply that property is negative from a religious perspective; wisdom literature as well as the final chapters of legal passages relate poverty explicitly to stupidity, laziness and divine punishment. It is impossible to speak of a 'sacrament of poverty' from a biblical perspective. Christians, however, must be aware of the fact that ownership of property entails an ethical duty (a fact enshrined in the German constitution!).

γ) Marxism may be appropriate as a methodological tool for the analysis of societal and economic processes, especially in countries with child labour, the prohibition of unions, and the oppression of political opposition. Still, it is difficult to separate these methodological tools from a Marxist world view that faces several systematic–theological problems: is religion merely comfort ('opium of the people'), is belief in God illusionary, or – even worse – the intentional deception

---

[232] See Oeming, M. (1990), *Das wahre Israel. Die genealogische 'Vorhalle' 1 Chronik 1-9*, BWANT 128, Stuttgart, pp. 206f.

[233] The title *kratiste* that refers to Theophilos (Luke 1:3) is used in the NT only for Roman procurators (Acts 22:26; 24:3; 26:25) and refers to a high-standing individual. See Merkel, H. (1997), 'Zu Bethlehem geboren...', in M. Oeming (ed), *Die fundamentalistische Versuchung*, Osnabrücker Hochschulschriften 17, Osnabrück, pp. 63-80, p. 73.

[234] See Merkel, H. (1982), Art. 'Eigentum', in *TRE* 9, pp. 410-413; ibid. (1992), 'Urchristlicher Liebeskommunismus? Zur historischen und theologischen Bedeutung von Apg 2:42-47 und 4:32-37', in H.G. Pöhlmann and B. Vrijdaghs (ed..), *Das Wort und das Schweigen* (FS K. Künkel), Osnabrück, pp. 130-142: 'The statements on this early practice of sharing are a part of salvation history. They say nothing about the appropriate social structure of Christianity. They do not try to portray a positive model, nor do they warn against a failed experiment' (139).

by a priestly class interested in maintaining their status quo?[235] A further huge problem is the assessment of violence: is revolutionary opposition to oppressive social structures 'self-defence'? Must the oppressed stick to passive protest or are the poor entitled to a 'just war'? Do we necessarily have to accept a dictatorship of the proletariat as an intermediate stage between a quasi feudalistic system and a just social order? The answers to these questions will certainly go in different directions.

f) Feminist Exegesis

A) The role of women in every area has changed drastically during the last century. Women rightfully refused to accept their limited access to education, career, and social power. Emancipation has fought successfully on all levels. It is primarily based on a new anthropological paradigm: women are a separate gender equipped with specific gifts equal to and in some cases better than men.

This general societal trend has influenced the church and the awareness of the Bible primarily since World War II. 'Feminist theology' has developed into an academic discipline that has become an increasing aspect of the academic enterprise in Europe and the USA since the 1980s.[236] Part of the driving force of feminist theology lies in a criticism of a male theology. The scientific methods and their results are questioned and often rejected. Patriarchal thinking is exposed for its role in elevating gender differences to a religious, cultural and social level, justifying the exclusion of women from these areas. Feminist thinking criticises unilaterally male images of God, emphasises the predominant role of women in the life of Jesus, recovers female traditions in the Bible and establishes a profile for female spirituality and holistic anthropology.

B) The wide scope of feminist interpretation can be classified in three groups that are different enough to warrant separate discussion.

α) The first approach can be described as the historical-critical study of female characters in the Bible. This group of feminist scholars emphasises that both men and women are created in the image of God by examining major female characters such as Deborah (Judge 4f) or the women surrounding David (Michal, Abigail,

---

[235] Some liberation theologians deny that Marx was truly this critical of religion. Marx knew how to appreciate the high potential for motivating political action that comes from religious conviction. Even in this view, we must ask whether religion is reduced to nothing more than a tool for positive political change and thus an illusion that ultimately should be overcome.

[236] Many faculties now have chairs for feminist theology; there is a growing call for topics specific to women. Some faculties have even established 'gender studies' as a separate discipline.

Bathsheba, to name three). This exegetical work describes how female characters function in biblical narratives. This important work has shown clearly that women play a much more important role in the Bible than reception history may have led us to believe over the past centuries.

β) A second group of feminist exegesis is guided by a *hermeneutics of suspicion*. It is based on the female perspective that biblical tradition cannot be trusted to have handed down the texts in their original form. A greater distinction must be made between divine word and human word. It is likely that a patriarchal tradition has edited texts with strong feminist impulses and weakened or distorted emancipatory content matter. The final canonical shape of the text can thus never be accepted as the normative text. The task of exegesis must be to recover the original pro-female content.

γ) A *hermeneutics of condemnation* informs a third group of feminist interpretation. It works on the assumption that the final canonical text, especially that of the Old Testament, is irreversibly and offensively biased against women. Following this argument, E. Schüssler-Fiorenza titles her book on the role of the women in the Old Testament *Texts of Terror*. No woman can interact constructively with these texts. Instead, women should draw a line and distance themselves from the incurable canonical (i.e. patriarchal) religion and search out their own spirituality in which femininity is respected appropriately. We need a *hermeneutic of creative actualisation* that no longer treats the Bible as a normative, 'unchanging archetype', but rather as a 'prototype' open to change and creative development.[237] This approach is not only open to, but demands that biblical narratives be retold from a feminist perspective, that approach biblical visions and commands be approached from a position of gender equality and expanded and embellished by emphasising the feminist traces that have survived biblical tradition.[238] Going back to religious ideas articulated by women (ideas that have left only rudimentary traces in the biblical texts), current interpretation should use great freedom and various types of media (i.e. dance, song, music, painting) to open new worlds of female religious experience. 'Revelation is not found in the biblical texts, but in the experience of women who are fighting for freedom from patriarchy; in this way, the Bible itself is liberated.'[239]

---

[237] Großmann, S. (1993), 'Feministische Hermeneutik', in *Das Christliche ABC heute und morgen*, Gruppe 4, pp. 177-192, p. 182.

[238] See Schüssler Fiorenza, E. (1989), 'Entscheiden aus freier Wahl. Wir setzen unsere kritische Arbeit fort', in M. Russell, *Befreien wir das Wort. Feministische Bibelauslegung*, München, pp. 148-161, p. 160.

[239] See Großmann, S. (1993), 'Hermeneutik', p. 183.

C) When giving examples for this approach, we will also deal with each group separately.[240]

α) The historical–critical feminist approach has produced numerous exegetical studies which *sine ira et studio* have highlighted the role of women in Old Testament texts. It is now clearer than ever how female characters made decisive, independent contributions at crucial moments in Israel's history: Eve in paradise, Sarah and Hagar in the patriarchal narratives, the Hebrew midwives and Pharaoh's daughter, Zipporah in the Moses narrative, the judge and prophet Deborah, the wives of David, Ruth, Esther or Judith. Each of these characters must be examined with the same diligence shown their male counterparts. Texts such as Prov 8 or Sir 24 with their depiction of wisdom as a woman, Prov 31 with its ode to the perfect wife,[241] or the Song of Songs show how the Old Testament speaks much more highly of women than a male-dominated reception history has often maintained.

This approach has also given us deeper insight into the situation of women in a patriarchal world. An analysis of Old Testament texts concerning the relation between fathers and daughters[242] shows that fathers had almost complete control over their female offspring as long as they were not transferred into the dominion of a husband. Lot's offer in Gen 19:8 to give up his virgin daughters in order to save his guests or Jephthah willingness to sacrifice his only daughter (Judg 11:34ff) are frightening examples of this fact.

β) These insights into underemphasized or overlooked female aspects of the biblical texts led to the hermeneutics of suspicion. This approach – as indicated above – assumes that texts were distorted during the process of tradition and that the original intentions were reinterpreted sexistically. A good example of this is the reception history of Gen 2:18.20: after God has created Adam as a single gender, he concludes: 'It is not good for man (*adam*) to be alone.' For this reason, he creates a 'helper'. A detailed analysis of the expression *'äzer k^enägdo* in this context shows that the text refers to something quite different from a servile

---

[240] Meyer-Williams, H. (1996), *Zwischen lila und lavendel. Schritte feministischer Theologie*, Regensburg, makes a similar distinction. She speaks of a '*Cinderella-hermeneutic*' that separates pro-feminist and anti-feminist texts, a '*Cassandra-hermeneutic*' that calls for the critical establishment of a female canon, and an '*Amanda-hermeneutic*' which critically examines the reception history of biblical texts and suggests alternative models.

[241] See the analysis by Hausmann, J. (1992), 'Beobachtungen zu Spr 31:10-31', in idem and H.-J. Zobel (ed.), *Alttestamentlicher Glaube und Biblische Theologie* (FS H. D. Preuß), Stuttgart, pp. 261-266.

[242] See Seifert, E. (1997), *Tochter und Vater im Alten Testament. Eine ideologiekritische Untersuchung zu Verfügungsgewalt von Vätern über ihre Töchter*, Neukirchner Theologische Dissertationen und Habilitationen 9, Neukirchen.

housekeeper.[243] The text shows clearly that the humanity of the individual is only complete in the togetherness of man and woman (even if the woman is not called 'image of God' as in the parallel text in Gen 1:27). In contrast to the animals, the woman is the only being who stands by Adam and fits him.[244] Without expansion by an independent personal 'other', equal and opposite (Gen 2:23), a human being is not what he or she is supposed to be. Both belong together not only on a linguistic level (*ish* and *isha*), but also on an ontological level (v. 23f.). The revolutionary and emancipatory force of this statement was hidden throughout the centuries and still remains to be understood fully.[245]

The narrative on David and Bathsheba in 2 Sam 11:2 relates how David observes Bathsheba who is *washing* herself. This story becomes a story of seduction in the imagination of most male interpreters: even though there is no indication in the text, exegetes insinuate that Bathsheba was intentionally bathing herself (which implies that she had shed her clothing). From being a victim of royal lust, Bathsheba herself becomes the perpetrator who deliberately uses her female charms to induce a hormonal reaction and take advantage of David's lack of self-control, using it to her own advantages.[246] Visual art has further advanced this interpretation. Various paintings depict Bathsheba as a 'vamp' in ever more seductive poses, with ever fewer textiles covering her body. David is the helpless victim who is 'remote-controlled' by this strong-willed woman. Batsheba's role in guaranteeing the succession of her son Salomon may have influenced this view. Feminist interpretation has correctly pointed to the male reinterpretation of *rachaz* = 'to wash' to mean 'to bathe naked', which has made it possible to excuse David's actions and shift the blame onto the woman.

Tradition has also obscured and diminished the important role played by women in early Christianity. Chauvinistic tendencies can be seen right down to textual criticism. Romans 16:7 states:

> Greet Andronicus and Junia, my relatives who were in prison with me; they are prominent among the apostles, and they were in Christ before I was.

---

[243] Kessler, R. (1987), 'Die Frau als Gehilfin des Mannes? Gen 2:18.20 und das biblische Verständnis von "Hilfe"', in *DBIAT* 24, pp. 120-126; Dohmen, Ch. (1993), 'Ebenbild Gottes oder Hilfe des Mannes? Die Frau im Kontext der anthropologischen Aussagen von Gen 1-3', in *JCWS* 24, pp. 152-164.

[244] See already Gunkel, H. (1901), *Genesis*, p. 11.

[245] See Schüngel-Straumann, H. (1990), 'Frau und Mann in den biblischen Schöpfungstexten', in P. Gordon (ed.), *Gott schuf den Menschen als Mann und Frau*, Graz, pp. 73-103.

[246] See Hertzberg, W. (1956), *Die Samuelbücher*, ATD 10, Göttingen, p. 359.

Junia is a female name occurring over 250 times in Latin texts.[247] The passage says clearly that Paul accepted a woman as apostle, not as one of the 12 'original' apostles, but as someone sent out by the power of God. This important fact has been suppressed by tradition. The name Junia mutated into Junias and became a male name, a distortion that persisted right up to the scientific editions of the New Testament! And even where Junia remained a female name, verse 7 was expanded by the comment that these two individuals were merely being praised by the true (meaning male) apostles.

Feminist criticism is fully justified in the face of such distortions; however, it can easily fall into one-sided mis-representations. An example is found in the study by E. Seifer mentioned above.[248] She pushes her comments so far as to include sexual domination of the daughter by the father. She basis her argument on the observation that the laws against incest (Lev 18) do not explicitly forbid sexual relations between fathers and daughters. It is not valid to conclude that fathers were given free rein in this area. This *argumentum e silentio* is an example where feminist criticism turns into feminist ideology. Deuteronomy 22:20f. threatens death by stoning should a woman not be a virgin going into marriage (see also Exod 22:15f.; Lev 21:7,13f.). This obviously implies that fathers would not have had sexual relations with their daughters. It is likely that such horrific acts may have occurred; however, the narrative of Lot and his daughters (Gen 19:30-38) displays incest in a very negative light, even if the text does not contain explicit condemnation: because of this narrative the rival nations of Moab and Ammon bear an eternal sacrilegious stigma.

γ) The development of an independent female spirituality usually takes place in a conscious rejection of biblical texts and a provocative reversal of male language. H. Sorge speaks of rediscovering the goddess and developing a 'theasophy'.[249] She creates the 'Our Mother' as a new prayer and rewords the Ten Commandments as ten permissions. The first permission states:

1. PERMISSION

I am wisdom and power over all. God sits beside me, the Son of Man who comes upon the clouds in the heaven. You may honour all of his names and all of my names which the peoples have invented. For I am not jealous and I do not punish innocent children for the iniquities of the parents to the third and fourth generation. (97)

---

[247] See Arzt, P. (1993), 'Iunia or Iunias? Zum textkritischen Hintergrund von Röm 16:7', in F.V. Reiterer (ed.), *Liebe zum Wort* (FS L. Bernhard), Salzburg and Wien, pp. 83-102; Thorley, J. (1996), 'Junia, a Woman Apostle'. in *NT* 38, pp. 18-29.

[248] Seifert, E. (1997), *Tochter und Vater*.

[249] Sorge, H. (1988), *Religion und Frau. Weibliche Spiritualität im Christentum*, Stuttgart.

This statement reverses the classic disputes within the Bible about true and false images of God. In her exegesis of Jer 44:15-29, H. Sorge openly takes the side of the Israelites who worshipped the queen of heaven:

> Let us suppose that the people were speaking the truth, that they lived peacefully, happily, and without hunger as long as they listened to their own judgement (Jer 44:17), a capital crime against Yahweh (see Gen 3), and sacrificed to the queen of heaven, a matriarchal goddess. Let us suppose further that they had been subject to hunger, war, and misfortune ever since they subjected themselves to the impossible legal demands of Yahweh (Jer 44:18). Would this not be a revolutionary insight for all of theology? If the people are speaking the truth (and everything seems to indicate this), then we have a simple formula to distinguish between matriarchy and patriarchy, namely the alternative peace *or* war, plenty *or* hunger, happiness *or* misery. If Jeremiah is trying to blame the people for their misfortune ('Why did you not believe more strongly in the Lord, so that you could accept the punishment you deserve for your lack of faith? Then you would be able to believe so much more strongly in the Lord who makes you miserable') then unbiased theologians should be able to see that Jeremiah's answer is not so much full of irony as it is of cold cynicism. (55)

The divining rod that is supposed to discover the hidden reservoirs of goddess-worship in the Bible leads H. Sorge especially to the Song of Songs, which she interprets as a matriarchal cultic liturgy for the goddess Ishtar (56). Even the New Testament contains theasophical traces, albeit more hidden than in the Old Testament:

> The goddess does not appear in the New Testament, or only in the form of the God-bearer Mary. Yet women, matriarchal wisdom, female symbols, action, and values are also important in the New Testament. A few examples: the dove, the matriarchal eros-symbol of the creation goddess Inanna, appears at the baptism of Jesus. Like the priestesses of the goddess, Mary of Bethany anoints Jesus as king; Jesus is born of a virgin, a matriarchal reminder of the virgin and goddess of love who gives birth to the hero; Jesus is compared to a snake (John 3:14), the symbol of female wisdom and matriarchal cultic practices. The Jesus-movement is primarily concerned with bringing back those who are lost (the poor, fringe-groups, the sick, children, women), achieving concrete physical and spiritual health, being comforted, saved, becoming whole. It is about giving life, integrating death into life (not the other way around!), and about resurrection ... The explicit form of the goddess appears in the New Testament only as Mary, the *servant*, or better: the *slave* douloi of the Lord as she is called in the Greek text (Luke 1:48). (59)

The interpretation of the Fall in Gen 2f is supposed to show that the 'dethronement of the matriarch' (110) stands at the beginning of all theology; this regrettable accident must be reversed. The snake is not the symbol of evil but – from a feminist point of view – the liberating symbol of female spirituality. Such free and self-dependent femininity drives out the controlling, punishing and prohibiting God. 'This God (and his representatives) is the sinner who removes autonomous identity from men and women, forbids them true knowledge and demands that they subject themselves to a strange will. This LORD desperately needs a renewed relationship with cosmic wisdom that continually gives birth to the true God. The theological concepts, especially paradise and kingdom, that support this patriarchal God must be revised drastically.' (117); these statements are based on a universal trust in love, an unchanging certainty that the goddess loves us, no matter what we do, and the belief that the power of love initiates the reign of God here and now. 'Jesus reveals the pagan truth that everything that remains is not created by those in power (no matter which god grants them this power), but by those who love and create a paradise on earth.' (149).

D) Any evaluation of feminist exegesis must be as differentiated as feminist theology itself.

α) The systematic study of women in the Bible is so obviously important, that nothing more needs to be said in this regard. On the one hand, it is important to show that the Bible is better than its reputation. On the other hand, we must realistically admit that the Bible itself is a product of a patriarchal culture and has certain sexist limitations. The texts, however, also contain many emancipatory impulses, so that the sexist limitations *of* the Bible can be overcome *by* the Bible. When Paul writes in Gal 3:28: 'There is no longer Jew or Greek, there is no longer slave or free, there is no longer male and female; for all of you are one in Christ Jesus', then all theologically important differences are removed. This gender equality is already a part of creation. Any exegesis that makes a value judgement based on the order Adam–Eve shows its own chauvinistic spirit, not that of the text.[250] In Christ every woman is fully equal to any man.[251]

β) The hermeutics of suspicion is first of all important in uncovering anti-feminist tendencies in the tradition of interpretation. It also works against one-sided male language in reference to God. Adressing God as 'Father' should not be tied to a specific gender.[252] Biblical theology must continually face critical feminist questioning and work towards the elimination of patriarchal distortion. The hermeneutics of suspicion can also fall into the trap of reductionism when it sees patriarchal thinking everywhere, even where the text does not warrant such a blanket approach. Such reductionism not only stands in danger of devaluing the

---

[250] This is already the case in 1 Tim 2:13, which connects this idea with the impossible theological concept that women gain salvation through childbirth (v.15).

[251] Kohelet's patriarchal advice to 'Enjoy life with the wife whom you love' (Eccles 9:9) can thus also be fully reversed 'Enjoy life with the husband whom you love'.

[252] See Monheim-Geffert, M. (1986), 'Abschied vom himmlischen Vater?', in C. Schaumberger (ed.), *Handbuch Feministiche Theologie*, Münster, pp. 323-331.

Old Testament[253], but also of reducing all of biblical hermeneutics as well as the varied theological statements in the Old Testament to feminist issues.

γ) What value can a creative, alternative, feminist re-writing of supposed biblical 'texts of terror' have for understanding the Bible? Can understanding be developed from this premise? This is hardly possible. This approach does not interpret the Bible; instead, war is declared on it. What refers to itself as a 'reading' of the Bible is in truth defamation and slander! The harsh judgements and attacks on the text can hardly be supported by historical argument. The thesis of an original matriarchy that was eradicated by devious men in the early history of Judaism and the early church is complete nonsense.[254] The theory that the Song of Songs is a cultic liturgy for Ishtar is not very likely.[255] The boundaries of what is acceptable are fully transgressed by the revival of exotic goddesses of love, witches, as well as primitive superstitions (i.e. the power of stones). This type of feminist theology establishes an anti-biblical neo-paganism in the name of female spirituality which cannot be supported by any Christian, male or female.

---

[253] See Wacker, M.Th. (1988), 'Matriarchale Bibelkritik – ein antijudaistisches Konzept?', in L. Siegele-Wenschkewitz, *Verdrängte Vergangenheit, die uns bedrängt. Feministische Theologie in Verantwortung für die Geschichte*, München, pp. 101-242; *Themaheft Kirche und Israel* 5/2 (1990).

[254] See Höffken, P. (1994), 'Matriarchat–Patriarchat. Überlegungen zu einer Sonderrichtung im Feminismus unter Berücksichtigung des AT', in *Das christliche ABC heute und morgen*, pp. 143-157.

[255] Most scholars agree meanwhile that the Song of Songs is a collection of secular love songs which was applied later to the relation between Israel and Yahweh.

Chapter 7

Methods Focused on the Reality behind the Text

The purpose of hermeneutics, according to Aristotle, is to describe the factual world by means of true sentences and to distinguish these from false sentences. The meaning of this postulate for biblical exegesis is indicated in the following quote, taken from a letter written in 1916 by K. Barth to his friend Eduard Thurneysen on the topic of his commentary on Romans:

> While I was working, it seemed a wind blew at me from Asia Minor, or Corinth carrying something ancient, fundamentally oriental, something indescribably sunny, wild, original that was hidden behind these sentences that allowed themselves to be interpreted in every generation new. Paul – what a man he must have been and what an audience he must have had so that he could hint at such succinct matters with a few fragmented thoughts! ... And then *behind* Paul: *what kind of realities* must have existed to set him in motion! And how secondary and derived what we write as a response to his statements of which we fail to understand 99%!'[256]

The surprising common element of the following three exegetical approaches consists in their focus on the actual subject matter located behind the texts and their search for the truth. They are interested in the true reality that touched the author, inspired the creation of the texts and is referred to by the texts, and that finally surrounds the reader as well. The basic hermeneutical rule that combines these three very different approaches states that a text can only be read and understood in light of the reality or subject matter that lies behind the text.[257] A level of knowledge must exist prior to reading the text which then critically determines all following steps of interpretation. The final criterion of every interpretation is its coherence with the reality that informed the text. We can even go one step further: the Bible is merely a witness to revelation, not revelation itself; the various biblical voices strive with human limitation to express the actual subject matter, namely God's revelation in Jesus Christ. Methods that merely strive to understand human aspects of the biblical text (authors, languages, readers) are considered superficial

---

[256] (1973), *Karl Barth–Eduard Thurneysen, Briefwechsel I, 1913-1921*, Gesamtausgabe V/15,1, Zürich, p. 236.

[257] See Barth, K. (1987), *Kirchliche Dogmatik*, I/2, Zürich, p. 505.

from this point of view. What combines the two testaments of the one Bible is their witness to the same divine reality, to the same basic subject matter found in them.[258]

a) Dogmatic Interpretation

The task of dogmatics (according to Schleiermacher and many after him) is the examination and presentation of what is true for the present. Its task also includes the plausible explanation and (re-)application of any talk about God to the current situation. In this task it must critically support the church in dealing with current issues.

Systematic–theological judgements are made in one of two ways:

a) On the one hand systematic theology can pursue coherent theological statements in analogy to philosophy and other academic disciplines. This approach is favoured by liberal theologians of the 19th century, Catholic foundational theology, or apologetics. This approach can lead to such an emphasis on the autonomy of human reason that the Bible becomes a relict of a heteronomous past with little or no relevance for the present.[259] At the very least, this approach speaks strongly against using the Bible as the basis for systematic–theological speech about God.[260]

---

[258] See Childs, B.S. (1996), *Die Theologie der einen Bibel, Band 2: Hauptthemen*, Freiburg, p. 446.

[259] A good example for a neo-liberal dismissal of the Bible in favour of human freedom and dignity is found in the theology of F. Wagner, who analyses the crisis of Scripture with brutal honesty and ends with the provocative summary: 'The normative demand of establishing a theology on the basis of Scripture proves to be ... unrealisable. Decisive dogmatic statements on current ethical and social issues as well as important social contexts are missing in biblical texts but absolutely vital for modern theology' (Wagner, F. (1994), 'Auch der Teufel zitiert die Bibel. Das Christentum zwischen Autoritätsanspruch und Krise des Schriftprinzips', in R Ziegert (ed.), *Die Zukunft des Schriftprinzips*, Bibel im Gespräch 2, Stuttgart, pp. 236-258). One can ask, whether biblical text have much more to say implicitly about current issues than Wagner allows. His theological programme seems like a soccer game where the players are no longer allowed to use the ball.

[260] See Pannenberg, W. (1967), 'Die Krise des Schriftprinzips', in idem., *Grundfragen systematischer Theologie*, Bd. 1, Göttingen, pp. 11-21; Wenz, G. (1988), 'Sola Scriptura? Erwägungen zum reformatorischen Schriftprinzip', in J. Rohls (ed.), *Vernunft des Glaubens* (FS W. Pannenberg), Göttingen, pp. 540-567; Schmid, H.H. and Mehlhausen, J. (1991), *Sola Scriptura. Das reformatorische Schriftprinzip in der säkularen Welt*, Gütersloh; Lessing, E. (1994), 'Theologischer Anspruch und faktische

b) On the other hand, dogmatics can establish a system of belief in conscious opposition to human reason, arguing on the basis of revelation found in the Bible, ecclesiastical tradition, or general religious experience. This system can present itself as the decisive rejection of the 'wisdom of this world' which is foolishness before God (see 1 Cor 1:18ff). In this model, typically found in reformational or dialectical theology, the Bible is highly important. Luther saw in the Bible the *principium*, the ultimate foundation on which all theology must be built. God has clearly revealed himself here and only here. *Sola scriptura!* With K. Barth, R. Bultmann and others, Scripture is the basic starting point, *the* medium through which God affects the world. Theology is interpretation![261] Still, it is de facto true that the principle of scripture as the sole basis of theology was never adhered to consistently in Protestant dogmatics. Many dogmatic programmes have applied and apply other criteria for judgement and evaluation, merely using biblical quotations as pious decorations for their dogmatic arguments (*dicta probantia*), thus eliminating the Bible as the foundational source and critical guide. In addition, the Bible is rarely considered in its entirety. Certain central passages, often printed in bold and collected at the end of catechisms, are often the only parts of the Bible that are taken seriously. These passages become the distillation of the entire Bible and present an illusory unity for instructional purposes. The newer dogmatic programmes, especially those close to dialectical theology, emphasise the importance of the Bible even more, at least in theory. The current discussion, however, has not yet achieved consensus on the precise relation between exegesis and dogmatics. Two models have emerged.

The first emphasizes the absolute importance of context, immediate textual context and the context of interpretation in the church, for the understanding of a specific biblical passage. The hermeneutical circle of the part and the whole necessitates that each passage be placed within the whole of ecclesiastical teaching in order to understand the text appropriately. This approach is to be found primarily (but not exclusively!) within Catholic circles. Protestant approaches tend to interpret Scripture around a certain centre, a canon within the canon (most often Paul's teaching on justification by faith in Roman 1-8), in order to establish guiding criteria for the evaluation of different topics.[262] Dogmatic reflection

---

Geltung des Schriftprinzips', in R. Ziegert (ed.), *Die Zukunft des Schriftprinzips*, Stuttgart, pp. 132-139.

[261] See Barth, K. (1987), *Kirchliche Dogmatik* I/1+2, Zürich, especially I/1, pp. 103ff.

[262] The theological committee of the Arnoldshaimer Konferenz, a gathering of the 16 churches of the EKD, stated succinctly: 'The Reformers stated clearly what they understood to be the *articulus stantis et cadentis ecclesia*: the teachings on justification through Jesus Christ by faith. According to Protestant insight, this is the centre of Scripture and thus the guide and goal of all interpretation. New ways of reading the Bible are to be evaluated whether they obscure this insight and promote an unbiblical view of human beings in their relation to God or distract from the true centre of Scripture'

decides what is central and binding and what stands at the periphery or is even to be rejected.

Dogmatic interpretation does stand out by placing exegesis within a broader horizon than other methods discussed so far. In addition, it strives to include the old properties of *sacra scriptura* (using new terminology and a modern arguments): the 'God-breathedness' or inspiration of Scripture, its *claritas* (comprehensibility), its *sufficientia* (its sufficiency for salvation), and its *perfectio* (the Bible cannot be improved). This argument goes hand in hand with a renewed emphasis on the importance of the Holy Spirit. By close identification of exegesis with pneumatology, biblical interpretation becomes an experience of the Holy Spirit. Appropriate understanding is the result of the *gratia spiritus sancti applicatrix*, the gift of the Holy Spirit that enables modern individuals to understand themselves in the face of the Bible and apply the teachings of the Bible to their current situation. This pneumatological exegesis leads to a revitalisation of a christological interpretation of the Old Testament: the entire Biblica Hebraica, not merely certain passages within it, is seen as witness to Christ.[263]

Unfortunately, these theories create the distorted picture that dogmatics overloads the Bible with external categories, making it a 'servant' of contemporary interests. Even if this may happen occasionally, G. Sauter and others show that this must not be true.[264] The systematic theologian who faces a (usually heated) debate on current societal or ecclesiastical issues must be able to find *theological* structures of argument and clarification. For Sauter, the first step must always be to *turn to the canon and start with the Bible*. The dogmatist may not avoid or bypass the Bible, she must instead move towards the Bible and walk alongside it. She must live in a *lectio contiunua* with the Bible in order to become aware of its variety even when it speaks against her own favourite theories. The Bible defines a 'principle of argumentation' and creates a space within which theological debate can take place.[265] The dogmatist faces the task of finding basic theological statements in the Bible (*dicta probantia* in the positive sense of finding basic principles of Scriptural theology that state clearly what is true). Marriage, for example, exists according to Scriptural witness in all its complexity within a special promise of God. From a Christian point of view, it cannot be defined as one of many contractual agreements between individuals.

((1992), *Das Buch Gottes. Fünf Zugänge zur Bibel*, Veröffentlichungen der Arnoldshainer Konferenz, Neukirchen-Vluyn, p. 23).

[263] See Becker, J. (1993), *Hermeneutik des Alten Testaments*, Frankfurt; R. Ziegert (ed.) (1994), *Die Zukunft des Schriftprinzips*, Stuttgart (especially the essay by F. Beißer); Childs, B.S. (1996), *Die Theologie der einen Bibel, Vol. 2: Hauptthemen*, Freiburg.

[264] Sauter, G. (1992), 'Die Kunst des Bibellesens', in *EvTh* 52, pp. 347-360; idem, 'Schrifttreue ist kein "Schriftprinzip"', in R. Ziegert, *Die Zukunft des Schriftprinzips*, Stuttgart, pp. 259-278.

[265] See Sauter, G. (1981), Art. 'Consensus', in *TRE* 8, pp. 212-223.

Disagreement in the face of what Scripture tells us: this is the beginning of sola scriptura. When honest and vital disagreement appears in the church, then it can only be resolved in a communal listening to Scripture. In other words, the only way out of an argument is to subject ourselves to God's judgement in the joint attempt to understand what is being said in the face of specific tasks, questions, and issues. The Word of God is the final court of appeal for all Christians – not what they think or feel about God, not their own inner voice as immediate connection to God, and not the church as God's representative on earth, the voice of Jesus, or the embodiment of the Holy Spirit. *Sola scriptura* is the correct choice against the alternatives of *sola ecclesia* (the church), *sola conscientia* (the individual conscience), *sola ratio* (human reason), or *solus affectus* (emotion).[266]

The Bible is not an arsenal ('It is written' – so there!), but an address ('It is said to you') in which God meets with us. Sauter recognises three aids in staying true to Scripture: the separation between spirit and letter, law and gospel, as well as promise and fulfilment. The classical distinctions are not static programmes, but guides to a complex reading of the Bible. The great strength of Sauter's theory lies in its ability to overcome rigid lines of prejudice. The fact that biblical studies and dogmatics find themselves as two separate disciplines is based primarily on a necessary division of labour. Biblical studies approaches its task from the socio-cultural conditions of the biblical world. Dogmatics works from the context of contemporary society; the two meet in their honest interaction with the common subject matter contained in the Bible.

C) A concrete example of dogmatic exegesis from a Catholic point of view is found in the Bible documents produced by the Papal biblical committee from 23 April 1993. The relation of dogmatics to exegesis is described as follows: 'Even if Scripture is not the only *locus theologicus*, it is the main foundation of the work of theology. In order to interpret Scripture with scholarly diligence, theologians depend on the work of exegetes.[267] Exegetes, on the other hand, must make sure that their "examination of Holy Scripture" becomes the "soul of theology" (Dei Verbum, 24). Their main focus must be on the theological content of biblical writings.' Dogmatic exegesis does not lose itself in historical irrelevancies, but concentrates instead on topics important for the teaching, proclamation and pastoral care of the church. Its prime tasks are the collection of biblical texts around a specific dogmatic theme, the preparation of sermon texts for the lectionary, and the focus on texts important for pastoral care. Biblical studies prepare the material for the questions which dogmatics must deal with in their effort to serve the church.

---

[266] Sauter, G. (1992), 'Schrifttreue ist kein "Schriftprinzip"', in R. Ziegert, *Die Zukunft des Schriftprinzips*, Stuttgart, pp. 266f.

[267] Notice the distinction between the two!

An example of dogmatic exegesis on the basis of dialectical theology is the interpretation of Gen 1:27 and 2:18 by Karl Barth.[268] Exegesis in general has often debated with great vigour how to understand the expression 'made in the image of God'. Over the course of history this has been understood to mean the upright stature of the human being, his capability for rational thought, or his domination over the animals. Barth approaches the issues from a strictly Trinitarian point of view. According to Barth, the plural expression in Gen 1:27 ('Let us create man') already points to God's conversation with himself. God's self-reference and his ability to relate to himself are at the core of a Trinitarian view of God. God appears not only in a single perspective; the true meaning of the Trinity is its understanding of God in his greatness and lowliness, his reign and his failure – all aspects of his vitality. By creating human beings in his image, God equips them for exactly this kind of relationality. 'For human beings to be created in the image of God thus means: God created them "male and female". This relation corresponds to the fact that God himself is in relation, that he is not alone and on his own.'[269]

D) It is very striking that the Trinitarian interpretation presented by Barth in his dogmatics, which viewed from a historical-critical approach is incorrect or at least inappropriate, has continued to impress learned exegetes.[270] Even though there is widespread agreement on the necessity to distinguish between *intentio auctoris*, *intentio operis* and *sensus in receptoribus*, we must admit that it is a positive result when interpretation becomes more than the efforts of comparative religious studies or the understanding of genetic hypotheses. When interpretation takes the leap into the reality of God it includes a truly indispensable aspect! This intensive care for the theological subject matter of the text is most probably the reason why Barthian interpretation of Scripture as been so influential.

The precise definition of the relation between dogmatics and exegesis remains a source of several problematic issues. An exegete who has taken the task of *interpreting* the Bible upon himself can only do justice to this task if, aside from all necessary history, philology and reception, he is also aware of the theological subject matter dealt with in the text; a text cannot be understood adequately without theological expertise. In other words: only a dogmatist can

---

[268] Barth, K. (1969), *Kirchliche Dogmatik III/1: Die Lehre von der Schöpfung*, Zürich, §41.

[269] Barth, K. (1969), *Kirchliche Dogmatik III/4*, Zürich p. 128. The fact that Christian readers fill the numerous gaps in the Old Testament with Christian concepts such as the trinity should not be seen as violence against the text from a Jewish perspective. Israel does the same when it finds later Jewish concepts contained implicitly in the Tenach.

[270] See Smend, R. (1988), 'Karl Barth als Ausleger der Heiligen Schrift', in H. Köckert and W. Krötke (eds), *Theologien als Christologie. Zum Werk und Leben Karl Barths. Ein Symposium*, Berlin, pp. 9-37; Childs, B.S. (1996), *Die Theologie der einen Bibel, Vol. 2: Hauptthemen*, Freiburg, p. 456 (the index contains over 60 references to Barth).

be an exegete.[271] The exegete is thus required to stay informed of current dogmatic trends and discussions. It is unfortunate that most specialists are more in favour of the strict separation of disciplines than interdisciplinary cooperation. Most often, exegetes consider it unwarranted interference when dogmatics tries to enter their territory. They harbour the suspicion that dogmatics favours an easy bridge to overcome the 'historical abyss' between ancient biblical texts and the present or uses cheap hermeneutical tricks to deny the existence of this abyss. The Papal committee on biblical interpretation is also intent on clearly separating exegesis and dogmatics by separating their areas of authority:

The task of the exegete is historical and descriptive and limits itself to interpreting the Bible. The dogmatist faces a more speculative and systematic task. For his purposes, he is interested in certain passages and aspects of the Bible; he also uses other non-biblical sources (patristic documents, conciliar definitions and other documents of teaching, liturgy, as well as philosophical systems and contemporary cultural, social, and political contexts) to inform his reflections. His task is not biblical interpretation, but a comprehensive examination and understanding of Christian faith in all its dimensions, particularly in regards to human existence. Due to its speculative character, systematic theology is often tempted to use the Bible as a reservoir of *dicta probantia*, in order to support a certain doctrinal position. Dogmatists today are more aware of the literary and historical context of biblical texts and their importance for correct interpretation thus, they make themselves more dependent on the work of exegetes. As the written Word of God, the Bible is so rich in meaning that is can never be fully exhausted and can never be fully represented in any systematic theology. A primary function of the Bible consists in challenging theological systems and reminding us of important aspects of divine revelation and human reality that are sometimes forgotten or neglected in systematic reflection. On the other hand, exegesis is dependent on theological research. Important questions that must be aimed at the text come from theology. These questions enable the texts to show their entire breadth and fruitfulness. Academic study of the Bible may not

---

[271] This view is illustrated beautifully by K. Barth in the preface to his commentary on Romans where he compares the exegesis of well-known historical-critical scholars to the exegesis of Calvin: 'How intensively does the latter go about his work of thinking "after" the text, having conscientiously determined what is in the text! He has dealt with the text until the wall between the 1st and the 16th century has become transparent, until Paul *speaks* there and the individual in the 16th century *listens* here, until the dialogue between document and reader is concentrated fully on the subject matter (which *cannot* be different here and there) ... Historical–critical scholars need to be more *critical*! ... In my search for understanding, I have to get to the point where I stand in front of the mystery of the subject matter and no longer only in front of the mystery of the text, where I almost forget that I am not the author, where I have understood him so well that I can let him speak in my name and I can speak in his name'. (XIf.)

be separated from either theological study, the spiritual experience or the judgment of the church. Exegesis does its best work, if it is connected to the living faith of the Christian community, which is aimed at salvation of the whole world.

In opposition to these voices I believe that the importance lies is clarifying the *inner connection between exegesis and dogmatics.* Neither Barth nor Bultmann would have ever considered the idea of abruptly interrupting their exegetical work and delegating the theological reflection of their results to a dogmatist. Dogmatic interpretation is concerned with systematising and thematically summarising the biblical witness in reference to contemporary human beings. This idea shows at least the beginning of the inner unity of theology. 'The history of interpretation is a continual warning that interpretation of the Bible has to be more than explanation because it always involves a serious struggle with the text. The history of interpretation shows clearly: Whenever exegesis was serious about this effort, it resulted in a true theological explosion in the church (Kierkegaard, Kähler, Barth, etc.).'[272] If exegesis is bound to urgent present issues it loses its distance, its academic dullness and museum-like quality. Dogmatics' call for relevance leads exegesis away from self-absorbed speculation. In this case, new theological questions could be approached on the basis of biblical theological models that do not occur in this form in the Bible (such as environmental issues, questions about world the economic order or genetic engineering).

Depite these important advantages and promising new approaches, there are also several dangers: the biblical canon contains several unconventional theological thinkers and even shocking eccentrics. The inner need for systematic coherence also carries the danger of violently bending texts to suit a certain dogmatic space when dogmatics selectively sees only what converges with dogmatic prejudices. The intensive debate on a 'canon within the canon'[273] shows clearly the problem of declaring one theological concept – be it even justification by faith – as the centre of the of Bible, thus silencing other voices. The necessary critical dialogue between dogmatics and the present age can lead easily to replacing the often troublesome and awkward biblical text by reckless theological pre-judgement.

---

[272] Childs, B.S. (1994), *Die Theologie der einen Bibel, Vol. 1: Grundstrukturen,* Freiburg, pp. 114f.

[273] Käsemann, E. (ed.) (1970), *Das Neue Testament als Kanon. Dokumentation und kritische Analyse zur gegenwärtigen Diskussion,* Göttingen; Lönning, I. (1972), *'Kanon im Kanon'. Zum dogmatischen Grundlagenproblem des neutestamentlichen Kanons,* Oslo/München.

b) Fundamentalist Biblical Interpretation

A) It is difficult to define the term 'fundamentalism'[274] clearly, especially as it has become a slogan with which to ridicule any belief in God or appreciation of tradition. Keeping the necessary differentiation in mind, it is possible to define fundamentalism *in the context of biblical hermeneutics* as an approach that believes the Bible to be verbally inspired by God, containing reliable facts with eternal authority. Any doubt or even criticism of biblical truth must be opposed (in the extreme even with violence). Fundamentalists strive to place their entire life in the service of biblical truth so that this movement is characterised by high ethical and political ideals. Because of its marked anti-historical bias and its conservative values, it might seem that the Middle Ages are reappearing in the form of fundamentalism; however, fundamentalism is a product of Modernism. The clear decision for the past can only be understood in opposition to the rise of modern or post-modern values. Fundamentalism sees itself as the only hope against a growing corruption of values and contemporary pluralistic relativism. In the eyes of fundamentalism, the lack of orientation leads the modern individual to catastrophic aberrations: the inability to love, loneliness, rudeness, abortion, gross materialism, environmental destruction, drugs, crime, pornography, AIDS, and many other evils. Fundamentalist Christians are called to fight the ruinous tendencies with the weapon of the one and only true and eternal Word of God. The unwavering belief of owning the truth, which exists outside of any historical relativism, leaves fundamentalism open to intolerance and militant action against abortion clinics or homosexuals (in extreme cases even against foreign tourists or secular states). On the basis of a clear relation to the truth of Scripture, fundamentalism radically rejects the decaying opinions of the age and revives virtues of the past. Fundamentalism as a societal and political force is growing ever more visible not only within Christianity, but also within Islam, Judaism and Hinduism. A basic tenet is the unity of Scripture and life: A highly moralistic life-style is seen as a decisive, serious and binding witness. The basis for the radical way of life is the belief that scriptural statements are valid outside of time. The biblical word is not separated from us by a wide historical abyss that must be overcome by hermeneutical tricks; it is possible to *simply follow* the Bible, obey its commandments. Paul, for example, did not write to the Romans; he wrote about *timeless truth* directly *to us*.

Another philosophical premise of fundamentalism is found in the belief that the Bible is a factual report. The Bible does not refer to the inner life of the author, to the linguistic structure of a text, or to the needs of current readers. The Bible

---

[274] The etymological root of the term is found in a series of publications titled *The Fundamentals*. These publications appeared from 1910 to 1915 and defended the Bible as tan inspired, inerrant and factual report (including the historical reality of the creation narrative, the fall into sin, the virgin birth, etc.).

simply refers to the real actions of God in the world. Miracles are not impossible for God, and God's elect are capable of the most astonishing things. This belief in miracles is not a sign of an unscientific or even anti-scientific attitude; on the contrary, many fundamentalists show a high interest in modern science and technology. Quantum physics and the theory of relativity are often used to show that our scientific view of the world is full of holes in which the miracles of God can be placed without problem. In addition, many miracles can be explained as natural phenomena with the help of scientific insight. Fundamentalism thus unifies moral and political conservatism, a serious dedication in applying the gospel to daily life, and a future-oriented fascination with technology and science.[275]

B) A fundamentalist reading of the Bible tries to show that contradictions in the biblical text can be explained meaningfully. Most often, it uses a model of salvation history which postulates that God revealed himself in stages according to the respective developmental state of humanity – ironically a model with roots in the Enlightenment. The harmonisation of biblical contradictions is accompanied by a harsh criticism of the historical–critical method.[276] Even when all attempts at harmonising conflicting passages fail, fundamentalism demands absolute obedience to the text, explaining these passages as tools with which God tests our faith.

C) A fundamentalist reading of the Bible, especially in first world countries, is not a naive reading that is in any way pre- or unscientific. Such reading has irrevocably been lost since the rise of the modern age. To a large degree, fundamentalist reading is a reaction against the insights of modern biblical scholarship.

An overview over the history of research into the person of Abraham in Gen 12-25 reveals the following tendency:[277] The dogmatic picture of Abraham as the factual–historical beginning of salvation history, as the real model of faith has crumbled bit by bit; instead, it has become clear

1. that the picture of Abraham in the final text is a composition made up of very different pieces
2. that the age of these pieces varies greatly
3. that the characterisation of Abraham contains definite fictional elements shaped by specific theological intentions

---

[275] See Marsden, G.M. (1980), *Fundamentalism and American Culture*, New York; Huth, W. (1995), *Flucht in die Gewißheit? Fundamentalismus und Moderne*, München.

[276] See Sierszyn, A. (1978), *Die Bibel im Griff? Historisch-kritische Denkweise und biblische Theologie*, Wuppertal.

[277] See Oeming, M. (1997), 'Tatsachenreportage oder Glaubenszeugnis. Zur geistigen Auseinandersetzung mit dem Fundamentalismus am Fallbeispiel Abraham', in M. Oeming, *Die fundamentalistische Versuchung*, Osnabrücker Hochschulschriften 17, Osnabrück, pp. 47-61.

4.   that the biblical tales about Abraham also contain dark sides and immoral actions
5.   that the point of the text is a witness to *faith* not to hard historical facts.

These scholarly insights have given rise to very different reactions. The fundamentalist reaction has been one of complete rejection. Not every rejection of critical (and perhaps hypercritical) hypotheses is automatically a fundamentalist rejection. We must differentiate clearly between different approaches:

a) One reaction comes from *conservative exegesis*. It stands on the same methodological foundation as its liberal opponents, but it tries to maintain an early date for the biblical sources as long as probably possible. For the case of the Abraham narratives this implies the position that the texts *most likely contain a historical core*. In this sense, conservative exegesis postulates that Abraham's origins from and relation to the Arameans, his semi-nomadic lifestyle, his relation to local sanctuaries, and his specific religion including the worship of the 'God of Abraham' are old facts that were not invented. This conservative assumption of a true historical core does little to preserve the historical truth of the concrete texts. The opinion that there were semi-nomadic individuals outside of fortified cities, proving the historicity of parts of the patriarchal narratives, cannot say whether any of these nomads were 'Mr.' Abraham who had the promise of God at his side.

b) A different reaction grows out of an *evangelical approach*. Evangelicals largely reject historical–critical scholarship as a tool for understanding the Bible.[278] One main criticism of the method is the accusation of atheism. Atheistic methods can never lead to correct results.[279] This criticism overlooks the fact that methods are not atheistic in principle, but only agnostic in their approach to the texts. The historical–critical method tries to determine the age and the intention of a text as much as possible with human reason. 'Interpreting the Bible is guided by the same conditions of understanding as interpreting all other literature... scholarly interpretation finds its goal in the understanding of human existence expressed in the texts.'[280] The method itself says nothing about the text's claim to truth. Whether the interpreter accepts the vision reflected in the text, whether he believes or not, does not determine his ability to understand the text. Evangelical interpretation is adamant in defending the inerrancy of the text.[281] Its basic

---

[278] Michel, K.H. (1982), *Sehen und Glauben. Schriftauslegung in der Auseinandersetzung mit Kerygmatheologie und historisch-kritischer Forschung*, Wuppertal; Cochlovius, J. and Zimmerling, P. (eds) (1987), *Evangelische Schriftauslegung*, Wuppertal, especially the essays 'Gegenkonzeptionen zur historischen Schriftauslegung' (pp. 295-328), 'Arbeitshilfen für exegetische Proseminararbeiten' (pp. 455-494), and 'Schriftauslegung im Dienst der Gemeinde' (pp. 495-516).

[279] See Maier, G. (1984), *Das Ende der historisch-kritischen Methode*, Wuppertal.

[280] Bultmann, R. (1968), 'Das Problem der Hermeneutik', in *GuV* II, pp. 211-235, pp. 231f.

[281] Marshall, H. (1986), *Biblische Inspirationen*, Wuppertal.

character is thus apologetic. Despite their loud protest against historical–critical scholarship, voiced especially in evangelical colleges, evangelicals frequently remove themselves from dialogue and fail to deal honestly with this method.

c) Fundamentalist understanding of Scripture approaches the biblical texts as factual reports of historical events given by God. Fundamentalists emphasise the verbal inerrancy of every detail to an even greater degree than evangelicals. The Abraham narratives, seen with fundamentalist eyes, relate historical facts as the unquestionable word of God. 'They hardly even consider the possibility of symbolic meaning.'[282] An interpretation that is 'merely' theological would not be sufficient. The reason for this fearful insistence on historical factuality is clear: B. Vawter states: 'If God did not covenant with ... Abraham ..., neither did the God of Abraham and Isaac and Jacob raise Jesus from the dead, for there is no fulfilment without a promise.'[283] Because salvation is dependent on the factual truth of every single 'report', it is only reasonable that critics of these 'reports' are damned. The whole stands and falls, lives and dies, with every detail; if the Bible errs in only one point or is only telling stories that never actually happened, who is to stop relativism from entering in and destroying everything? Fundamentalists are thus forced to construct theories that enable them to understand every biblical tradition as a historical report. For the stories of Abraham, this pressure leads to the following theory:[284] the patriarchs preserved their own experiences on personal clay tablets and carried these continually with them. These tablets contain nothing, absolutely nothing, that was not based on the experiences of the patriarchs. These autobiographical witnesses finally ended up in the hands of Moses. 'There is no in principle argument against the belief that Moses ... had access to written documents which he redacted into a final text.'[285] This theory raises several obvious questions: why did Abraham not write in first-person narrative? Why did he contradict himself? Why did he change his style so drastically while alternating his use of the name of God? Why does Moses never indicate his role as redactor? This dogmatic theory does show the great care with which even small details are considered, because if one detail were to remain unexplained, the entire theory would collapse. In this manner, fundamentalism mistakes the final text of tradition as the original text.

A special problem with fundamentalism is its blindness towards the historical abyss between past and present. Individual passages are understood and defended

---

[282] Papal Bible Commission (1993), *Die Interpretation der Bibel in der Kirche*, Vatikanstadt, p. 73.

[283] Vawter, B. (1965), *A Path through Genesis*, London, p. 8.

[284] See the widely read book Wiseman, P.J. (1987), *Entstehung der Genesis. Das erste Buch der Bibel im Licht der archäologischen Forschung*, Wuppertal, 4th edition.

[285] Beck, H.W. (1991), 'Was sagt die Archäologie zur Entstehung der Genesis?', in S. Scherer (ed.), *Die Suche nach Eden. Wege zur alternativen Deutung der menschlichen Frühgeschichte*, Neuhain-Stuttgart, pp. 126-135, p. 131.

as eternal truths. When all apologetical manoeuvres fail, there is always the safety net of stating that Scripture can only be understood by those who believe. This epistemological system allows the rejection of any insight not gained by (their) faith.

The fundamentalist interpretation of the burning bush in Exod 3 is a good example for fundamentalist understanding of miracles. The factual truth of the report is supported by the fact that

> biological research has now enabled us to fully understand the text. A glow worm of the species *Luciola* exists in Africa and the Middle East. Different from the central European fireflies both male and female Luciolae are able to fly. During dusk thousands of these glow worms meet in the branches of a bush, chosen for reasons not known to us. They quickly run back and forth, blinking with the lights on their lower abdomen. In the dark, the bush starts to glow with a ghostly light that can be seen as a yellow-green torch in an area of several hundred square metres. Scores of additional glow worms are attracted to this 'light-house', and join the others. Soon the bush is transformed into a pyramid of wavering light: a large 'mating' scene for animals that are following their mating urge ... The miracles of God reported in the Bible are different from the so-called miracles of quacks and magicians in that they do not work with illusion. Instead, they occur within a realistic framework which is itself given by the miracle of creation.[286]

D) An evaluation of fundamentalism is not as easy as it may seem. The questions which fundamentalism asks deserve to be treated seriously – especially because many scholars believe that the 21st century threatens to become the century of religions and religious wars. Fundamentalism has many aspects – moral, political, cultural and academic; it influences universities and schools and demands differentiated treatment. It is not enough to reject the phenomenon as reactionary, authoritative, passé, frightening, etc. Many students and teachers show sympathy for basic fundamentalist beliefs. This sympathy expresses itself in a sceptical rejection of critical biblical scholarship that examines the intention of Scripture free from dogmatic ties. From the fundamentalist point of view, biblical interpretation demands an a priori certainty of faith, thus eliminating any historical–critical dissection. If theology gives up the unquestionable special status of the Bible as God's special revelation, it cuts off the branch on which it is sitting: this is what many students as well as many ministers are worried about. In this case, theology within its academic enterprise would dig faith's grave and initiate the destruction of Christianity's foundations. In this light, the retreat into fundamentalist certainty is highly attractive; many are in danger (often subconsciously) of withdrawing from open dialogue and falling back onto rigorous spiritual foundations that promise comfort, guidance and meaning. The intensive

---

[286] Dröscher, V.B. (1987), *'... und der Wal schleuderte Jona an Land.' Die Tierwunder der Bibel naturwissenschaftlich erklärt*, Hamburg, pp. 18f.

desire to live according to Scriptural principles is a desire worthy of respect. An undoubtedly positive aspect of fundamentalism is its re-introduction of a sense of the sacredness of the texts into academic theology that stands in healthy opposition to an all too easy dissection of biblical texts. We must also heed its demand for a unity of teaching and living, of scholarship and ethos.

Despite these observations, the dangers of fundamentalist interpretation must be articulated clearly. Even if postmodern developments in society give rise to understandable anxiety, it is hard to see how one can biblically justify a rejection of any change in values. The naive fundamentalist belief that present issues find clear unambiguous answers in the Bible cannot be brought into harmony with biblical testimony, which itself includes changes in value as well as a lively discussion on which values are important.[287] In a final evaluation, fundamentalist interpretation leads to a rigid legalism which opposes the biblical spirit of freedom and love. Even the voluntary surrender of critical thinking that flees into the illusionary certainty of verbally inspired divine revelation is not a witness to the spirit of the Bible. The Bible opens a space in which human beings are called to decide how to live and realise God's love. The biblical message does not relieve us of our responsibility, but creates room – within clear boundaries (such as the Decalogue) – that must be filled by each individual according to his or her capability.[288] The existing shape of the Word of God demands continual reflection; by fixing a canon that does not gloss over and weaken contradictions and differences, the church has institutionalised a continual theological discussion. Current ethical issues cannot be solved as easily as fundamentalist circles would like us to believe.

We must strongly oppose the hermeneutical immunisation created by the theory that true faith is a prerequisite for correct understanding. This theory turns fundamentalism into a hermetically closed system. The danger created by such closure is seen in the willingness of fundamentalist circles to use *violence* to guarantee what they see as the only correct way of life. Even if violence is the exception and not part of the general appearance of Christian fundamentalism (at least not at the moment), it is a basic and integral possibility built into the system; other forms of fundamentalism show us what could happen within Christianity at any time. Jigal Amir, the assassin of Jitzchak Rabin, declared after his bloody crime that he had acted in the name of God. God had promised the land to Abraham and no Israeli politician was allowed to give this promised land to Arabs. Amir, and all those who think like him, forget that the biblical promise of land itself has a history! The giving of the land is an *act of God* balanced by the threat

---

[287] See Barton, J. (1978), 'Understanding Old Testament Ethics', in *JSOT* 9, pp. 44-46; Otto, E. (1991), 'Forschungsgeschichte der Entwürfe einer Ethik im Alten Testament', in *VuF* 36, pp. 3-37.

[288] See Schmithals, W. (1983), *Bekenntnis und Gewissen. Theologische Studien zur Ethik*, Berlin.

that this land can be taken away should Israel break the Torah and cease doing the will of God (Amos 4:1ff.; Jer 4:5ff.; Deut 28:63ff. a.o.); this balance should at least provide the basis for critically evaluating any human politics. The methodical mistake consists in treating a specific biblical passage as an eternal truth without bringing it into dialogue with other biblical voices, using instead it as the basis for actions. The fundamentalist loyalty to the Bible is thus far removed from the biblical witness. In the face of a frightening critique of their sacred book, fundamentalism retreats into a longing for a new naivety, a direct and firm way of believing. But once we have tasted from the tree of historical insight, our eyes are opened and we must recognise that we are naked, i.e. that we cannot find ultimate proof for the security of our faith.

It hurts to have to argue about the Bible with people who strive to live their life according to the Bible. But we must take *their* Bible out of their hands in order to give them *the* Bible back as it truly is. In the continuing debate with fundamentalism we must always insist on the basic maxim: Read the Bible! Read it closely, very closely. The example of Jigal Amir shows that a fundamentalist treatment of Abraham can be incredibly tragic. The idealisation of Abraham as a model for contemporary action misses the point of the text. Even if fundamentalism claims to have the most intensive connection to the verbal details of the text, it is in truth the approach that is furthest removed from them because it refuses to read *what is actually written*. Fundamentalism refuses to acknowledge any symbolic meaning of the texts. It thus closes itself to the possibility of discovering the *faith* that is expressed in the Bible. Fundamentalist interpretation moves the argument to an area that the Bible does not see as that important. Whether the various facts can be proven archaeologically or not, whether Abraham, seen from the eyes of critical historical scholarship, was a real person or not – all this is not the real issue. The recognition that later *theological* interests added fictional elements to the figure of Abraham is not a negative truth![289] Faith is not the insistence on historical reality in the face of good arguments to the contrary; faith is the personal appropriation of the view of existence displayed in the texts. In this sense, faith is independent of historical verification or falsification Stated in the extreme: even if Abraham never existed, then the definition of existence unfolded in the Abraham narratives still retains the status of revelation![290] The Abraham cycle speaks to the justification of the sinner and

---

[289] See Oeming, M. (1984), 'Bedeutung und Funktionen von Fiktionen in der alttestamentlichen Geschichtsschreibung', in *EvTh* 44, pp. 254-266.

[290] The issue is different, and there we can agree with fundamentalists, concerning the death and resurrection of Jesus Christ. If Christ's death were fictional, his resurrection an illusion, then Christians would indeed be 'of all people most to be pitied' (1 Cor 15,19); still, this is a statement of *faith* that can never be proven by scientific argument. The concrete reports of Christ's passion and resurrection contained in the four gospels are theological narratives, literary constructs created by good theologians. By keeping this

shows that faith can never become a possession, but must be understood as a continual relationship to God; Abraham stands for hope as radical openness to the future, a hope that continues to hold on to God even in the face of severe temptation, as in the sacrifice of his son. Abraham reminds us that faith trusts in God beyond all human probability. It was the much-maligned historical–critical method that showed that not morals, but unreserved living in reliance on God is at the centre of religion as described in the Abraham narratives. It thus opens an understanding of these texts that must remain closed to a approach bent on moralistic meaning and historical realism.

A similar case is the ethical demand in early Israelite religion that a man who has intercourse with a woman must take that woman to be his wife:

> When a man seduces a virgin who is not engaged to be married, and lies with her, he shall give the bride-price for her and make her his wife. (Exod 22:16)

This statement is not an eternal truth independent of historical contexts; it must be interpreted as the combination of several legal concepts: the unmarried woman is seen as the possession of the father who releases her only after a certain price has been paid;[291] the woman plays no active role. This reflects the chauvinist (mis-) understanding that the woman becomes the possession of the husband and thus may not have 'belonged' to someone else.[292] Two other aspects are also involved: women who were seduced or sexually abused could not simply be cast out; the seducer (and even the rapist) must assume an ongoing *responsibility*. A further *responsibility* arises in light of children that may be born as the result of intercourse. Is feminist theology not correct when it attacks this 'role-play' – fathers and husbands as owners and protectors of passive women – as the expression of sexist limitation that must be overcome by means of the Bible itself in light of such passages as Gen 1:27f. and 2:18ff.?[293] Can the protection of female

---

fact in mind, the reoccurring sensational reports about an 'empty grave' make their only positive contribution.

[291] For various current interpretations of this custom see Otto, E. (1994), *Theologische Ethik des Alten Testaments*, Stuttgart, pp. 51-54; the element of a 'purchased bride' remains despite Otto's suggestions.

[292] See as contrast the continual elevation of the woman in tradition of the Decalogue where the woman gains the status of an independent person (Schmidt, W.H., Delkurt, H. and Graupner, A. (1993), *Die Zehngebote im Rahmen alttestamentlicher Ethik*, EdF 281, Darmstadt, p. 133).

[293] Fundamentalist circles would certainly oppose this approach; see Neuer, W. (1982), *Mann und Frau in christlicher Sicht*, Gießen and Basel; Neuer states: 'The biblical understanding of gender roles consists in defining the man as the *head* of the woman and the woman as the *helper* of the man ... This status of helper means for the woman that she must a. submit herself in love to the guidance of the man. b. complement the man

honour and the responsibility for potential children not be accomplished in any way other than by a forced marriage? Is the text not overloaded with meaning when used by fundamentalist and evangelical circles as the basis for equating sexual intercourse with marriage?[294] Can the responsibility for potential children not be met by preventive contraception? If we see marriage as a deeply considered, voluntary, and long-term partnership of mature equals that stands under a special blessing from God, could it not be a Christian duty to also explore erotic compatibility before marriage? Is marriage not diminished by a rushed and irresponsible decision to enter into a life-long relationship with a partner without knowing a decisively important aspect of that person?

As a last point, fundamentalism completely misses that miracles are also *intended* to be understood symbolically when it insists on their factual reality (such as the unbroken hymen of Mary up to the birth of Jesus). A positivist insistence that language only relates facts is hermeneutically fatal. This can also be seen when obviously incorrect cosmological theories (such as a three-storey view of the earth as dwelling place of human beings, hell as dwelling place of sinners, and heaven as the dwelling place of God, his heavenly court, and good souls; or the creation of the earth *in six days* with the human being as final element in the chain of creation) are stubbornly defended. This negates the human and historical aspects of the Bible and turns minor topics into major considerations. The 'explanation' of miracles by means of natural science cannot do justice to the biblical character of these events; the Bible sees these actions as proofs of the mighty power of God which is even capable of acting outside of natural laws. Whoever 'proves' that miracles can be explained naturally, accuses the Bible of error.

The only appropriate response to fundamentalism is close study of the Bible and insistence on the selective and narrow avoidance of certain aspects of this study.

c) Existential Interpretation

A) In his analysis of being, Heidegger developed certain basic concepts aimed at describing human existence (being cast out (*'Geworfensein'*), temporality, worry, journey towards death, leap into actuality (*'Sprung in die Eigentlichkeit'*), etc.). Bultmann saw the potential of these concepts for the interpretation of the Bible.[295] He used Heidegger's terminology to explain the biblical message more precisely. The 'unquestioned a priori interpretation of existence', the dictatorship of the 'you should', and the lack of actual existence were understood as descriptions of an

---

with her special gifts as a woman' (168). Neuer infers a harsh rejection of women in any type of leadership position such as female ministry (161-167).

[294] This identification can most probably be explained by psychological factors such as the fear of failure, loneliness, rejection or irresponsible promiscuity.

[295] And not vice versa, as he has been accused of by his opponents.

'existence in sin' appropriate to the modern age. The 'fruit of sin' is the experience of death. Faced with the tragedy of temporal existence, redemption becomes a necessary fact. Here Bultmann's theology departs from Heidegger's philosophy. By describing redemption from death and the release into true existence as the action of God, the theologian Bultmann follows a very different path from the (partly gnostic) self-redemption of the philosopher.

B) The application of existential philosophy to the interpretation of biblical texts[296] is based on the conviction that every biblical text mirrors the basic structures of human existence. Every text must be examined in order to find the understanding of existence contained in it. Bultmann called this specific inquiry 'existential interpretation'. Its goal is to move beyond the surface structure of historically varied texts and reach the sub-structure and the interpretation of human existence contained on that level. Worry and concern, for example, is a basic element of human reality, yet it appears in a million different forms. The German poet J.W. Goethe captured the essence of this reality by having the personified 'Worry' speak the following words to Faust:

> Whoever belongs to me
> To him the world is nothing;
> Eternal darkness descends.
> With senses all turned outward
> Complete darkness dwells within.
> And he knows not of these treasures
> How to gain their possession
> Happiness and despair become the grasshopper
> Who starved in the midst of plenty;
> Be it joy, be it plague,
> He postpones it to another day,
> Is aware only of the future
> And thus is never done. [...]
> He loses himself ever more deeply,
> Looks at all things ever more slanted,
> Becomes a burden on self and others,
> With shallow breath and lack of air; [...]
> Sometimes freedom, sometimes oppression,
> Half asleep in restless resting,
> I nail him on the spot
> And prepare him for hell.

---

[296] See Schmithals, W. (1967), *Die Theologie Rudolf Bultmanns*, Tübingen, pp. 226-277, which is still the best presentation of Bultmann's theology.

Following this speech, 'Worry' breathes on the derisive Faust and he becomes blind.[297]

Understanding becomes possible because both author and reader are connected to a common subject matter that finds its expression in a text.[298] Without prior understanding on the part of the reader, be it unreflected or mistaken, there can be no encounter between reader and author. Understanding without preconditions does not exist. The basic subject matter of the Old and the New Testaments is the true nature of existence.[299] The true nature of existence is defined by proclaiming and sharing (through study and especially through preaching) a view of human nature, lived in faith and based on God's Word. According to Bultmann, the Bible presents us with models for understanding self, the world, and God. These models can be analysed by scientific method; the acceptance of these models as a personal reality is not a matter of science but of faith. It occurs under the guidance of the Holy Spirit and cannot be grasped methodologically. Faith is thus not the belief in certain supernatural tenets or pious phrases, but life and perseverance within a certain understanding of reality. This existential concern is also the primary concern of the biblical authors and their texts. The symbolic, mythical descriptions of creation in six days, of angels and devils and their armies, or of a virgin birth, are elements of an ancient world view that are not important in and of themselves. These mythical elements must not be eliminated or explained away. They are instead the objects of existential *interpretation*. The primary task of academic theology consists in uncovering and explicating the biblical view of existence in its meaning for individuals today. *Historical–critical scholarship, existential interpretation and application must coincide.* It must become clear in the course of interpretation that the biblical texts deal with the same subjects as current philosophy and poetry.

> We have finally found the appropriate question for the interpretation of the Bible. The question is: How is human existence understood in the Bible? I approach biblical texts with this question for the same reason that guides all historical research and all interpretation of historical documents. Understanding history provides me with models

---

[297] Goethe, J.W. von (1829), *Faust, Zweiter Teil, Fünfter Akt, Mitternacht*, lines 11452-11500.

[298] See Bultmann, R. (1968), 'Das Problem der Hermeneutik', in *GuV* II, p. 217.

[299] 'The Old Testament portrays the individual as subject to time and history. He is able to understand himself not by recurring to the universal, the cosmos, in order to see his part in the whole, or to the logos in order to find true being outside of time. He is instead confronted with his own particular history, its past and future as well as its present which envelops him within a community of "neighbors" and the concrete needs of the moment ... This understanding of existence is the same in the New Testament' (Bultmann, R. (1966), 'Die Bedeutung des Alten Testaments für den christlichen Glauben', in *GuV* I, pp. 313-336, p. 324).

for understanding human life and thus my own life. The final reason for studying history is the resulting awareness of possibilities for human existence.'[300] '

Faith is the renewed understanding of personal existence. In other words, God's actions grant us a new understanding of ourselves.'[301] According to Bultmann, the New Testament (and the Old!) communicate a specific view of personal existence, God, and the world. Because of my sin, I cannot discern the true nature of reality by myself or on the basis of the world around me. It can only be given to me from the outside, from God. *This* is the scandal, the provoking element contained in the Bible. This *extra nos* of faith is what is meant by the ambiguous term 'otherworldliness': understanding does not come from this world (from reason, emotion, nature or whatever), but from the transcendent. Asking about God is the same as asking about the foundations of my own existence as well as my appropriate interaction with the world. The images contained in the biblical texts should not be allowed to cover up its provocative message; mythical language needs not be avoided, but it must be deciphered according to what is says about human existence. *'Demythologising'* is nothing but the concrete application of existential interpretation.

C) a) An example based on the seemingly simple Psalm 93 can help clarify the issue:

1 The LORD is king, he is robed in majesty; the LORD is robed, he is girded with strength. He has established the world; it shall never be moved;
2 your throne is established from of old; you are from everlasting.
3 The floods have lifted up, O LORD, the floods have lifted up their voice; the floods lift up their roaring.
4 More majestic than the thunders of mighty waters, more majestic than the waves of the sea, majestic on high is the LORD!
5 Your decrees are very sure; holiness befits your house, O LORD, for evermore.

The Psalm and its central topic of the 'kingdom of God' has been the object of several studies with varied results. A comparison with Ugaritic texts from the 14th century B.C. suggests the following interpretation of the phrase 'Yahweh is king': Yahweh is king of the *gods*. The royal title probably indicates a pantheon, arguing the issue of who is the king over all of the gods. The phrase is thus highly mythical.[302] In critically distancing itself from surrounding nations, Israel stopped emphasising the dynamic struggle between Yahweh and other gods and developed the concept of an eternal kingdom of God; the early royal psalms transformed the

---

[300] Bultmann, R. (1965), 'Jesus Christus und die Mythologie', in *GuV* IV, Tübingen, p. 168.
[301] Ibid., p. 181.
[302] See Schmidt, W.H. (1966), *Königtum Gottes in Ugarit und Israel*, BZAW 80, Berlin.

original myth in a process of nominalization.[303] The combination of the cosmic reign of Yahweh, who was seated on the throne of Zion while creating and sustaining the world, with the particular history of the people of Israel and their post-exilic projections about the future (Psalm 145) was a relatively late stage in the history of tradition.[304] In the later stages of history, the kingdom of God was interpreted either as a gift of the law (Ps 93:5; 99:7; Deut 33:4) or as a current reality of grace.[305]

Contrasting this approach, H.J. Gunneweg has suggested an existential interpretation. He rejects the possibility of a pre-exilic feast of Yahweh's enthronement as long as an earthly king from the Davidic dynasty resided in Jerusalem. In accordance with ancient oriental ideology, the Davidic king would have claimed the position of royal mediator for himself. The statement 'Yahweh is king' could only have been possible following the end of the Davidic dynasty, and then only in a polemical sense: any human kingdom would be confronted with the 'totally other' kingdom of God (a statement foreshadowing Luther's teaching on two kingdoms).[306] 'Monarchies, governments, and constitutions are functions of this world – the *regnum mundi* – that exist alongside others. They are meant to guarantee the highest degree of justice possible and eliminate grave injustice. Like the created world as a whole with all of its occupations and institutions, they are part of God's will, but definitely not designed to stand in God's place and bring about eschatological salvation. Only this realisation can resolve the exemplary and typical conflict which is part of Israel's history. The important realisation that temporary realities can only have temporary authority is only given to those who have heard of God's eschatological salvation.'[307] The understanding of God, world

---

[303] Jeremias, J. (1987), *Das Königtum Gottes in den Psalmen*, FRLANT 141, Göttingen.

[304] Spieckermann, H. (1989), *Heilsgegenwart. Eine Theologie der Psalmen*, FRLANT 148, Göttingen, convicingly described the absence of any historical traditions in pre-exilic psalms.

[305] This interpretation has been criticised on the basis of the grammatical form of the verbs involved. The dynamic description of Yahweh ascending and seating himself on his throne goes against a static understanding of a particular divine status quo (see Otto, E. (1988), 'Mythos und Geschichte im Alten Testament – Zur Diskussion einer neuen Arbeit von Jörg Jeremias', in *BN* 42, pp. 93-102; Janowski, B. (1989), 'Das Königtum Gottes im den Psalmen Bemerkungen zu einem neuen Gesamtentwurf', in *ZThK* 86, pp. 389-454).

[306] See Gunneweg, A.H.J. (1992), 'Herrschaft Gottes im Alten Testament', in A.H.J. Gunneweg, *Sola Scriptura*, Vol. 2, Göttingen, pp. 37-54.

[307] Gunneweg, A.H.J. (1993), *Biblische Theologie des Alten Testaments*, Stuttgart, pp. 114-120, p. 119.

and the individual expressed in the statement 'God is king!' (instead of any human being) implies a criticism of any human form of government.[308]

b) In his commentary on the Gospel according to Mark, W. Schmithals has presented an existential interpretation of an entire biblical book. The question behind his approach is: why do we find no reference to the writings of Paul in the earliest synoptic traditions? Paul relates very few sayings of Jesus and seems to know nothing of miracles or long sermons that go back to the historical Jesus. Paul's Jesus consists of the terse elements also found in the Apostles' creed: 'born of the virgin Mary, suffered under Pontius Pilate, crucified, died.' Schmithals concludes somewhat surprisingly that Paul did not include any elements of synoptic tradition because they did not yet exist at the time he wrote his epistles. Prior to the written texts of the gospel writers there was no oral tradition pertaining to the deeds of Jesus. The synoptic tradition, in the controversial suggestion by Schmithals, is the product of an ingenious author who wrote the original core of the Gospel according to Mark some years after Paul. The goal of this author was to rework Pauline theology in narrative form for the purposes of communication and comprehension. This author did not collect prior narrative traditions; he invented them in order to explicate Pauline thinking.

> When the original form of the Gospel continually states that Jesus *taught* the people without actually relating what Jesus *said*, it becomes obvious that the *narratives themselves* are a presentation of the teachings of Jesus, and that these teachings therefore have Jesus himself as the primary subject matter. These narratives, especially the miracle narratives, thus often contain a high degree of metaphor and symbol. One can speak in this context of 'allegory' as part of the narrator's intention. The narrator shapes the narratives according to the same principles that guide the creation of the parables which are also characterised by a high degree of metaphor. The *interpreter* must not create allegories himself. He must explain and decipher the metaphoric speech of the narrator. The key for deciphering this speech is found in basic statements on Christological and ecclesiological kerygma.[309]

The miracle narratives, for example, do not intend to relate mighty deeds of the historical Jesus. They aim to describe an understanding of reality which must interpreted by the exegete. The blind person whose eyes are opened is not a person of past history, he is a picture of myself; the deaf person who learns to hear the words of Jesus also refers to me. The mute person given speech, the possessed freed from demons, the lame walking once again: all these individuals are images for the journey out of unbelieving existence into the truth. Without faith, existence is diseased, deficient and steeped in error; only faith can bring healing (Mark

---

[308] See also Dietrich, W. (1980), 'Gott als König. Zur Frage nach der theologischen und politischen Legitimität religiöser Begriffsbildung', in *ZThK* 77, pp. 251-268.

[309] Schmithals, W. (1986), *Das Evangelium nach Markus*, ÖTK 2/1+2, Gütersloh, p. 45.

10:52). All miracle narratives illustrate the basic Pauline concept: 'because if you confess with your lips that Jesus is Lord and believe in your heart that God raised him from the dead, you will be saved' (Rom 10:9). In his interpretation of Mark 4:35-41[310] (Jesus calms the storm), Schmithals combines source criticism,[311] form criticism, comparative religion and tradition history in a manner typical of his whole approach. He even includes the history of theology and philosophy as well as a profound knowledge of hymnology. By referring to Luther, Goethe, Kierkegaard and Heidegger, he shows how this particular miracle illuminates the human being in a state of fear. The key to understanding this narrative is found in the realisation that many of its aspects are meant as parable and must be understood as such. To speak of the 'storms of life' has meanwhile become commonplace. Everyone can understand the metaphoric elements of this passage without the need for too much explanation. We must constantly experience how the journey of our life is interrupted by obstacles and redirected onto unexpected paths. We find ourselves thrown onto shores we never wanted to arrive at. We talk of strokes of fate and failure, we are thrown off course, we stand up to our necks in water and must start all over again. Philosophers speak of being thrown and pushed around as basic aspects of human existence.[312] The interpretation of a historical text and of current reality flow together as one.

The close connection of exegesis and preaching can be illustrated by the following sermon given by A.H.J. Gunneweg on the basis of Schmithals' commentary:

> Travelling with Jesus towards the opposite shore on a stormy lake. And along the way the miracle of calming the storm. A so-called natural miracle is told to us by the gospel writers; miracles – faith's favourite child. For this reason they have been subjected again and again to various explanations: what really happened on that lake? The question was asked and the following answers given: perhaps the storm disappeared as quickly as it came, and pious imagination later expanded on what it had witnessed. Or the first disciples were simple, naive fishermen, and thus as susceptible to miracles as children. Or: we should not explain the miracle away, for it shows that Jesus was not only concerned with saving our souls, but also with saving us in a material sense. The narrative thus motivates us to follow him and also work towards material well-being. Yet what exactly does this work look like? Should we build dikes and dams? Do we really need the story in Mark 4:35ff to know that? – Let us turn to the meaning of the story!
>
> Individuals are on the move, with or without Jesus, but they are definitely on the move, from one shore to the other, from age-group to age-group, from child-like trust to their first steps of independence and towards full maturity, discerning good and evil.

---

[310] Ibid., pp. 254-264.

[311] Schmithals distinguishes between an assumed basic text by an ingenious author and a later redaction by Mark.

[312] Schmithals, *Das Evangelium nach Markus*, p. 259.

Following maturity we enter the autumn of our life – then – just as leaves fall to the earth, human beings once again become dust to dust, ashes to ashes: this, too, leads us to a different shore. People travel to different shores – with changing moods.

This story means us. No one goes through life without 'storms of life'. We are not spared the experience of storms that push our boat off the intended course and throw it onto strange shores that were never intended when we made plans for our life. Who among us in this church today can say that she has never been thrown onto an unintended shore – and is already moving on again, who knows where? Storms are frightening, but a complete lack of wind is equally frightening: periods of contemplation when we ask ourselves: where am I, where are we headed, as individuals, as a nation, as humanity – that also move to places never intended? What do we mean by: the other shore?

This is what our story is about, it is about us, about the boat that no one can leave, and about our fear of storms or of the lack of wind, the repressed fear of the void, of sinking into the bottomless abyss, into destruction. The story tells us all about this, but it mainly tells us about Him. We have not yet spoken about Him. We are on the move alone, this is what we often think, alone with our fear. The story seems to agree with us: in the moment of greatest desperation, He is asleep! How incomprehensible, how panic-ridden is a situation when the sleeping saviour draws back into divine disinterest: 'Does it not matter to you that we are sinking, that we are plunging into the abyss?'

And then the miracle that cannot be explained, when he answers – not to our prayer, that was not a prayer – to our accusation and calms the storms: 'and there was a great silence'. He stands up, and speaks a word, His word. And the situation changes completely, we change completely: Now the accusing questioners must themselves face questioning: 'Why are you so afraid? Why have you no faith?' Have you never heard of the great deeds of God who made the cosmos of life from the hullabaloo of the primal flood, who performs miracles? Have you heard it, but forgotten it all? 'Master, do you not care that we are perishing?' 'Why have you no faith?' And there was a great silence.

And they were afraid and said: 'Who is he? For even the wind and the sea are obedient to him.' Fear of destruction has been transformed into fear, appropriate fear of God that takes God's miracles seriously, even without explanation. There the story ends, the story that is about us, whose story is not yet over. But perhaps we now remember various storms and fears in our life that were transformed into great and wonderful stillness and we recognise in hindsight: It was He who performed miracles. Wind and waves were obedient to him. And some of us may add: and I did not recognize that it was Him.

One thing is for sure: we all still face one final storm and one final fear. Will He still perform miracles, or will our boat sink and drag us into the abyss? – Whoever can say: Jesus is with us and beside us in our boat, even if the storm does not end and the boat sinks, that person can also say: On the final shore – on the other side – He will be there waiting for us – on the unknown shore we will meet him, who has revealed himself to us as the one whom we know and trust and who is with us even today, revealing himself in his entire goodness in the words of our gospel.[313]

D) The primary contribution made by existential interpretation to the theory of hermeneutics is the recognition that author and interpreter must share basic aspects of reality. Without a common approach to the subject matter or without at least single points of agreement, understanding becomes impossible. This realisation has many consequences for religious pedagogy, homiletics and theology in general. Understanding the Bible is connected to a rich personality capable of bringing a vast reservoir of experiences to the understanding of biblical texts. Exegetical training must be wide in scope, maintaining close contact to current issues. The text remains mute if we do not direct questions at it. Existential interpretation is able to overcome the abyss of history by uncovering the structural similarities between past and present existence while showing: *tua res agitur* ('It is about you!').

Existential interpretation emerged as the main trend primarily in German New Testament scholarship following World War II, yet the last twenty years have been rather quiet in this area. Several points of criticism were articulated in response to existential interpretation: the reduction of concrete history to abstract concepts of existence was seen as a weakness; many rejected the artificial and somewhat stilted terminology derived from Heidegger's philosophy; others articulated the danger of constant repetition when each Sunday the congregation was led on a journey from illusion to true existence. The most effective criticism was probably the accusation that existential interpretation was escapist, withdrawing from the world of politics into a sphere of private inwardness. It was argued that the concept of 'otherworldliness' pulled individuals away from concrete interaction with the world, which could also be seen in a marked *anti-Judaism*.[314]

These criticisms are highly inappropriate as they are based on profound misunderstandings. The concept of 'otherworldliness', which Bultmann used in complete analogy to Paul and St John, does not refer to an escapist withdrawal into the inner self, but rather to a critical distance to the seemingly necessary laws of the world that resulted from divine renewal (see John 18:36f; Rom 12:2). Bultmann is intent on distinguishing between mere human political action and the reign of God (see the short exegesis on Psalm 93). Politics always falls short of completion; even work for social betterment cannot be equated with God's work of salvation. Situational ethics may allow ethical decisions as to what is good and appropriate to faith, love, and hope to be based on the individual conscience in the

---

[313] Gunneweg,. A.H.J. (1996) 'Predigt zu Mk 4,35ff', in R. Landauer (ed.), *Calwer Predigtbibliothek*, Vol. 1, Stuttgart, pp. 106-108.

[314] See Osten-Sacken, P. von der (1978), 'Rückzug ins Wesen und aus der Geschichte. Antijudaismus bei Adolf von Harnack und Rudolf Bultmann', in *WuPKG* 67, pp. 106-122.

face of specific circumstances. Situational ethics, however, does not relieve individuals of responsible action. Instead, it protects the freedom found in faith. It is hard to understand how it is possible to accuse Bultmann of anti-Judaism in light of his public protest against racial laws in 1934, and his close connections to Jewish friends such as Hans Jonas. The mere fact that Bultmann clearly recognised and articulated the differences between Christianity and Judaism would not be understood as anti-Judaism from a Jewish perspective.[315]

Heidegger's language is not wrong as such; it is merely a tool for explication which could be replaced and expanded at any time by terminology more suited to the subject matter. The fact that methods devolop their own jargon is an unavoidable state of affairs and cannot be used against the validity of existential intepretation as such. The danger of monotony and repetition can surely be avoided by a close connection to the polyphony of the texts. In contrast to the allegorical interpretation of Homer, in which external concepts are brought to the text that were never intended by it, existential interpretation strives to clarify the subject matter contained in the text itself by separating secondary aspects of the text from its main message. Demythologising is not an alienation effect thrown over the text, but rather a valid method of interpreting the text's subject matter. It is also not the point of existential interpretation to follow the enlightenment goal of establishing the one eternal truth of the text as 'kerygma'. '*The* kerygma', in any case, cannot exist outside of history as a distilled essence; there is no philosophical foundation for such a view. In summary, existential exegesis appears as a wonderful instrument for combining differentiated historical–critical exegesis with a theological understanding and explanation of present issues.

---

[315] See Gräßer, E. (1985), 'Antijudaismus bei Bultmann?', in E. Gräßer, *Der Alte Bund im Neuen*, WUNT 35, Tübingen.

PART III:
SUMMARY:
FULLNESS OR FLOOD OF
MEANING?

Chapter 8

The Bible and the Current Plethora of Methods

The question guiding our introduction was: when can I say that I have understood the Bible? A phenomenological description of the process of understanding led to the description of four corners of a hermeneutical square that can be distinguished but not separated from each other. This model enabled us to explain and organise the many ways the Bible is understood today. The explanation included case studies that were intended to highlight the strengths and weaknesses of each of the seventeen approaches. We saw that each method was able to emphasise a particular aspect of the biblical text, but that each method also included its share of blind spots. Each method thus has a claim to relative validity while also standing in need of critical supplementation. The following graphic summarises the richness resulting from the various approaches (Figure 4).

The 'newer approaches to the Bible should not be understood as alternatives to the historical–critical method. We are dealing with different questions aimed at the text that complement each other hermeneutically and methodologically. The exact nature of the interaction between these methods is still in need of clarification.'[316] It is becoming clear that the vision of a holistic understanding of of the Bible serves important *regulative* functions, but that it can never be fully attained. One consequence of this insight is a negative statement: *none of the methods can fully make the claim of having understood the Bible.* This criticism limiting exegetical prowess is an important defence against exegetical arrogance. No single method can be said to have a monopoly on understanding. The hermeneutical discussion in this book should have shown instead that there *has* to be a wide scope of different understandings. A 'holistic understanding of the Bible'[317] as the ideal goal of research is only possible in a synopsis of the various facets balancing each other. This requires that exegetes must undergo careful training and maintain a continual aptitude for interdisciplinary cooperation. So far, there have only been a few projects that attempt to combine the wide scope of possible approaches to the Bible. One example is found in K. Grünwald and H. Schröter, Was suchst du hier,

---

[316] Merklein, H. (1989), 'Integrative Bibelauslegung? Methodische und hermeneutische Aspekte', in *BiKi* 44, pp. 117-123, p. 122.

[317] See Fischer, R. (1996), *Die Kunst des Bibellesens. Theologische Ästhetik am Beispiel des Schriftverständnisses*, Beiträge zur theologischen Urteilsbildung 1, Frankfurt.

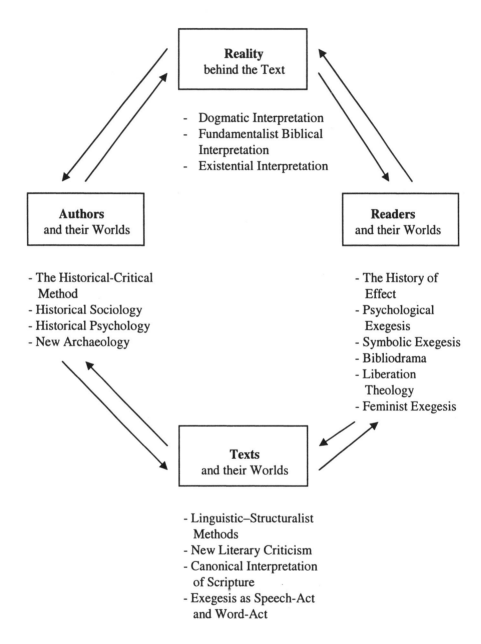

Figure 4   The hermeneutical square and the various methodological approaches

Elia?,[318] which gathers more than 30 contributions to the figure of Elijah, covering almost all of the methodological approaches discussed above. This is an ideal example of how exegesis can present an adequately complex picture of biblical interpretation.

The current diversity of methods and the resulting flood of biblical meanings is *not* a new phenomenon; nor should it be a cause for concern. The diversity is a *necessary* aspect of the process of understanding and can be seen in analogy to the medieval teaching on the four-fold meaning of Scripture: the four-fold interpretative task should no longer concentrate on: literal meaning + faith + love + hope (historical + dogmatic + ethical + eschatological meaning), but rather on: author + text + reader + subject matter.

This insight leads to the following unavoidable conclusion: biblical interpretation must never be one-dimensional, but must remain open for the existing richness of possible interpretations! Stated positively: the manifold approaches to the Bible enable us to uncover and see the richness contained in the Word of God. The complexity of the process of understanding contains and legitimises the multiplicity of approaches from the very beginning as a *fundamentum in re*![319]

The hermeneutical arguments are supported by the plurality within contemporary society and the resulting necessity for various different approaches to the biblical text. We live in a world in which different groups co-exist, all with their own religious attitudes and requirements. It seems pointless to try to regulate these factions through prohibitions and taboos. Any attempt at gathering all Bible readers under one normative methodological umbrella is doomed to failure. We should instead rejoice in the attention and interest the Bible still has in our pluralistic society.

Many colleagues react with sorrow and shock at the diffuse situation of biblical interpretation: 'The great unifying concepts and ideas have disappeared. This is also true for biblical interpretation.'[320] Many fear that methodical rigour, objectivity, intersubjectivity, and the interdisciplinary reputation of biblical interpretation will be lost by opening the doors to pluralism. With J. Hermand we could suspect that 'the widespread willingness for reconciliation is merely an indication of our total lack of perspective, leaving us open to a liberal anarchy of

---

[318] Grünwald, K. and Schröter, H. (1995), *Was suchst du hier Elia? Ein hermeneutisches Arbeitsbuch*, Hermeneutica 4, Rheinbach-Merzbach.

[319] See Dalferth, I. (1994), 'Von der Vieldeutbarkeit der Schrift und der Eindeutigkeit des Wortes Gottes', in R. Ziegert (ed.), *Die Zukunft des Schriftprinzips*, Stuttgart, pp. 155-173.

[320] Dienst, K. (1994), 'In Zukunft ganz pluralistisch? Zur Legitimität des eigenen Blicks auf die Bibel', in R. Ziegert (ed.), *Die Zukunft des Schriftprinzips*, Stuttgart, pp. 207-221, p. 207.

allowing everything ... Are we heading into a democratic "be nice to each other?" agnosticism?, ignorance?'[321]

These are important critical challenges; however, they do not negate the need for an appreciation of plurality. In regards to the interdisciplinary reputation of biblical interpretation, even within theological faculties (!), it must be said that this reputation has already suffered for a long time:

> The exegetical disciplines have largely replaced ... an open, critical awareness of the text with a clean and peaceful division of labour. *The specialists in half- and quarter-verses who can no longer be understood by anyone outside their area of specialisation have no impact on those who are trying to come to terms with new models for biblical theology.* This *inconsequential exegetical game* is crowned by the attempt to cut back the importance of Hellenism in favour of the Old Testament and early Judaism. It is clear that these efforts are also guided by a guilty conscience about the frequently disqualified later forms of Judaism. Answering Auschwitz and the Holocaust by reducing Christianity to its beginnings, especially its early Jewish beginnings, is unreflected systematic nonsense ... These attempts also contribute to the *eradication of the profile of Protestant exegesis through a mishmash of exegetical confusion.*[322]

We must ask whether an interdisciplinary interaction between biblical interpretation and general literary and cultural research might not even rebuild some of the reputation of biblical exegesis through the inclusion of multiple interpretations. Biblical research must face the challenge of analysing and describing the multiple effects and plurality of discourse and language games involving the Bible and contemporary society. Fundamental opposition of approaches – such as synchronic versus diachronic interpretation – have already proved to be mere theoretical constructs that disappear in day-to-day exegetical work. Good exegesis will always deal with historical matters of text-production and reception, timeless matters of textual structure, and even issues of reader-response.[323] These aspects are often supplemented (albeit with a certain degree of shyness) by theological reflection. The actual process of exegesis in action deviates to a large degree from one-sided theory. This deviation is a positive situation that should reflected upon more carefully.

---

[321] Hormand, J. (1978), *Synthetisches Interpretieren. Zur Methodik der Literaturwissenschaft*, München, p. 187.

[322] Wagner, F. (1994), 'Auch der Teufel zitiert die Bibel. Das Christentum zwischen Autoritätsanspruch und Krise des Schriftprinzips', in R. Ziegert (ed.), *Die Zukunft des Schriftprinzips*, p. 251 (emphasis M.O.).

[323] See Moor, J.C. de (ed.) (1995), *Synchronic or Diachronic? A Debate on Method in Old Testament Exegesis. Papers from the Ninth Joint Meeting of Het Oudtestamentlisch Werkgezelshap in Nederland en Belgie and the Society for Old Testament Study, held at Kampen 1994*, OTS 34, Leiden/New York.

Many who would support an acceptance of pluralism *in principle* voice the concern that it is not *feasible*. In the face of the already stringent preconditions for professional exegesis, exegetes are simply not capable of a careful, comprehensive study of interpretation in past and present. This concern cannot in principle negate the need for such study. Biblical research is called to continually face new intellectual and cultural trends, even if these may seem confusingly complex at first. The goal must always be to develop adequate approaches to the Bible.[324] The complexity of the material requires a type of exegete who is also willing and able to see beyond the boundaries of his or her exegetical discipline. The great exegetes of the past have always shown this trait.

Despite the many problems that undoubtedly exist, of which some even seem to defy resolution, the arguments stand clearly in favour of an acceptance of methodological plurality! Six limitations, however, are necessary:

α) The choice of method appropriate to a certain text is very dependent on *context*. This context is determined by three aspects: *the idiosyncrasy of the interpreter, the idiosyncrasy of the text, and the purpose of the exegesis*. Not every method is suited for every interpreter; the degree of education as well as other aspects will determine whether an academic approach or a meditative, pragmatic approach to the text is more appropriate. The Bible contains several different textual genres that must each be dealt with separately. Psychological interpretation of a legal text or liberation exegesis on a genealogy will seem overly artificial. The purpose of the interpretation is a very important aspect. It would be nonsense to present the result of historical–critical scholarship in Sunday school or a Sunday school story in a university classroom.

The exegete must develop a careful sense of which method may be appropriate for which situation. This requires experience, sensitivity, an awareness of one's audience as well as a good measure of plain common sense.

β) It is important to *distinguish between the original sense of the text and its later reception* (including one's own). The meaning of a text at the time of its production, or at least at the time of its canonisation, must remain at the centre of the *academic* study of the Bible. *Sub specie scientiae*, the methods are not equal but are arranged hierarchically. The historical-critical method is a powerful tool for the description of the original meaning(s) of the text which has a strong regulative function within the process of understanding as a whole. This method is also capable of correcting itself as well as integrating new insights and important aspects from other methods. In the context of understanding as a whole, however, the historical–critical method cannot lay claim to any kind of monopoly.

γ) Bridging the historical abyss between ancient texts and modern readers is a prime task of biblical hermeneutics. While each method solves this problem in a different manner, we must recognise the pre-eminence of existential interpretation!

---

[324] H. Timm has made several constructive suggestions in this area: Timm, H. (1995), *Sage und Schreibe. Inszenierungen religiöser Lesekultur*, Innen & Außen 2, Kampen.

The fact that biblical authors articulate an understanding of human existence, with which they also speak to modern readers, seems to be the principal prerequisite for the basic possibility of understanding. Existential interpretation does justice both to the idiosyncrasies of the Bible as well as the idiosyncrasies of present recipients.

δ) The programmatic proclamation of such plurality leads *de facto* to the increased development of particular special interests. Individual scholars, along with their students and colleagues address a certain area of specialization and pursue their personal strategies and ideologies in a very regional context. A true synthesis of methodologies does not occur at all! As a pluralistic context allows every one to find salvation according to their own design, biblical scholarship is increasingly fragmented instead of bound together with its various aspects. Interdisciplinary research must mean more that bringing experts together who then merely continue to think along their own predisposed paths.[325]

ε) The plurality of methods calls for the establishment of a scholarly *ethos*. 'In the end, exegesis is an act of obedience, an act of listening to the text. The interpreter must focus on the text and not on himself. This should be the goal of reflective methodological work on the text ... this also involves the ability of seeing through the hermeneutical implications of the various methods.'[326]

ζ) Aristotle describes ethics as a path created by continually walking on it as a practical habit. 'An "ethics of interpretation" thus entails living in and remaining in an interpretation.'[327] The most important ethical axiom is habitually dealing with the Bible, living together with the Bible, even living in the Bible. Whoever lives in a house will know the important interactions within that house, will appreciate the functional design and interrelation of the various rooms, and will be able to move freely and securely in that house; individual rooms are not seen in isolation or ever mixed up with each other. 'If you continue in my word, you are truly my disciples; and you will know the truth, and the truth will make you free' (John 8:31f.).

η) We must relativise our passion for objectivity, so often combined with the use of the term 'method'. Which approaches to the Bible even deserve the high status of being referred to as 'method'? The humanities differ from the sciences in one basic regard: they are not primarily interested in *explanations* that can be measured and intersubjectively verified; instead, they focus on subjectively coloured and complex *understanding* that can be measured only to a degree and only with great difficulty. This is the goal of hermeneutics.[328] For this reason, we cannot precisely define methods of biblical interpretation (as is true for all

---

[325] Grünwald and Schröter's highly acclaimed book on Elijah (see note 318) also shows that the individual contributions stand in isolation without working towards a true synthesis.

[326] Merklein, H. (1989), 'Integrative Bibelauslegung?', p. 123.

[327] Sini, C. (1993), 'Die Ethik der Auslegung', in F. Bianco (ed.), *Beiträge zur Hermeneutik aus Italien*, Alber-Reihe Philosophie, Freiburg/München, pp. 141-157, p. 146.

[328] See Riedel, M. (1978), *Verstehen oder Erklären? Zur Theorie der hermeneutischen Wissenschaft*, Stuttgart.

disciplines in the humanities), nor can we use them mechanically. A person can execute a series of laboratory experiments with the goal of collecting data without a deeper understanding of what it is he is measuring. This is impossible when dealing with the Bible. Without dealing with the Bible on an existential level and being at home in it, it is impossible to come to appropriate and fruitful observations of its content. We must thus be careful about placing too much faith in method. True understanding is not primarily dependent on the method chosen; it is rather dependent on the intensity developed in dealing with the object under consideration.

The six limitations mentioned above lead in the end to a hopeful affirmation of the plurality of approaches to understanding the Bible.

When can I say: I have understood the biblical text? Understanding the Bible – like all understanding – is 'condemned' to change because of the historicity of our existence. There can be no definitive conclusion. This basic insight should not lead to resignation. In each generation and age, human beings face the promising challenge of discovering the texts through a lively interaction with the Bible in the context of ever new categories of thought and experience. This will always reveal a new facet of the biblical message: interpretation will always open a new room, or closet, or at least a drawer not yet known to previous dwellers in the same house. Depression, apologetics and fear are not appropriate as a reaction to postmodernism, neither is an illusionary search for an all-new, all-encompassing 'transversal rationality'[329] that would combine all exegesis, but a living interaction with the Bible, carried by the trust that the Bible can stand up for itself (*sacra scriptura sui ipsius interpres*). Whenever the Bible comes into play, we will experience a hermeneutical transformation as the interpreted text becomes the interpreter. Scripture illuminates our existence.

In conclusion, I will allow myself the following metaphor: A few years ago, a certain manufacturer of up-market watches started an impressive advertising campaign: the commercials showed how the watch was 'mis-used' under extreme circumstances; it was attached to a ski and driven down a hard-packed slope. The watch was thrown back and forth and violently slammed against the ground. Upon arrival in the valley, the skier removed the watch from the ski, brushed the snow off, and the watch was still working, displaying the correct time. The situation with the Bible is similar. Through history, it has been 'tested' under the extremest circumstances: at the beginning of the modern era it was subjected to the Enlightenment and dealt with by Marxism; Freud attacked it, historical–critical exegesis has pushed and kicked it, and it was made to suffer under various forms of reception. Yet when we brush away yesterday's snow and today's dust and open the Bible and look at it closely, we will see: it still works and displays precisely what we need to know for our times! Readers of the Bible know more.

---

[329] See Welsch, W. (1995), *Die transversale Vernunft*, Frankfurt.

Bibliography

A. Basic Texts

Aurelius Augustinus (1997), *De doctrine christiana. On Christian teaching. St. Augustine,* ed., trans. with an introd. and notes by R.P.H. Green, Oxford.

Bengel, J.A. (1877), *Gnomon of the New Testament, revised and ed. by Rev. A.R. Fausset,* Edinburgh.

Matthias Flacius Illyricus (1567), *Clavis scripturae sacrae seu de Sermone Sacrarum literarum [...].* = Geldsetzer, L. (ed.) (1968), *Über den Erkenntnisgrund der heiligen Schrift,* Düsseldorf.

Luther, M.(1989), *Luthers Vorreden zur Bibel,* KVR 1550, 3rd edition, Göttingen.

Origenes (1966), *On first principles; being Koetschau's text of the De principiis, trans. into English, ed. by Henry De Lubac,* New York.

Reimarus, H.S. (1972), *Apologie oder Schutzschrift für die vernünftigen Verehrer Gottes (Fragmente eines Ungenannten, posthum von Ephraim Lessing 1774ff. hrsg.),* Frankfurt.

B. Summaries and Overviews

Becker, J. (1993), *Grundzüge einer Hermeneutik des Alten Testaments,* Frankfurt.

Berg, H.K. (1991), *Ein Wort wie Feuer. Wege lebendiger Bibelauslegung,* München and Stuttgart.

Berger, K. (1988), *Hermeneutik des Neuen Testaments,* Gütersloh.

Branson, M.L. and Padilla, C.R. (eds) (1986), *Conflict and Context: Hermeneutics in the Americas,* Grand Rapids.

Bühler, P. and Karakash, C. (eds) (1995), *Quand interpréter c'est changer. Pragmatique et lectures de la parole. Actes du Congrès International d'Hermeneutique (Neuchâtel, 12.-14. Septembre 1994),* Lieux théologiques 28, Genf.

CERIT sous la direction de Claude Coulot (1994), *Exegèse et herméneutique: comment lire la Bible,* Lectio divina 158, Paris.

Coggins, R.J. and Houlden, J.L. (1990), *A Dictionary of Biblical Interpretation,* London.

Dohmen, Ch. and Söding, Th. (eds) (1995), *Eine Bibel – zwei Testamente,* UTB 1893, Paderborn.

Fabry, H.J. (ed.) (1993), *Bibel und Bibelauslegung. Das immer neue Bemühen um die Botschaft Gottes,* Regensburg.

Gunneweg, A.H.J. (1978), *Understanding the Old Testament, trans. by J. Bowden,* London.

Hochgrebe, V. and Meesmann, H. (eds.) (1989), *Warum versteht ihr meine Bibel nicht? Wege zu befreitem Leben,* Freiburg.

Joest, W. (1988), 'Fundamentaltheologie', in *ThW* 11, Stuttgart, pp. 135-255.

Knight, D.A. and Tucker, G.M. (eds.) (1985), *The Hebrew Bible and its Modern Interpreters*, Chicago.

Körtner, U.H.J. (1994), *Der inspirierte Leser. Zentrale Aspekte biblischer Hermeneutik*, Göttingen.

Langer, W. (1987), *Handbuch der Bibelarbeit*, München.

Lapointe, R. (1967), *Les trois dimensions de l'herméneutique*, CRB 8, Paris.

Luz, U. (1993), *Zankapfel Bibel. Eine Bibel – viele Zugänge*, 2nd edition, Zürich.

Maier, G. (1992), *Biblische Hermeneutik*, 2nd edition, Wuppertal.

McKim, K.D. (ed.) (1986), *A Guide to Contemporary Hermeneutics. Major Trends in Biblical Interpretation*, Grand Rapids.

Morgan, R. and Barton J. (1989), *Biblical Interpretation*, Oxford Bible Series, 2nd edition, Oxford.

Müller, P. (1994), *'Verstehst du auch, was du liest?' Lesen und Verstehen im Neuen Testament*, Darmstadt.

Oeming, M. (1987), *Gesamtbiblische Theologien der Gegenwart. Das Verhältnis von AT und NT in der hermeneutischen Diskussion seit Gerhard von Rad*, 2nd edition, Stuttgart.

Raddatz, W., Sauter, G. and Ulrich, H.G. (1970), 'Verstehen', in G. Otto (ed.), *Praktisch-theologisches Handbuch*, Hamburg, pp. 483-513.

Seebass, H. (1974), *Biblische Hermeneutik*, UB 199, Stuttgart.

Söding, Th. (1995), *Mehr als ein Buch. Die Bibel begreifen*, Freiburg.

Sternberg, Th. (ed.) (1992), *Neue Formen der Schriftauslegung?*, QD 140, Freiburg.

Stuhlmacher, P. (1986), *Vom Verstehen des Neuen Testaments. Eine Hermeneutik*, GNT 6, 2nd edition, Göttingen.

Timm, H. (1995), *Sage und Schreibe. Inszenierungen religiöser Lesekultur*, Innen und Außen 2, Kampen.

Weder, H. (1989), *Neutestamentliche Hermeneutik*, 2nd edition, Zürich.

C. Secondary Literature on the Various Methodological Approaches

1. Methods Focused on Authors and their Worlds

a) The Historical–Critical Method

Baldermann, I. (1987), 'Der leidenschaftliche Gott und die Leidenschaftslosigkeit der Enogooo. Anfragon ou oinom exogotischen Defizit', in *IBTh 2*, pp. 137-150

Chevallier, M.-A. (1984), *L'exégèse du Nouveau Testament. Initiation à la méthode*, Genf.

Ebeling, G. (1963), *Word and faith*, London.

Egger, W. (1996), *How to read the New Testament. An introduction to linguistic and historico-critical methodology*, ed. by H. Boers, trans. by P. Heinegg, Peabody.

Fohrer, G. (ed.) (1993), *Exegese des Alten Testaments. Einführung in die Methodik*, 6th edition, Heidelberg.

Gese, H. (1977), 'Das biblische Schriftverständnis: Vom Sinai zum Zion', in *BEvTh 78*, pp. 9-30.

Raffelt, A. (ed.) (1991), *Begegnung mit Jesus? Was die historisch-kritische Methode leistet*, Düsseldorf.

Riedlinger, H. (ed.) (1985), *Die historisch-kritische Methode und die heutige Suche nach einem lebendigen Verständnis der Bibel*, München and Zürich.

Rose, M. (1988), 'Approches classiques de l'Ancien Testament: Techniques exégétiques et implications theologiques', in *ETR* 63, pp. 337-360.

Ruppert, L. (1994), 'Die historisch-kritische Methode in der Bibelexegese im deutschen Sprachraum: Vorgeschichte, gegenwärtige Entwicklungen, Tendenzen, Neuaufbrüche', in L. Ruppert, *Studien zur Literaturgeschichte des Alten Testaments*, SBAB 18, Stuttgart, pp. 266-307.

Schmidt, W.H. (1996), 'Grenzen und Vorzüge historisch-kritischer Exegese', in W.H. Schmidt, *Vielfalt und Einheit alttestamentlichen Glaubens 1*, Neukirchen-Vluyn, pp. 21-33.

Schnelle, U. (1988), 'Sachgemäße Schriftauslegung', in *NT* 30, pp. 115-131.

Söding, Th. (1995), 'Wissenschaftliche und kirchliche Schriftauslegung. Hermeneutische Überlegungen zur Verbindlichkeit der Heiligen Schrift', in W. Pannenberg and Th. Schneider (eds), *Verbindliches Zeugnis II*, DiKi 9, Göttingen, Freiburg, pp. 72-121.

Steck, O.H. (1993), *Exegese des Alten Testaments. Leitfaden der Methodik*, 13th edition, Neukirchen-Vluyn.

Wink, W. (1973), *The Bible in human transformation. Toward a new paradigm for Biblical study*, Philadelphia.

Zimmermann, H. (1982), *Neutestamentliche Methodenlehre. Darstellung der historisch-kritischen Methode*, 7th edition, Stuttgart.

b) Historical Sociology

Casalis, G. (1984), *Correct ideas don't fall from the skies. Elements for an inductive theology, trans. from the French by Sister J.M. Lyons and M. John*, New York.

Clévenot, M. (1985), *Materialist approaches to the Bible, trans. by W.J. Nottingham*, Maryknoll.

Crüsemann, F. (1983), 'Grundfragen sozialgeschichtlicher Exegese', in *EvErz* 35, pp. 273-286.

Füssel, K. (1985), 'Materialistische Lektüre der Bibel', in *ThBer* 13, pp. 123-163.

Gottwald, N.K. (ed.) (1983), *The Bible and Liberation*, Maryknoll.

Gottwald. N.K. (1985), *The Hebrew Bible. A Socio-Literary Introduction*, Philadelphia.

Holmberg, B. (1990), *Sociology and the New Testament. An Appraisal*, Minneapolis.

Kee, H.C. (1989), *Knowing the Truth. A Sociological Approach to New Testament Interpretation*, Minneapolis.

Laub, F. (1989), 'Sozialgeschichtliche Exegese. Anmerkungen zu einer neuen Fragestellung in der historisch-kritischen Arbeit am Neuen Testament', in *MThZ* 40, pp. 39-50.

Schottroff, W. and Stegemann, W. (eds.) (1979), *Der Gott der kleinen Leute. Sozialgeschichtliche Bibelauslegungen, Vol. 1: Altes Testament; Vol. 2: Neues Testament*, München, and Gelnhausen.

Schottroff, W. and Stegemann, W. (1984), *God of the lowly. Socio-historical interpretations of the Bible, trans. from the German by M.J. O'Conell*, Maryknoll.

Staden, P. van and Aarde, A.G. van (1991), 'Social Description or Social-Scientific Interpretation? A Survey of Modern Scholarship', in *HTS* 47, pp. 55-87.

Stegemann, E. and Stegemann, W. (1999), *Jesus movement: a social history of the first century, trans. by O.C. Dean Jr.*, Minneapolis.

Theißen, G. (1978), *The first followers of Jesus. A sociological analysis of the earliest Christianity, trans. from the German by J. Bowden*, London.

Welten, P. (1989), 'Ansätze sozialgeschichtlicher Betrachtungsweise des Alten Testaments im 20. Jahrhundert', in *BThZ* 6, pp. 207-221.

Wilson, R.R. (1984), *Sociological Approaches to the Old Testament*, Philadelphia.

c) Historical Psychology

Berger, K. (1991), *Historische Psychologie des Neuen Testaments*, SBS 146/147, Stuttgart.

Journal (1991ff), *Psychologie und Geschichte 1ff.*

Jüttemann, G. (ed.) (1986), *Die Geschichtlichkeit des Seelischen*, Weinheim.

Jüttemann, G. (ed.) (1988), *Wegbereiter der Historischen Psychologie*, München and Weinheim.

Jüttemann, G., Sonntag M. and Wulf, Ch. (eds) (1991), *Die Seele. Ihre Geschichte im Abendland*, Weinheim.

Leiner, M. (1995), *Psychologie und Exegese. Grundfragen einer textpsychologischen Exegese des Neuen Testaments*, Gütersloh.

Oeming, M. (1995), 'Altes Testament und Tiefenpsychologie. Aufklärung oder Freudsche Fehlleistung', in *ThLZ* 120, pp. 107-120.

Sonntag, M. and Jüttemann, G. (eds) (1993), *Individuum und Geschichte. Beiträge zur Diskussion um eine 'Historische Psychologie'*, Heidelberg.

Theißen, G. (1987), *Psychological aspects of Pauline theology, trans. by J.P. Galvin*, Philadelphia.

d) New Archaeology

Crüsemann, F. (1979), 'Alttestamentliche Exegese und Archäologie', in *ZAW* 91, pp. 177-193.

Dever, W.G. (1981), 'The Impact of the "New Archaeology" on Syro-Palestinian Archaeology', in *BASOR* 242, pp. 14-29.

Dever, W.G. (1992), 'Archaeology', in *AncB Dictionary 1*, pp. 354-367.

Fritz, V. (1987), *Kleines Lexikon der Biblischen Archäologie*, Konstanz.

Fritz, V. (1990), *Die Stadt im alten Israel*, München.

Fritz, V. (1994), *Introduction to biblical archaeology*, Sheffield.

Keel, O. and Küchler, M. (1984), *Orte und Landschaften der Bibel Vol. I*, Göttingen.

Noort, E. (1979), *Biblisch-archäologische Hermeneutik und alttestamentliche Exegese*, Kampen.

Perdue, L.G., Toombs, L.E. and Johnson, G. (eds) (1987), *Archaeology and Biblical Interpretation*, Atlanta.

Theißen, G. (1991), *The gospels in context: social and political history in the synoptic tradition, trans. by L.M. Maloney*, Minneapolis.

Wright, G.E. (1974), 'The "New Archaeology"', in *BA* 38, pp. 104-115.

Zwickel, W. (1995), *Bilder zur biblischen Welt in Religionsbüchern. Eine Problemanzeige*, Wechselwirkungen 16, Waltrop.

2. Methods Focused on Texts and their Worlds

a) Linguistic–Structuralist Methods

Brinker, K. (1988), *Linguistische Textanalyse. Eine Einführung in ihre Grundbegriffe und Methoden*, Germ 29, Berlin.

Güttgemanns, E. (1982), 'Semiotik und Theologie. Thesen zu Geschichte und Funktion der Semiotik in der Bibel', in *Semiotik* 4, pp. 151-168.

Güttgemanns, E. (1983), *Fragmenta semiotico-hermeneutica. Eine Texthermeneutik für den Umgang mit der Hl. Schrift*, FThL 9, Bonn.

Patte, D. (1990), *Structural Exegesis for New Testament Critics*, Minneapolis.

Poland, L.M. (1985), *Literary Criticism and Biblical Hermeneutics: A Critique of Formalist Approaches*, Chicago.

Preuss, H.D. (1982), 'Linguistik – Literaturwissenschaft – Altes Testament', in *VF* 27, pp. 2-28.

Richter, W. (1971), *Exegese als Literaturwissenschaft. Entwurf einer alttestamentlichen Literaturtheorie und Methodologie*, Göttingen.

Schweizer, H. (1986), *Biblische Texte verstehen. Arbeitsbuch zur Hermeneutik und Methodik der Bibelinterpretation*, Stuttgart.

b) New Literary Criticism

Alter, R. (1981), *The Art of Biblical Narrative*, London and New York.

Alter, R. (1985), *The Art of Biblical Poetry*, New York.

Alter, R. and Kermode, F. (eds) (1987), *The Literary Guide to the Bible*, Glasgow (London. 1989)

Bar-Efrat, T.S. (1989), *Narrative Art in the Bible*, JSOT.S 70, Sheffield.

Barton, J. (1984), *Reading the Old Testament*, Oxford, especially pp. 140-179.

Berlin, A. (1983), *Poetics and Interpretation of Biblical Narrative*, BiLiSe 17, Sheffield.

Fokkelman, J.P. (1981-1990), *Narrative Art and Poetry in the Books of Samuel*, 3 Vols., Assen.

Long, B.O. (1990), 'Some Difficulties in the New Poetics of Biblical Narrative', in D. Assaf (ed.), *Proceedings of the Tenth World Congress of Jewish Studies. The Bible and its World*, Jerusalem, pp. 59-66.

Ska, J.-L. (1990), *Our Fathers. Introduction to the Analysis of Hebrew Narratives*, SubBi 13, Rome.

Sternberg, M. (1985), *The Poetics of Biblical Narrative. Ideological Literature and the Drama of Reading*, Indiana literary biblical series, Bloomington, Indiana.

c) Canonical Interpretation of Scripture

Barr, J. (1983), *Holy Scripture. Canon, Authority, Criticism*, Oxford.

Barton, J. (1996), 'The Significance of a Fixed Canon of the Hebrew Bible', in M. Saebø (ed.), *Hebrew Bible – Old Testament. The History of its Interpretation I/1: Antiquity*, Göttingen, pp. 67-83.

Brett, M.G. (1991), *Biblical Criticism in Crisis? The Impact of the Canonical Approach on Old Testament Studies*, Cambridge.

Childs, B.S. (1979), *Introduction to the Old Testament as Scripture*, Philadelphia and London.

Childs, B.S. (1985), *Old Testament Theology in a Canonical Context*, Philadelphia and London.

Childs, B.S. (1992), *Biblical Theology of the Old and New Testaments*, Philadelphia and London.

Childs, B.S. (1994), *The New Testament as Canon*, 2nd edition Philadelphia and London.

Dohmen, Ch. and Oeming, M. (1992), *Biblischer Kanon – warum und wozu? Eine Kanontheologie*, QD 127, Freiburg.

Dohmen, Ch. (1995), 'Der Biblische Kanon in der Diskussion', in *ThRev* 91, pp. 451-460.

Lohfink, N. (1988), 'Was wird anders bei kanonischer Schriftauslegung? Beobachtungen am Beispiel von Psalm 6', in *JBTh* 3, pp. 29-53.

Miller Jr, P.D. (1988), 'Der Kanon in der gegenwärtigen amerikanischen Diskussion', in *JBTh 3*, pp. 217-239.

Oeming, M. (1996), 'Kanonische Schriftauslegung. Vorzüge und Grenzen eines neuen Zugangs zur Bibel', in *BiLi* 69, pp. 199-208.

Rendtorff, R. (1994), '"Canonical Interpretation" – a New Approach to Biblical Texts', in *StTh* 48, pp. 3-14.

Sanders, J.A. (1984), *Canon and Community. A Guide to Canonical Criticism*, Philadelphia.

Sanders, J.A. (1987), *From Sacred Story to Sacred Text: Canon as Paradigm*, Phildelphia.

d) Exegesis as Speech-Act and Word-Act

Brantschen, J. (1980), *Zeit des Glaubens. Ein Versuch, um Ernst Fuchs zu verstehen*, Zürich.

Ebeling, G. (1973), *Introduction to a theological theory of language, trans. by R.A. Wilson*, London.

Fuchs, E. (1968), *Marburger Hermeneutik*, Tübingen.

Fuchs, E. (1970), *Hermeneutik*, 4th edition, Bad Cannstatt.

Jüngel, E. (1983), *God as the mystery of the world: on the foundation of the theology of the crucified one in the dispute between theism and atheism, trans. by D.L Guder*, Grand Rapids, Michigan.

Meurer, H.-J. (1997), *Die Gleichnisse Jesu als Metaphern. Paul Ricoeurs Hermeneutik der Gleichniserzählung Jesu im Horizont des Symbols 'Gottesherrschaft/Reich Gottes'*, BBB 111, Weinheim.

Ricoeur, P. and Jüngel, E. (1974), *Metapher. Zur Hermeneutik religiöser Sprache*, EvTh.Sonderheft, München.

Weder, H. (1989), *Neutestamentliche Hermeneutik*, 2nd edition, Zürich.

Weder, H. (1990), *Die Gleichnisse Jesu als Metapher*, FRLANT 120, 4th edition, Göttingen.

3. Methods Focused on Readers and their Worlds

a) The History of Effect (Wirkungsgeschichtliche Exegese)

Dohmen, Ch. (1987), 'Rezeptionsforschung und Glaubensgeschichte. Anstöße für eine neue Annäherung von Exegese und Systematischer Theologie', in *TThZ* 96, pp. 123-134.

Frankemölle, H. (1991), 'Evangelium und Wirkungsgeschichte. Das Problem der Vermittlung von Methodik und Hermeneutik in den neuesten Auslegungen zum Matthäusevangelium', in L. Oberlinner and P. Fiedler (eds), *Salz der Erde – Licht der Welt. FS A. Vögtle*, Stuttgart, pp. 31-89.

Gnilka, J. (1989), 'Die Wirkungsgeschichte als Zugang zum Verständnis der Bibel', in *MThZ 40*, pp. 51-62.

Huizing, K. (1996), *Homo legens. Vom Ursprung der Theologie im Lesen*, TBT 75, Berlin and New York.

Huizing, K., Körtner, U. and Müller, P. (1997), *Lesen und Leben – Drei Essays zur Grundlegung einer Lesetheologie*, Bielefeld.

Iser, W. (1974), *The implied reader: patterns of communication in prose fiction from Bunyan to Beckett*, Baltimore.

Iser, W. (1978), *The Act of reading: a theory of aesthetic response*, Baltimore.

McKnight, E.V. (1988), *Post-Modern Use of the Bible. The Emergence of Reader-Oriented Criticism*, Nashville.

Koch, K. (1991), 'Rezeptionsgeschichte als notwendige Voraussetzung einer biblischen Theologie – oder: Protestantische Verlegenheit angesichts der Geschichtlichkeit des Kanons', in H.H.Schmid and J. Mehlhausen (eds), *Sola Scriptura*, Gütersloh, pp. 143-155.

Link, H. (1980), *Rezeptionsforschung*, UTB 215, 2nd edition, Stuttgart.

Luz, U. (1985), 'Wirkungsgeschichtliche Exegese. Ein programmatischer Arbeitsbericht mit Beispielen aus der Bergpredigtexegese', in *BThZ* 2, pp. 18-32.

Räisänen, H. (1992), 'Die Wirkungsgeschichte der Bibel. Eine Herausforderung für die exegetische Forschgung', in *EvTh* 52, pp. 337-347.

Schenk, W. (1988), 'Die Rollen der Leser oder der Mythos des Lesers', in *LingBibl* 60, pp. 61-84.

Warning, R. (ed.) (1979), *Rezeptionsästhetik. Theorie und Praxis*, UTB 303, 2nd edition, München.

b) Jewish Exegesis

Berg, H.K. (1988), 'Die Schrift im Dialog verstehen. Vorarbeiten für ein Gespräch mit der jüdischen Hermeneutik', in G. Büttner and J. Thierfelder (eds), *Religionspädagogische Grenzgänge. FS E. Bochinger u. M. Widmann*, Stuttgart, pp. 15-34.

Brewer, D.I. (1992), *Techniques and assumptions in Jewish exegesis before 70 CE*, TSAJ 30, Tübingen.

Brocke, E. (1972), 'Von jüdischer Weise, die Schrift auszulegen', in *LZ* 32, pp. 109-124.

Brooks, R. and Collins, J.J. (eds) (1990), *Hebrew Bible or Old Testament? Studying the Bible in Judaism and Christianity*, CJAn 5, Notre Dame, Indiana.

Dahan, B. (1990), *Les intellectuels chrétiens et les juifs au moyen age*, Paris.

Dauber, K. (1985), 'The Bible as Literature: Reading Like the Rabbis', in *Semeia* 31, pp. 27-48.

Dohmen, Ch. and Stemberger, G. (1996), *Hermeneutik der Jüdischen Bibel und des Alten Testaments*, Studienbücher Theologie 1,2, Stuttgart.

Fishbane, M. (1992), *The Garments of Torah. Essays in Biblical Hermeneutics*, 2nd edition, Bloomington, Indiana.

Fishbane, M. (ed.) (1993), *The Midrashic Imagination. Jewish Exegesis, Thought and History*, Albany.

Goshen-Gottstein, M. (1975), 'Christianity, Judaism, and Modern Bible Study', in *VT.S* 28, pp. 69-88.

Gradwohl, R. (1987ff), *Bibelauslegungen aus jüdischen Quellen Vols. 1-4*, Stuttgart.

Heide, A. van der (1983), 'PARDES: Methodological Reflections on the Theory of the Four Senses', in *JJS* 34, pp. 147-159.

Hengel, M. and Löhr, H. (1994), *Schriftauslegung im antiken Judentum und im Urchristentum*, WUNT 73, Tübingen.

Hengel, M. and Schwemer, A.M. (eds) (1994), *Die Septuaginta zwischen Judentum und Christentum*, WUNT 72, Tübingen.

Kamin, S. (1992), *Jews and Christians interpret the Bible*, Jerusalem.

Levinson, N.P. (1982), *Ein Rabbiner erklärt die Bibel*, München.

Magonet, J. (1994), *A Rabbi reads the Psalms*, London.

Mulder, M.J. (ed.) (1988ff), *Mikra. Reading and Interpretation of the Hebrew Bible in Ancient Judaism and Early Christianity*, Assen.

Petuchowski, J.J. (1982), *Wie unsere Meister die Schrift erklärten. Beispielhafte Bibelauslegungen aus dem Judentum*, Freiburg.

Rendtorff, R. (1991), 'Wege zu einem gemeinsamen jüdisch-christlichen Umgang mit dem Alten Testament', in *EvTh* 51, pp. 431-444.

Saebø, M. (ed.) (1996), *Hebrew Bible, Old Testament. The History of its Interpretation, Vol. 1,1: From the Beginnings to the Middle Ages (until 1300)*, Göttingen.

Simon, U. (1985), 'Von der religiösen Bedeutung des Wortsinns der Schrift heute', in *Jud* 41, pp. 217-237.

Stemberger, G. (1989), *Midrasch. Vom Umgang der Rabbinen mit der Bibel*, München.

Uffenheimer, B. and Reventlow, Graf H. (eds) (1988), *Creative Biblical Exegesis. Christian and Jewish Hermeneutics through the Centuries*, JSOT.S 59, Sheffield.

Weiss, M. (1987), 'Zur Frage einer jüdischen Hermeneutik in der Tanach-Forschung', in M. Klopfenstein (ed.), *Mitte der Schrift?*, Judaica et Christiana 11, Bern, pp. 29-43.

Zenger, E. (1995), *Das Erste Testament. Die jüdische Bibel und die Christen*, 5th edition, Düsseldorf.

c) Psychological Exegesis

Bucher, A.A. (1992), *Bibelpsychologie. Psychologische Zugänge zu biblischen Texten*, Stuttgart.

Drewermann, E. (1984), *Tiefenpsychologie und Exegese, Vol. 1: Traum, Mythos, Märchen, Sage und Legende*, 2nd edition, Olten and Freiburg.

Drewermann, E. (1986), *Tiefenpsychologie und Exegese, Vol. 2: Wunder, Vision, Weissagung, Apokalypse, Geschichte, Gleichnis*, 2nd edition, Olten and Freiburg.

Kassel, M. (1980), *Biblische Urbilder. Tiefenpsychologische Auslegung nach C.G.Jung*, München.

Kassel, M. (1987), *Das Auge im Bauch*, 3rd edition, Olten and Freiburg.

Leiner, M. (1995), *Psychologie und Exegese. Grundfragen einer textpsychologischen Exegese des Neuen Testaments*, Gütersloh.

Lohfink, G. and Persch, R. (1987), *Tiefenpsychologie und keine Exegese. Eine Auseinandersetzung mit Eugen Drewermann*, SBS 129, Stuttgart.

Oeming, M. (1995), 'Altes Testament und Tiefenpsychologie. Aufklärung oder Freudsche Fehlleistung', in *ThLZ* 120, pp. 107-120.

Raguse, H. (1993), *Psychoanalytische und biblische Interpretation. Eine Auseinandersetzung mit Eugen Drewermann's Auslegung der Johannes-Apokalypse*, Stuttgart.

d) Symbolic Exegesis

Balderman, I. (1992), *Wer hört mein Weinen? Kinder entdecken sich selbst in den Psalmen*, WdL 4, 3rd edition, Neukirchen-Vluyn.

Betz, O. (1987), *Elementare Symbole. Zur tieferen Wahrnehmung des Lebens*, Freiburg.

Biehl, P. and Baudler, G. (1980), *Erfahrung – Symbol – Glaube. Grundfragen des Religionsunterrichts*, RPäH 29, Aachen.

Biehl, P. (1991), *Symbole geben zu lernen, Vol. 1: Einführung in die Symboldidaktik anhand der Symbole Hand, Haus und Weg*, WdL 6, 2nd edition, Neukirchen.

Biehl, P. (1993), *Symbole geben zu lernen, Vol. 2: Zum Beispiel: Brot, Wasser und Kreuz. Beiträge zur Symbol- und Sakramentsdidaktik*, WdL 9, Neukirchen.

Bucher, A.A. (1990), *Symbol - Symbolbildung – Symbolerziehung*, St Ottilien.

Halbfas, H. (1982), *Das dritte Auge. Religionsdidaktische Anstöße*, Düsseldorf.

Oelkers, J. and Wegenast, K. (eds) (1991), *Das Symbol – Brücke des Verstehens*, Stuttgart.

Timm, H. (1993), *Gib mir ein Zeichen*, Stuttgart.

Volp, R. (ed.) (1982), *Zeichen. Semiotik in Theologie und Gottesdienst*, München and Mainz.

Weidinger, N. (1990), *Elemente einer Symboldidaktik. 1. Elemente einer Symbolhermeneutik und -didaktik*, St. Ottilien.

e) Bibliodrama

Andriessen, H and Derksen N. (1989), *Lebendige Glaubensvermittlung im Bibliodrama. Eine Einführung*, Mainz.

Bobrowski, J. (1991), *Bibliodramapraxis. Biblische Symbole im Spiel erfahren*, Hamburg.

Keßler, H (1995), *Bibliodrama und Leiblichkeit. Leibhafte Textauslegung im theologischen und therapeutischen Diskurs*, Stuttgart, Berlin and Köln.

Kiehn, A. (ed.) (1989), *Bibliodrama*, 2nd edition, Stuttgart.

Laeuchli, S. (1987), *Das Spiel vor dem dunklen Gott. 'Mimesis' – ein Beitrag zur Entwicklung des Bibliodramas*, Neukirchen-Vluyn.

Langer, H. (1991), *Vielleicht sogar Wunder. Heilungsgeschichten im Bibliodrama*, Stuttgart.

Martin, G.M. (1995), *Sachbuch Bibliodrama. Praxis und Theorie*, Stuttgart.

Warns, N. and Fallner, H. (eds) (1994), *Bibliodrama als Prozeß*, Bielefeld.

f) Liberation Theology and Exegesis

Boff, L. (1990), *Wie treibt man Theolgie der Befreiung*, 4th edition, Düsseldorf.

Cardenal, E. (1976-1982), *The Gospel in Solentiname, trans. By D.D. Walsh*, Maryknoll.

Casalis, G. (ed.) (1985), *Bibel und Befreiung. Beiträge zu einer nichtidealistischen Bibellektüre*, Edition Exodus/edition liberación, Freiburg (Swiss) and Münster.

Castillo, F. (1983). *La Iglesia de los pobes en America Latina*, Santiago.

Croatto, J.S. (1989), *Die Bibel gehört den Armen. Perspektiven einer befreiungstheologischen Hermeneutik*, ÖEH 5, München.

Crüsemann, F. (1990), 'Anstöße. Befreiungstheologische Hermeneutik und die Exegese in Deutschland', in *EvTh* 50, pp. 535-545.

Fricke, M. (1997), *Bibelauslegung in Nicaragua. Jorge Pixley im Spannungsfeld von Befreiungstheologie, historisch-kritischer Exegese und baptistischer Tradition*, EuZ 2, Münster.

Goldingay, J. (1982/83), 'The Hermeneutics of Liberation Theology', in *HBT* 4/5, pp. 133-161.

Gudorf, C.E. (1987), 'Liberation Theology's Use of Scripture. A Response to First World Critics', in *Interp.* 41, pp. 5-18.

Gutierrez, G. (1988), *A theology of liberation: history, politics and salvation, trans. and ed. by Sister Caridad Inda and J. Eagleson*, Maryknoll.

Hofmann, M. (1978), *Identifikation mit dem anderen. Theologische Themen und ihr hermeneutischer Ort bei lateinamerikanischen Theologen der Befreiung*, Göttingen.

Kessler, R., Ulrich, K., Schwantes, M. and Stansel, G. (eds) (1997), *'Ihr Völker alle, klatscht in die Hände.' FS für E.S. Gerstenberger*, EuZ 3, Münster.

Lohfink, N. (1986), 'Von der "Anawim-Partei" zur "Kirche der Armen". Die bibelwissenschaftliche Ahnentafel eines Hauptbegriffs der "Theologie der Befreiung"', in *Bibl.* 67, pp. 153-175.

Mesters, C. (1983), *Vom Leben zur Bibel – von der Bibel zum Leben. Ein Bibelkurs aus Brasilien für uns*, 2 vols., Mainz and München.

Pieris, A. (1988), *Asian theology of liberation*, Maryknoll.

Richard, P. (1991), 'Bibellektüre durch das Volk in Lateinamerika. Hermeneutik der Befreiung', in *EvTh* 51, pp. 20-39.

Schottroff, L. and Schottroff, W. (eds) (1986), *Wer ist unser Gott? Beiträge zu einer Befreiungstheologie im Kontext der ersten Welt*, München.

Schottroff, W. and Stegemann, W. (eds) (1980), *Traditionen der Befreiung. Sozialgeschichtliche Bibelauslegungen*, 2 vols., München and Gelnhausen.

g) Feminist Exegesis

Dawson Scanzoni, L. and Hardesty, N.A. (1986), *All We're Meant to Be. Biblical Feminism for Today*, Nashville.

Fischer, I. (1995), *Gottesstreiterinnen*, Stuttgart.

Friebe-Baron, Ch. (1988), *Ferne Schwestern, ihr seid mir nah. Begegnungen mit Frauen aus biblischer Zeit*, Stuttgart.

Gerber, U. (1987), *Die feministische Eroberung der Theologie*, Beck'sche Reihe 335, München.

Halkes, C.M. (1980), *Gott hat nicht nur starke Söhne. Grundzüge einer feministischen Theologie*, GTBS 371, Gütersloh.

Heine, S. (1988), *Woman and early Christianity: a reappraisal*, trans. by J. Bowden, Minneapolis.

Heister, M.-S. (1986), *Frauen in der biblischen Glaubensgeschichte*, 2nd edition, Göttingen.

Jahnow, H. (ed.) (1994), *Feministische Hermeneutik und Erstes Testament. Analysen und Interpretationen*, Stuttgart.

Moltmann-Wendel, E. (1986), *A land flowing with milk and honey: perspectives on feminist theology*, trans. J. Bowden, New York.

Ruether, R.R. (1993), *Sexism and God-talk: toward a feminist theology*, Boston.

Russell, L.M. (1985), *Feminist interpretation of the Bible*, Philadelphia.

Schottroff, L., Schroer, S. and Wacker, M.-Th. (1998), *Feminist interpretation: the Bible in women's perspective*, trans. by M. and B. Rumscheidt, Minneapolis.

Schüngel-Straumann, H. (1989), *Die Frau am Anfang. Eva und die Folgen*, Freiburg.

Schüssler Fiorenza, E. (1995), *Bread not stone: the challenge of feminist biblical interpretation*, Boston.

Schüssler Fiorenza, E. (1994), *In memory of her: a feminist theological reconstruction of Christian origins*, New York.

Sorge, E. (1988), *Religion und Frau. Weibliche Spiritualität im Christentum*, 5th edition Stuttgart.

Trible, P. (1978), *God and the rhetoric of sexuality*, Philadelphia.

Trible, P. (1984), *Texts of terror: literary-feminist readings of Biblical narratives*, Philadelphia.

Trible, Ph. (1995), *Mein Gott, warum hast du mich vergessen! Frauenschicksale im Alten Testament*, GTBS 491, 3rd edition, Gütersloh.

Wacker, M.-Th. (1988), 'Gefährliche Erinnerungen. Feministische Blicke auf die hebräische Bibel', Wacker, M.-Th. (ed.), *Theologie feministisch. Disziplinen, Schwerpunkte, Richtungen*, Düsseldorf, pp. 14-58.

4. Methods Focused on the Reality behind the Text

a) Dogmatic Interpretation

Bächli, O. (1986), *Das Alte Testament in Karl Barths Kirchlicher Dogmatik*, Neukirchen-Vlyn.

Ebeling, G. (1995), 'Dogmatik und Exegese (1980)', in Ebeling, G., *Wort und Glaube IV*, Tübingen, pp. 492-509.

Küng, H. (1979), 'Historisch-kritische Exegese als Provokation für die Dogmatik', in *ThQ 159*, pp. 24-35.

Mildenberger, F. (1991-93), *Biblische Dogmatik. Eine biblische Theologie in dogmatischer Perspektive. Vols. 1-3*, Stuttgart.

Pannenberg, W. and Schneider, Th. (eds) (1995), *Schriftauslegung – Lehramt – Rezeption: Verbindliches Zeugnis II*, Freiburg and Göttingen.

Pottier, B. (1986), 'La "Lettre aux Romains" de K. Barth et les quatre senns de l'écriture', in *NRTh* 108, pp. 823-844.

Smend, R. (1988), 'Karl Barth als Ausleger der Heiligen Schrift', in H. Köckert and W. Krötke (eds), *Theologie als Christologie. Zum Werk und Leben Karl Barths. Ein Symposium*, Berlin, pp. 9-37.

Vorgrimmler, H. (ed.) (1962), *Exegese und Dogmatik*, Mainz.

Weder, H. (1987), 'Exegese und Dogmatik. Überlegungen zur Bedeutung der Dogmatik für die Arbeit des Exegeten', in *ZThK* 84, pp. 137-161.

b) Fundamentalist Biblical Interpretation

Barr, J. (1978), *Fundamentalism*, Philadelphia.

Maier, G. (1983), *Heiliger Geist und Schriftauslegung*, Wuppertal.

Marshall, H. (1986), *Biblische Inspirationen*, Wuppertal.

Michel, K.H. (1982), *Sehen und Glauben. Schriftauslegung in der Auseinandersetzung mit Kerygmatheologie und historisch-kritischer Forschung*, Wuppertal.

Niewiadomski, J. (ed.) (1988), *Findeutige Antworten? Fundamentalistische Versuchung in Religion und Gesellschaft*, Theologische Trends 1, Thaur.

Oeming, M. (ed.) (1997), *Die fundamentalistische Versuchung*, Osnabrücker Hochschulschriften 17, Osnabrück.

Tibi, B. (1995), *Krieg der Zivilisationen. Politik und Religion zwischen Vernunft und Fundamentalismus*, Hamburg.

Weinrich, M. (1990), 'Die demütigen Sieger. Fundamentalistische und evangelikale Bibelauslegung', in *Einwürfe* 6, München, pp. 48-93.

c) Existential Interpretation

Bornkamm, G. (1963), 'Die Theologie Rudolf Bultmanns in der neueren Diskussion', in *ThR 29*, pp. 33-141.

Bultmann, R. (1958), *Jesus Christ and mythology*, New York.

Gräßer, E. (1994), 'Notwendigkeit und Möglichkeiten heutiger Bultmannrezeption', in *ZThK* 91, pp. 272-284.

Gunneweg, A.H.J. (1992), 'Altes Testament und existentiale Interpretation (1984)', in H.H. Schmid and J. Mehlhausen (eds.), *Sola Scriptura. Vol. 2*, Göttingen, pp. 66-81.

Lorenzmeier, T. (1968), *Exegese und Hermeneutik. Eine vergleichende Darstellung der Theologie Rudolf Bultmanns, Herbert Brauns und Gerhard Ebelings*, Hamburg.

Schmithals, W. (1968), *An introduction to the theology of Rudolf Bultmann, trans. by J. Bowden*, London.

Sölle, D. (1974), *Political theology, trans. by J. Bowden*, Philadelphia.

D. The Bible and the Current Plethora of Methods

Dalferth, I. (1994), 'Von der Vieldeutbarkeit der Schrift und der Eindeutigkeit des Wortes Gottes', in R. Ziegert (ed.), *Die Zukunft des Schriftprinzips*, Stuttgart, pp. 155-173.

Fischer, A. (1996), *Die Kunst des Bibellesens: theologische Ästhetik am Beispiel des Schriftverständnisses*, Beiträge zur theologischen Urteilsbildung 1, Frankfurt.

Fowl, S.E. (1990), 'The Ethics of Interpretation or What's Left Over After the Elimination of Meaning', in D.J.A. Clines (ed.), *The Bible in Three Dimensions*, JSOT.S, Sheffield, pp. 379-398.

Fuchs, O. (1989), 'Umgang mit der Bibel als Lernschule der Pluralität', in *US* 44, pp. 208-214.

Harsch, H. and Voss, G. (1972), *Versuche mehrdimensionaler Schriftauslegung*, Stuttgart and München.

Kruz, H. (1986), 'Mehrdimensionale Schriftauslegung. Ein Überblick für Religionslehrer', in *KatBl* 111, pp. 576-590.

Merklein, H. (1989), 'Integrative Bibelauslegung? Methodische und hermeneutische Aspekte', in *BiKi* 44, pp. 117-123.

Raguse, H. (1995), *Der Raum des Textes. Elemente einer transdisziplinären theologischen Hermeneutik*, Stuttgart.

Index A: Authors

Index B: Biblical Names

Index C: Scriptures